VISIT...G

SMALL-TOWN

FLORIDA

4TH EDITION

BRUCE HUNT

PINEAPPLE PRESS

Palm Beach, Florida

For Gerry Hunt

Pineapple Press
An imprint of Globe Pequot, the trade division of
The Rowman & Littlefield Publishing Group, Inc.
4501 Forbes Boulevard, Suite 200, Lanham, Maryland 20706
www.rowman.com

Distributed by NATIONAL BOOK NETWORK

British Library Cataloguing in Publication Information Available

Library of Congress Cataloging-in-Publication Data Available

Library of Congress Control Number: 2021008245
ISBN 978-1-68334-271-7 (paper : alk. paper)
ISBN 978-1-68334-260-1 (electronic)

♾™ The paper used in this publication meets the minimum requirements of
American National Standard for Information Sciences—Permanence of Paper
for Printed Library Materials, ANSI/NISO Z39.48-1992.

ACKNOWLEDGMENTS

First and foremost, thank you to all the wonderful folks at Pineapple Press for your commitment to and enthusiasm for my books over the last twenty-five years. All my Pineapple Press books have been a team effort, and it is a terrific team to be on. In addition, there are countless Florida small-town residents, shop owners, B&B owners, restaurateurs, museum curators, historians, and journalists who have been most helpful and supportive in my research over the years—far too many to list but I could not have written the *Visiting Small-Town Florida* books without them. For this edition there are two people that I want to thank for their invaluable help: The first is Nancy Pepper, road trip navigator, companion, and restaurant-tester. Nancy traveled with me to most towns featured in this book. Second is Dr. Leslie Poole, my original writing mentor, and the best source for all things Florida history.

CONTENTS

CENTRAL REGION

SOUTH REGION

INTRODUCTION

*M*y first published book, *Adventure Sports in Florida* (Pineapple Press, 1996) enjoyed moderate success, but it started a relationship with June and David Cussen, founders of Pineapple Press, that would go on to significantly impact my life for decades. June and David showed interest in my writing, and in a way took me under their wing. Shortly after *Adventure Sports in Florida* was published, they asked if I had any other Florida travel book ideas. I did, but I prefaced my pitch with a caution: it would probably be a niche market book. I liked exploring off the beaten path places and tiny towns, but I did not know if there was enough of an audience to justify a guidebook to Florida's small towns. June and David said they thought it was worth a shot. They were right. The level of interest in *Visiting Small-Town Florida* (1997) surprised everybody, and a year later June and David asked me to write a second edition that included additional towns. It was published in 1999. A revised (second) edition, combing the two previous volumes and updated with some new additions, was published in 2003. The third edition came out in 2011. It's been ten years since the last edition, so the fourth edition has been a long time coming. (Although this is the fourth edition, it is my fifth *Visiting Small-Town Florida* book.)

Although far too young to appreciate the value of it at the time, I had the good fortune to grow up in South Tampa, a place that, in the 1960s and early 1970s functioned very much as a small town. Our small commercial center included Pardo's Market, Martin's Drugs, and Jake's Barbershop. We had two grocery stores: Publix and B&B. Agliano's Seafood, Kalupa's Bakery, Schiller's Delicatessen, and Chan's Toy Shop were just a few blocks away. The elementary school and junior high were close enough to walk to. Our family dentist, pediatrician, and veterinarian were all less than a half-mile from our home. On Saturday mornings my friends and I would ride our 10-speed bikes right down the middle of Kennedy Boulevard (Tampa's main east-west thoroughfare) to downtown, without stopping or encountering traffic.

We played sandlot football in vacant lots, organized bicycle races that circumnavigated our neighborhood, and built tree houses in our backyards from discarded wood collected from construction site scrap piles.

Today, we're bombarded on a daily basis with messages that say the world has changed. Nothing will ever be the same. What we once knew and cherished, what we once endeavored to achieve, no longer applies. However, in sharp contrast, what I saw in my neighborhood in this chaos-filled time were families riding bicycles, tossing baseballs or footballs to each other, and pulling lawn chairs out at the end of the day to sit in their front yards and chat with neighbors. They were being careful to maintain some distance, but clearly the craving for community has not just survived, but maybe has been revitalized.

Certainly, Tampa has grown into a big city, with much of the trappings that entails. And one of the reasons I first wrote *Visiting Small-Town Florida* was to provide a guidebook for those wishing to get away from the city and to experience places that function at a different pace. Even so I am heartened to still see a glimmer of small-town-ness in my hometown.

I thought it might be useful to go back twenty-four years and see what I had written in the first edition's introduction. Had those desires and attitudes really changed? Are the things that seemed important then different from what is important now?

Here's an excerpt from that introduction:

We seem to have come to a time in society (and even more acutely so in Florida) when people are starved for simpler lifestyles—lifestyles that are still commonplace in the little hamlets and boroughs that are fortunate enough to be inconvenient to Florida's main thoroughfares. Most people have to live in the large population centers because that's where their jobs are. That's a fact of life. However, big cities represent sometimes overwhelming complications. Life can make unreasonable demands on the city dweller. Crime, crowds, traffic jams, long lines, and rude people (who don't care because they'll probably never see you again) are things that they have to deal with on a daily basis. In the middle of all this mayhem, they are daydreaming about Mayberry: "If only my life were as simple as Andy and Aunt Bea's."

A big city works hard to homogenize the personalities of its residents. It stifles individuality. It makes it too easy for people to blend in with the background and exist without affecting their surroundings—a whole life can pass by without ever making a mark. In a small town, even the meekest find a purpose, or they are given one. A small town requires the inclusion of each one of its residents—there is no anonymity. Individuals make up its character, which breeds a sense of community and responsibility. A big city's personality is diluted by its vast population. Small towns have a richness and eccentricity that can only come when a small enough group of people, who almost all know each other, live in relative isolation from mass-produced society. People develop more distinct identities when they are not such small morsels in a giant stew.

I think that message rings as true today as it did then. So, from my viewpoint, I feel confident that our core human needs, desires, and goals have not been altered. Thankfully. In some cases, how we achieve them has evolved, though. For instance, it is no longer necessary to live in a large metropolitan area in order to work. That means more people are putting down roots in smaller, more livable communities, which means small-town populations are growing. But this did not just happen. It has been going on for a while. Previously, as a parameter for the purpose of inclusion, I tried to include towns with populations of ten thousand or less. In this volume, I am including towns of fifteen thousand or less because there are many great Florida small towns that fit into that range that I want to include.

Florida is an odd-shaped state, and to make *Visiting Small-Town Florida* most useful I have separated it into three regions: North, Central, and South.

The North Region contains the Florida Panhandle, which is located between the northern coast of the Gulf of Mexico and the Alabama and Georgia state lines. This region has more in common with those two states, both geologically and culturally, than it does with the rest of Florida. Locals fondly refer to the Panhandle's coast as the "Redneck Riviera." Here beach towns sit among wind-blown sand dunes and overlook pristine, glistening white beaches with sand made of quartz washed down from the Appalachian Mountains over thousands of years. Inland—up closer to Alabama and Georgia, rolling hills, river crossings, and pastureland dominate the landscape. Meandering two-lane roads navigate elevation changes and connect the dots between isolated communities. The northeast coast bills itself as the "First Coast," and for good reason. Although Christopher Columbus is routinely credited with "discovering" America, he never got any farther than the Bahamas and the Caribbean. Columbus never actually set foot on mainland America. It was another European explorer (who had sailed with Columbus on earlier expeditions), Spaniard Juan Ponce de Leon, who first landed on Florida's beaches on April 2, 1513. There is some argument about the exact location where de Leon landed. Depending on which historian you talk to, it was either a bit north of where St. Augustine is now, or just south of Daytona, at Ponce Inlet, or just south of Cape Canaveral near Melbourne. Two of Florida's most significant small towns are here: Fernandina Beach (on the north tip of Amelia Island, near the Florida-Georgia state line) and St. Augustine.

The Central Region (which contains my hometown, Tampa) is a marvelous mix of the state's much varied culture and ethnicity. From Greek influences springing from Tarpon Springs, to Cuban, Spanish, and Italian influences originating in Tampa, to rural interior "Florida Cracker" influences, you will find it all here.

The South Region takes on an entirely different flavor—far more Caribbean and South American.

Within each region I have ordered the towns geographically: generally, west to east, and then north to south. Many people like to road trip and visit a variety of towns in one outing, so this was the most logical way to arrange the book. It has allowed me to group towns, which road-trippers are likely to visit on one trip, in a logical order, like: Grayton Beach, Seaside, and Rosemary; Apalachicola, St. George Island, and Carrabelle; Micanopy, Cross Creek, and Evinston; Floral City, Pineola, and Istachatta; Crystal River, Ozello, and Homosassa; Sebring, Lake Placid, and Arcadia; Matlacha, Bokeelia, Pineland, and St. James City; and Everglades City, Chokoloskee, and Ochopee.

In this edition I cover seventy-nine small towns, spreading from Florida's far northwest at Perdido Key on the Florida-Alabama border, to the far northeast corner at Fernandina Beach on Amelia Island, down to Big Pine Key in Florida's far southern keys. I will delve into the history of each, seek out and dine at their best local eateries, stay at their quaint inns and bed and breakfasts, and browse their shops, galleries, and museums. Some are mere crossroads, offbeat places like Two Egg, or historically significant like Rosewood. Some are bustling towns with centuries of history, like St. Augustine. In-between there are quirky artist communities, like Matlacha, and places to unwind and soak in the sun and breathe in the salt air, like St. George Island.

For me, experiencing local cuisine is a major component to travel. Sometimes I travel just for the purpose of finding great food. With Florida's rich melting pot of ethnic influences—Spanish, Cuban, Bahamian, Greek, Italian, and Puerto Rican (to name just a few)—its small towns have much to offer. And then of course there is the seafood. You are never far from fresh seafood in Florida. With the Gulf of Mexico on the west and the Atlantic Ocean on the east, the most landlocked spot in Florida is still less than ninety miles from the sea. Small-town Florida's restaurants often feature fresh-caught fish, shrimp, lobster, and the state's own delicacies like stone crab claws, bay scallops, and oysters. Apalachicola, Fernandina Beach, Mount Dora, Anna Maria, and Islamorada may all be small, but they are all spectacularly good restaurant towns.

Readers will note that, on occasion, I give my opinion and say, "My favorite . . .," "I recommend . . . ," and "I can vouch for . . . " repeatedly. So, yes, I love barbecue, comfort food, soul food, and seafood. If you do too, you will likely enjoy those that I have noted.

All the towns in this edition of *Visiting Small-Town Florida* were chosen because I found something captivating there: an enchanting story in its history, inviting lodging, or exceptional local cuisine. Many are vacation destinations worthy of long weekend or even week-long stays, like Seaside, Apalachicola, St. George Island, Fernandina Beach, St. Augustine, Mount Dora, Boca Grande, Sanibel, and Captiva. At the other end of that spectrum are some tiny spots where you are more likely to spend just an hour (or less) but that are worth detouring through just to see. These merit mention because they have intriguing stories, like Two Egg, Sopchoppy, Cross Creek, Briny Breezes, Rosewood, or Ochopee.

Lastly, I have devoted a good bit of space to historical anecdotes in most of my chapters. Why? Most people drive through these towns without slowing down, but if they knew the stories behind these places they might be persuaded to stop and visit for a while.

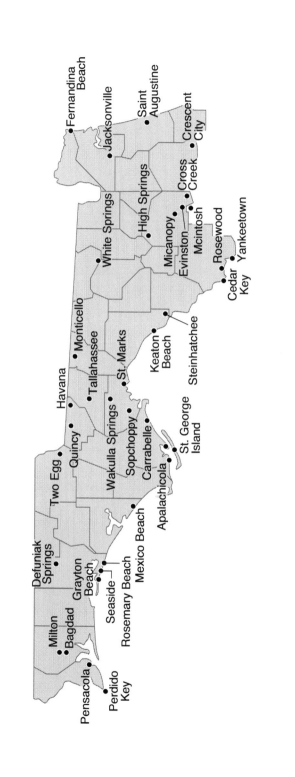

NORTH REGION

The Flora-Bama Lounge on Perdido Key

FLORA-BAMA/ PERDIDO KEY

Population not listed on census

I know. Flora-Bama is not actually a town. Neither is Perdido Key, the barrier island that stretches about twenty-five miles from Johnson Beach National Seashore (in Florida) to Orange Beach (in Alabama). I first heard about the Flora-Bama Lounge and Perdido Key in the late 1970s while I was a student at Auburn University. Although ostensibly majoring in business/marketing, I will confess I devoted much of my time to skydiving. I was president of the university's skydiving club (the oldest such collegiate club in the country), and head instructor. I would skydive every weekend and fellow skydivers formed my circle of college friends. Occasionally, we would do exhibition jumps at football games, lake parties, and sometimes a clandestine sunset jump onto campus. A gang of my L. A. (that's "Lower Alabama" not California) skydiving buddies told me about a jump that takes place at a big annual party, something they called "The Mullet Toss," at the Flora-Bama Lounge on Perdido Key. The Flora-Bama was a ramshackle dive beach bar—locally famous back then. It's still a ramshackle dive beach bar but it's internationally famous now.

Perdido Key stretches along the Gulf Coast, across the Florida/Alabama state border, southwest of Pensacola. Stilt houses overlook beach sand dunes and the emerald green water of the Gulf of Mexico. Although not commercially overbuilt, it is mostly residential; Perdido has long been a popular summer vacation spot for families from Alabama, Mississippi, and Florida.

In 1964, Ted and Ellen Tampary, along with their two sons Tony and Connie, had planned to debut the Flora-Bama Lounge in time for the start of summer. But the just completed building caught fire and burned down before they could open. Undeterred, they rebuilt and opened in October. It was (and still is) the quintessential beach roadhouse. What makes the Flora-Bama unique is that it straddles the Florida-Alabama state line. Perdido Key was a near-desolate barrier island back then. A bridge (from the Alabama side) had just been built in 1962.

The Flora-Bama Lounge on Perdido Key

In 1978, the Tamparys sold to Joe Gilchrist and Pat McClellan, who knew a good thing when they saw it and changed nothing about the décor but thought some live entertainment might lure more customers. They also came up with something that ultimately put the Flora-Bama on the national map: The Interstate Mullet Toss, an annual contest and beach party that takes place on the last weekend in April. It is just what it sounds like—a contest that sees who can throw a mullet the farthest, from one state to the next. The first time I visited the Flora-Bama (back in the mid-1990s) it was still a one-story building. The state line was painted down the middle of the bar's floor. I ordered a dozen oysters on the half shell and a beer in one state and consumed them in the other. In 2004, Florida experienced its every-four-decades rash of hurricanes. Four slammed the state in a six-week period. Number three, Ivan, was one of those that hung out in the Atlantic and Caribbean for a couple weeks before driving up into the Gulf of Mexico as a Category 5. It had weakened to a Category 3 by the time it made landfall, but it was still a monster—with a fifty-mile-wide eye, and it landed right on the Florida-Alabama border. Some of the Flora-Bama withstood the onslaught but a massive storm surge gutted it beyond repair. Ivan stands as one of the most devastating hurricanes ever to strike the Alabama/West Florida coast, so everyone assumed that this was the end of the Flora-Bama. But, just like forty years prior, eventually it re-opened.

In 2011, Gilchrist and McClellan added a third partner, John McKinnis. In 2012, the Flora-Bama underwent a major renovation building it three stories tall. The new owners salvaged much of the original bar and installed it on the third floor. To make the (now) multiple bars function more efficiently, they built a special "liquor room" with an automated system that pumps booze from hundreds of bottles, on demand, directly to the bars.

Today, the once lonely roadhouse is one of the most popular stops in this region and one of the best places in Florida to just hang out. Well-known musicians like Kenny Chesney and Jimmy Buffet are regularly booked. In addition, the Flora-Bama serves up some outstanding fresh-out-of-the-Gulf seafood: oysters—raw, Cajun-spicy, or "McClellan" (with bacon, onions, and Gouda cheese); and shrimp—peel-and-eat or coconut-fried.

DON'T MISS
The Interstate Mullet Toss if you
are there the last weekend in April

On September 16, 2020, just a few months away from my *Visiting Small-Town Florida*, fourth edition, manuscript deadline, Category 2 Hurricane Sally made landfall near Gulf Shores, Alabama, just west of the Flora-Bama. This was not something new for them. They boarded up and sand bagged as needed. Although there was first-floor flooding, they cleaned up, repaired, and reopened just days later. Ironically, Hurricane Sally hit on the sixteenth anniversary of Hurricane Ivan.

Milton Railroad Depot Museum

MILTON, BAGDAD

Population: Milton 10,523; Bagdad 3,474

*T*he question on the mind of nearly every golf fan in May 2012 was, "Where the heck is Bagdad, Florida?" The tiny town received some instant national attention when professional golfer and Bagdad resident Bubba Watson won that year's Masters Tournament. Two years later he won again. Watson was born, raised, and lived in Bagdad until 2015 when he and his family moved to nearby Pensacola. He currently owns a Chevrolet dealership in Milton (across Pond Creek from Bagdad).

The two towns of Bagdad and Milton seem very much like one. They are separated only by Pond Creek, a tributary of the Blackwater River (which passes by both towns). Milton is popular with paddlers, rafters, and tubers, and claims the title of Canoe Capital of Florida. There is easy access to those waterways in addition to the Coldwater and Sweetwater rivers. Overlooking the banks of the Blackwater

Bagdad Village Museum

River, downtown Milton is a designated Florida Main Street community and is listed on the National Register of Historic Places. The Milton Museum of Local History is a great place to explore the area's history and culture.

Pine logging and milling in the Milton/Bagdad area traces back to the early 1800s. The two towns grew side by side. Today, each have embraced its heritage and done much to preserve it, making them an interesting visit for history buffs.

In 1817, the king of Spain granted land along Pond Creek to Juan de la Rua. De la Rua built and operated a lumber mill there for ten years before becoming discouraged with the local laborers. In 1828, he sold his property to Joseph Forsyth, who took on partners Ezekiel and Andrew Simpson. They built the dam-driven Arcadia Mill, and a village began to grow around it. The vast forests of this region were thick with valuable long-leaf yellow pine, and the Blackwater River provided a ready highway for floating logs down to Pensacola Bay. Forsyth and the Simpsons prospered and took on additional partner Benjamin Thompson. In 1840, they moved the mill a couple of miles downstream to the juncture of Pond Creek and the Blackwater River. A village grew around it again. Joseph Forsyth chose the name Bagdad—perhaps because, like its Middle Eastern namesake, it was wedged between two important rivers. (By the way, that is not a typo. Forsyth spelled the town's name without the "h.")

Bagdad was on the south side of Pond Creek and Milton on the north side. About the same time that Joseph Forsyth and the Simpson brothers were getting the Arcadia Mill into full swing, Benjamin and Margaret Jernigan were starting a mill of their own. People began to refer to the area around it as Jernigan's Landing and also as Scratch Ankle, presumably because of the dense briars that grew along the banks of the Blackwater River. Neither of those names stuck, but a more definitive one, Milltown, did, and it eventually evolved into Milton, which was incorporated in 1844.

More sawmills opened over the following decades. By the turn of the century, Milton and Bagdad had become the most industrialized towns in Florida. The lumber barons thought the bounty was endless, but they were short-sighted. The Great Depression in the 1930s hit both towns hard. Plus, the once-plentiful pine forests had become depleted. The last of the mills, the Bagdad Land & Lumber Company, closed in 1939.

Santa Rosa County Road 191 becomes Forsyth Street as it rolls into Bagdad from the south. On the right, behind a hedge, is the stately, pre-Civil War (1847) Thompson House. Arcadia Mill partner Benjamin Thompson built this palatial two-story antebellum mansion, with double front porches supported by twelve white columns. During the Civil War, invading Union troops commandeered the house. While there they scrawled a taunting message in charcoal across the parlor wall, which is still there today: "Mr. Thompson, Spurling's First Cavalry camped in your house on the 26th of October 1864." Originally, the house overlooked the Blackwater River, a few blocks to the east, but in 1913 the owners must have wanted a change of scenery. They jacked the house up onto log rollers, turned it around 180 degrees, and pulled it by mule to its present location. In 2009, the Thompson House finally got its own Florida Heritage Site/State Historic marker.

Four blocks away, at the corner of Bushnell and Church Streets, the Bagdad Village Preservation Association operates the Bagdad Historical Museum in a restored circa 1880s church building that was Bagdad's first African American church. Displays there tell the story of Bagdad's and the surrounding area's early days and particularly of Bagdad's involvement in the Civil War. During one battle of note that took place here in October 1864, the aforementioned Union colonel Thomas Spurling and some two hundred troops raided a

Bagdad logging operation. Confederate troops engaged them in a battle that lasted two hours.

Across Pond Creek Bridge, Milton has grown into a sizable town. The downtown district has been nicely renovated, particularly Caroline Street (Highway 90) and Willing Street, which parallels the Blackwater River. Downtown reminds me of a miniature Savannah or New Orleans French Quarter. Riverwalk Park—with its pink-blossoming crepe myrtle trees, brick walkways, wrought iron and wood park benches, and gas lamp-style streetlights, occupies the waterfront behind Willing Street. Visitors will find some good places to eat here. For doughnuts, muffins, pastries, and pies the Milton Quality Bakery, a family-owned business for more than fifty years, is a must stop. For upscale dining and entertainment try the Blackwater Bistro.

Devastating fires swept through downtown Milton in 1909 and again in 1911, leveling much of the district. But this was boom time, and the town was rebuilt bigger and better than before. Two notable brick buildings—the three-story Imogene Theater on Caroline Street and the Exchange Hotel at the corner of Caroline and Elmira Streets—were part of Milton's rebirth.

Architect Walker Willis designed the theater. It was originally called the Milton Opera House when it opened in 1912. When the Gootch family bought it in 1920, they renamed it after their eleven-year-old daughter, Imogene. A post office and a store shared the first floor. The upstairs theater ran vaudeville shows, silent movies, and "talkies" until it closed in 1946. The Santa Rosa Historical Society restored it in 1987 and turned it into the Milton Opera House Museum of Local History. Unfortunately, fire struck again in January 2009. So, once again, the Historical Society went to work on restoration, which still continues today.

Charles Sudmall, who operated the local telephone exchange in the early 1900s, was so impressed with the new Milton Opera House that he hired the same contractor, S. F. Fulguhm Company of Pensacola, to build the Exchange Hotel in 1913. Sudmall insisted that the hotel architecturally match the opera house. The hotel closed around 1946, but it was restored in 1984 and is now the First Judicial Circuit State Attorney's Office.

Another restored Milton historical structure, the 1909 Milton Railroad Depot, sits next to railroad tracks just across the Pond Creek Bridge on County Road 191. Although trains still run on these tracks, they no longer stop here. The original depot, built in 1882, burned in 1907. The 1909 depot was part of the Louisville and Nashville Railroad system. When passenger trains were discontinued in 1973, the depot closed and fell quickly into disrepair. The following year, the Santa Rosa Historical Society formed to save it. The depot reopened on July 4, 1976. It now houses the West Florida Railroad Museum.

Just west of Milton and Bagdad (off Highway 90) you'll find the Arcadia Mill Archaeological Site and Simpson House museum. Local historian Warren Weekes found the remains of the original mill while canoeing up Pond Creek in 1964 and spearheaded its archaeological excavation. When I spoke to Warren Weekes in 1998 (he was the museum curator at the time), he told me about Arcadia in the 1840s. "Back then, you were not allowed to acquire property and then turn right around to resell it. When Juan de la Rua got this property from the king of Spain, he had to keep it, improve it, and work it for a minimum of seven years. He paid the king of Spain one shipload of square lumber per year in taxes. When de la Rua sold the property to John Forsyth for four hundred dollars, he was glad to get rid of it. Apparently, he was less interested in running a mill and more interested in politics. Later he would become mayor of Pensacola. The Arcadia Mill ran off two big water wheels driven by Pond Creek. The mill made square lumber with straight saws—the round saw was not invented until after 1840. They would cut the long-leaf yellow pine lengthwise, flip it on its side, and then cut it again so that it came out square." Sadly, Warren Weekes has since passed away, but the work that he began still goes on. On display at the museum is a collection of old photographs from the mill's era, as well as artifacts excavated from the Arcadia site by the University of West Florida's (UWF) archaeology department. Today, students from UWF are conducting extensive field research and digs. From the museum, a trail leads through the woods and down into a ravine where it crosses a swinging wooden bridge spanning Pond Creek. This was the site of the Arcadia Mill dam and water wheels, discovered by Weekes. Beneath the clear water of Pond Creek, you can still see the remains of the foundation of the dam.

The Little Big Store, DeFuniak Springs

DEFUNIAK SPRINGS

Population: 6,968

*L*ike many of Florida's historic small towns, DeFuniak Springs (established in 1881) began as a railroad stop. But in this case, the railroad company saw it as more than just a stopover. Along with rail line charter rights, the state of Florida had granted Pensacola and Atlantic (a subsidiary of Louisville and Nashville Railroad [L&N Railroad]) property ownership covering what today encompasses more than five counties. The rail line recognized that the area surrounding what is now Lake DeFuniak and Chipley Park, had promise as a scenic community with recreational offerings. It was a special enough place that they named it for Frederick DeFuniak, L&N Railroad president.

In 1884, the Chautauqua Association, based in Lake Chautauqua, New York, chose DeFuniak Springs as its Florida Chautauqua winter assembly location. The association promoted a combination of adult education, recreation, and religion. It would have a substantial, long-term influence on education and society in DeFuniak Springs.

In 1886, a group of local women in DeFuniak Springs started a library to support the needs of the Florida Chautauqua Association. Renamed the Walton-DeFuniak Library in 1975, it is the oldest continuously operated library in Florida. Located on the inside of Circle Drive, it sits overlooking Lake DeFuniak about one-quarter of the way around from downtown. The hardwood-frame building is simply designed with some pleasing exterior motifs typical for the late nineteenth century, such as the diagonal slats on the upper portion of the outside walls and scalloped shingles in the front gable over the entranceway. The original building was completed in 1887 at a cost of only $580. A rear addition was added in 1984 but blends so well architecturally that it appears to have been a part of the original.

Inside, polished wood floors and large oval throw rugs give the library a warm feeling. An amazing display of old swords, spears, battle axes, crossbows, and muskets hang on the walls. The collection originally belonged to Professor Kenneth Bruce from Palmer College in DeFuniak Springs, who left the armaments to the college in his will. When Palmer College closed its doors in the 1930s, the collection was given to the city and then later passed on to the library. Many of the weapons are European and date back to the Crusades (AD 1100–1300), while some pieces come from Malaysia, Persia, and Japan. The Kentucky muskets date from the mid- to late 1700s.

Additional historic buildings and Victorian homes surround the near perfectly round spring-fed Lake DeFuniak. Just past the library is the 1909 Chautauqua Building, originally the Chautauqua Hall of Brotherhood. Today it houses the Walton County Chamber of Commerce. Circle Drive continues past St. Agatha's Episcopal Church, with its ornate stained-glass windows. Built in 1896, it is the oldest church on the circle. On the next block, at 219 Circle Drive, you'll find the Bullard House, a three-story turn of the century Victorian complete with bay windows, a turret, and steeple.

Baldwin Avenue is the main street of DeFuniak Springs' historic district. It runs east/west just across the railroad tracks from Lake DeFuniak. Renovated brick storefronts face south and overlook the lake and the restored L&N train depot, now home to the Walton County Heritage Museum. Chipley Park, on the north side of Lake DeFuniak,

DeFuniak Springs Library

has an open-air amphitheater and band shell that was constructed by the city in 1988, which fits beautifully with the town's turn of the century charm. And it is an idyllic setting for concerts.

Antique and curio shops fill the restored buildings on and around Baldwin Avenue. The Big Store, in a century-old building fronting Baldwin, is now closed, but just around the corner you'll find the Little Big Store—an old-fashion country general store and mercantile. There is an assortment of antique shops here, but my favorite is the Nook & Cranny, with a vast inventory of collectibles and whimsical art pieces.

I found two good downtown eateries: Bogey's Bar & Restaurant at the east end of Baldwin Avenue and Café Nola at the Hotel DeFuniak. Sadly, an old favorite, The Busy Bee Café (which had been there since 1916) has closed. But I found something new. The Perla Baking Company, which opened in 2019, is an outstanding fresh-baked goods (buttery croissants, cinnamon, blueberry, and cheese Danish pastries, plus cakes and cupcakes) and gourmet espresso shop. Perla has quickly become DeFuniak Springs' coffee hangout.

There is historic lodging here as well. The elegant 1920 Hotel DeFuniak underwent extensive restoration in 1997. Today, it offers elegant period-themed rooms and suites. This charming two-story hotel was originally built as a Masonic lodge in 1920. The Masons held meetings upstairs and rented the downstairs to a furniture store. Following the collapse of the Florida real estate boom, in 1929 the building sold at a foreclosure auction to attorney Stealie Preacher, who opened his law office downstairs. Preacher's wife turned the upstairs into the Lake Hotel. In the 1940s it sold again—this time to pharmacist Marshall Lightfoot, who kept the hotel upstairs and opened a drugstore downstairs. But like so many of America's downtown historic structures, by

Perla Baking Company, DeFuniak Springs

the 1970s the building had fallen into disrepair. It wasn't until 1996 that a local group purchased it, spent a year restoring it, and then reopened it as the Hotel DeFuniak.

One hundred years ago, DeFuniak Springs was a place that successfully combined southern small-town charm with sophistication, culture, and education. Today's residents continue to do an exceptional job of maintaining that heritage.

DON'T MISS
The historic Walton-DeFuniak Library

The Lawrence Grocery Store, Two Egg, 1998 and 2020

TWO EGG

Population not listed on census

*I*t may have been a stretch to call two little country stores, the Lawrence Grocery and the Pittman Store, across the road from each other and out in the middle of nowhere, a town, but Two Egg has a story that no one can resist. I first stopped into Lawrence Grocery and met the owner Nell Lawrence King in 1998.

Nell King had owned the Lawrence Grocery since 1988. Prior to 1988 King's father, her uncle, and her brothers had all owned it at one time or another.

"I've lived within a couple miles of here all my life," Nell told me. "This is the entire town of Two Egg. Let me count up for a second and I'll tell you what the population is." For about five seconds Nell mentally ticked off in her head who had had babies lately. "Should be twenty-eight right now. Yeah, we may be a small town but people do know we are here. The Florida Department of Transportation folks over in Tallahassee tell us that the Two Egg road sign out on County Road 69 is the most stolen road sign in the whole state."

Of course, I had to ask her about the story behind the name Two Egg. Originally, it was called Allison. Back in the 1890s, a salesman who frequently stopped into the store on his route started calling it Two Egg. Every time he would come into the store, he would see the little children of a local farming family, the Williams's, bringing in eggs to trade for sodas or candy. It was a large family. Each child had a chicken to care for, and in lieu of an allowance they could use the eggs from their chickens to barter with. The smaller children could just manage one egg in each hand, hence the name.

The Lawrence Grocery Store closed for good in 2007 and now sits sadly boarded up and surrounded by a chain-link fence. The Pittman Store is long gone, now just a vacant lot.

Two other interesting side notes: actress Faye Dunaway grew up a couple miles from Two Egg in the community of Bascom and reportedly visited the Lawrence Grocery often as a child. Also, Two Egg has its own skunk ape/bigfoot, the Stump Jumper.

Gadsden Arts Center and Museum, Quincy

QUINCY

Population: 6,827

*S*cenic Highway 12 glides over rolling hills and past oak trees spider-webbed with kudzu on my drive from Havana to Quincy. It is a reminder that the topography at this northern end of the state blends seamlessly with southern Alabama and southern Georgia. The town of Quincy does the same thing. It is the county seat of Gadsden, and consistent with small-town county seats throughout the south, it has a stately dome-topped courthouse in the middle of the town square with four massive white columns. The courthouse has been in continuous use since 1827.

All of downtown Quincy and most of the surrounding residential area have been designated a National Register Historic District. One of the fifty-five historic structures in the district is the 1912 Bell & Bates Hardware Store Building on North Madison Street, on the east side of the town square. When the Bates family moved their store in 1997, they donated the original 1912 building to Gadsden Arts, Inc., which restored and opened it in 2000 as the Gadsden Art Center, a beautiful gallery and educational center with continuously revolving new exhibits of art and sculpture from Florida, national, and world-famous artists. In 2009, Gadsden Art Center expanded into the adjacent Fletcher Building, greatly enlarging their exhibit space and as of 2016 they have been renamed the Gadsden Art Center & Museum.

Another historic building of note found on East Washington Street is the 1949 Leaf Theatre Building. It was originally a movie theater named in honor of the shade tobacco that was grown in this area for cigar wrappers (see next chapter on Havana). The movie theater closed in 1980. Through private donations and grants, it was restored and reopened in 1983 as a performing arts theater. It has fifteen rows of seats plus a bal-

Leaf Theatre Building, Quincy

cony, and its deep-set stage includes a revolving center. Currently, the theater is not hosting any programs, but hopes are that it will reopen at a future date.

The surrounding neighborhood is filled with both pre– and post–Civil War homes. A historic walking tour pamphlet, available at the Gadsden Art Center, is the best guide to finding these gems. Three of these historic homes have been turned into bed-and-breakfasts: the Queen Anne Victorian McFarlin House, built by tobacco planter John McFarlin in 1895; the Allison House, built in 1843 by General Abraham K. Allison who would also serve as governor of Florida in 1865; and the circa 1898 White Squirrel Inn.

There is an interesting historical side note that connects Quincy with the Coca-Cola Company. In the early 1900s, patrons of the Quincy

State Bank, Florida's first chartered state bank, were told by Mark Munroe, the bank's president, that purchasing stock in a fledgling drink company might prove to be a good investment. Lots of Quincyites took his advice and became wealthy. For many years, residents in Quincy held more than half of Coca-Cola's outstanding shares.

DON'T MISS
The Gadsden Art Center & Museum

Pedestrian-friendly Havana

HAVANA

Population: 1,708

*B*y the early 1970s, tiny Havana had become a boarded-up ghost town. That is Havana, Florida, twelve miles north of Tallahassee. Locals pronounce it "Hay-van-ah."

Havana incorporated in 1906 and was named in honor of the Cuban tobacco that had been widely cultivated there during the previous three-quarters of a century. In later years, tobacco farmers in Havana specialized in growing "shade tobacco," the leaves of which cigar makers used as the outer wrapper. They called it shade tobacco because it grew under cheesecloth tarps, which let just the right amount of light through in order to grow perfect leaves. The harvested leaves were then carefully dried over charcoal pit fires. The entire operation was a delicate process.

In the mid-1960s, under a foreign goodwill program sponsored by the US government, North Florida shade tobacco growers special farming and harvesting techniques were taught to workers in several South

American countries. Within just a couple of years, these countries were producing shade tobacco at a significantly lower cost, and the growing industry around Havana (and, consequently, the town itself) died.

It would be almost two more decades before Tallahassee antique dealers Keith Henderson and Lee Hotchkiss, in search of a more affordable location, would come along and begin CPR on Havana's downtown district.

When I interviewed them in 1998, Lee told me, "We originally were just interested in the one corner building, but the owners wanted to sell the whole block and made us such an attractive offer that we bought it all. We talked to all our antique-business friends in Tallahassee about the idea of an antique district in downtown Havana. They loved it, and four of them decided to move their stores here and rent space in the block." The Hotchkiss's spent that entire summer and fall gutting the interior of their store, sandblasting away old paint, pulling out the drop ceiling, and stripping drywall to expose the original brick interior walls. Their shop, H & H Antiques, became H & H Furniture and Design and filled the whole bottom floor of their newly restored 1908 two-story brick building. The first weekend of their opening, four other shops opened on the block as well.

From 1981 on, Havana was a town reborn. A restoration revival began in the downtown district and spread to the surrounding neighborhood. Antique shops, art galleries, and quaint cafés began to open, turning Havana into a destination for visitors from all over the south.

In the 1990s, Keith and Lee took on another project—the mid-1800s McLauchlin House—a large dogtrot floor plan farmhouse, now located one block west of H & H Furniture and Design. It has a wide, shaded wraparound porch with ornate gingerbread trim. Inside are a variety of shops that sell antiques, furniture, gifts, and apparel. When I asked Keith about the house, a smile formed on his face. "That's an interesting story," he told me. "The McLauchlin House was built in the 1840s. It was on a farm about twenty miles north of here in Decatur County, Georgia. One of the residents here in Havana, Nellie McLauchlin Cantey, was born in the house in 1899. She married her husband, Joe Cantey, in the house in 1919. When Nellie's brother passed away, the family considered selling the farm. Lee and I went

McLauchlin House, Havana

up there to buy some of the furniture, and we just fell in love with the house. We talked to them about buying it, along with some of the acreage. It turns out that the family really wanted to keep the property, but no one was going to live in the house. Then Nellie came up with a wonderful plan. She offered to give us the house on two conditions: one, that we pay the expense to move the house, and two, that we move it to Havana, where she could be near it. We accepted her offer. The house movers had to cut it into three sections to transport it. In 1994, not long after we finished fixing it up, Nellie and Joe celebrated their seventy-fifth wedding anniversary in the house."

Over the last three decades there has been store turnover, naturally. H & H Antiques/H & H Furniture and Design is no longer there, and the building that the Hotchkiss's had purchased is currently being renovated once again.

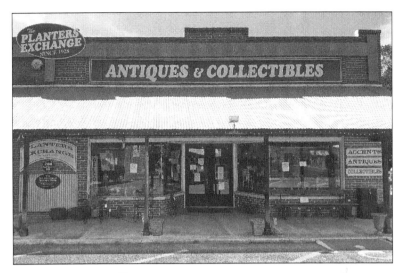

Planters Exchange, Havana

Today, the McLauchlin House's main tenant is Weezies Cottage Home Décor. One block behind the McLauchlin House is the Planters Exchange, where a couple dozen antique and collectibles dealers share space in a historic building that was designated a National Historic Landmark in 1999. The Havana History & Heritage Society Museum can be found here as well. Around the corner, Wanderings Décor & More features eclectic custom furniture, as well as jewelry and artsy décor items. In 2019, they added Poppy's Coffee & More to one corner of the store. Poppy's is a terrific gourmet coffee shop with fresh baked pastries, muffins, and cakes (I can vouch for their terrific tres leche cake!). At the other end of First Street visitors will find Oscar's Pizza, which in addition to pizza also serves a variety of pasta dishes, paninis, and salads. For deli sandwiches and ice cream try Gocki's at the Havana Trading Company gift store.

The town of Havana has done a remarkable job of continually reinventing itself, creating something fresh out of the remains of what was almost lost forever while still paying homage to the town's heritage.

DON'T MISS
The Planters Exchange

Monticello Opera House, Monticello

MONTICELLO

Population: 2,409

*M*onticello, the county seat of Jefferson County, is named after President Thomas Jefferson's home in Virginia. However, locals pronounce the "c" like an "s" whereas Jefferson's home is pronounced with a "ch." It was chartered in 1827, twenty-three years before Florida became a state. Monticello takes pride in its historic structures. It is a Florida Main Street community, and the Monticello Historic District (downtown) is listed on the National Register of Historic Places. Downtown has several notable historic buildings, including the Monticello Opera House (built in 1890), where musical events and theater performances are still performed, and the recently restored 1906 Jefferson County Courthouse.

There is historic lodging as well, like the 1897 Daffodale House Bed & Breakfast. If you want to spend the night in a historic haunted house this might be your best bet. Daffodale House was built by a prominent banker and politician. Cathy and Scotty Ebberbach, owners since

Jefferson County Courthouse, Monticello

2006, first detected spooky goings-on during their initial renovations. According to them, strange music can sometimes be heard from the Safari room, patrons occasionally catch a whiff of pipe smoke in the vicinity of the elevator, and also hear footsteps up in the attic. But the spookiest may be the ethereal woman dressed in white seen walking about the premises. Paranormal investigators claim to sense the presence of a family and young child in the home.

If ghosts are not your thing, consider the 1872 John Denham Inn or The Cottage Bed & Breakfast.

I found an excellent lunch spot in downtown Monticello, the Rev Café, where I enjoyed superb blackened redfish with collard greens. Their jambalaya and shrimp and grits looked equally tasty.

DON'T MISS
Lunch at the Rev Café

At Tribe Kelly Surf Post Shop, Grayton Beach

GRAYTON BEACH

Population not listed on census

*L*ong before there was a Seaside, a Watercolor Resort, or a Rosemary Beach on the now-famous byway County Road 30A, there was Grayton Beach. The town was founded in 1890 and named for an army major Charles Gray, who had homesteaded here five years prior. The little beach town nestles up next to sand dune-filled, picturesque Grayton Beach State Park, which opened in 1968. The town, cherished by locals, existed in relative obscurity for a century until discovered by visitors to Seaside. The quaint Florida cracker beach cottage architectural style made famous by Seaside borrowed heavily from Grayton Beach, according to architects at Arquitectonica, the designers of Seaside's original town layout.

Grayton Beach is mostly residential, but for two blocks along Hotz Street (one block from the Gulf beach) there are a couple of art and surf shops, plus two restaurant/bars. The most iconic of these is the Red Bar, which opened on Super Bowl Sunday in 1995. Early on the

Sign at Grayton Beach, Grayton Beach

morning of February 13, 2019, the Red Bar burned to the ground, but owners Oli and Philippe Petit rebuilt and reopened ahead of schedule on July 15, 2020. Comfy overstuffed couches and musician posters and artwork cover the walls and ceilings that comprise the Red Bar's interior decorating. Their menu features "beach food" items like blackened grouper, shrimp, crawfish, seafood gumbo, crab cakes, and oysters, plus the requisite hamburgers. Its best known for hosting exceptional local rock and roll, blues, and jazz musicians. Regular house bands include the Red Bar Jazz Band and Dread Clampitt, a Louisiana funk-blues-rock band. Across the street you will find the somewhat quieter Chiringo, where classic cocktails and good bar food and pizza are served. My favorite Grayton Beach shop is The Zoo Gallery opened in 1979 by Chris and Roxie Wilson. It specializes in eclectic art, pottery, jewelry, home decor, and beach apparel. Tribe Kelly Surf Post next door features an exclusive line of beach and surf wear.

On the north edge of town, the friendly Hibiscus Guest House is comprised of a cluster of pine tree-shaded two-story houses with thirteen rooms and its own coffee shop, Hibiscus Cafe. I stayed in their Art Deco room, which had a few odd decorations—like a 1950s free-standing salon hair dryer. The room's screened front porch shares space with the coffee shop. The backyard garden can be used for small concerts or weddings.

DON'T MISS
The Zoo Gallery

House used in The Truman Show movie, Seaside

SEASIDE

Population not listed on census

*H*ighway 98 is the Florida Panhandle's main coastal east-west thruway. However, there is a detour just east of Destin, Walton County Road 30A, that dips down and winds along an idyllic coastline for twenty miles, where it follows a stretch of beach consistently rated among the most beautiful in the United States. The beach's blinding white sand consists of powdered quartz from the Appalachian Mountains, washed down over the eons. It squeaks when you walk on it.

In 1978, developer Robert Davis inherited eighty acres of undeveloped land nestled between Grayton Beach State Park and Seagrove along County Road 30A that had belonged to his grandfather. Davis envisioned a small beach town there with sand-and-shell walkways winding between pastel-shaded wood-frame bungalows—a reminder of his childhood summers spent on the beach at Seagrove. In 1981, he began building Seaside. At that time, he did not know it would evolve into the model for New Urbanism—the now much-heralded (and much copied) community design concept. New Urbanism seeks to promote the interaction of neighbors with pedestrian and bicycle-friendly pathways, and homes with front porches, all within walking distance of the town's commercial center. It is an old idea, reborn as something new.

Davis went to architects Andres Duany and Elizabeth Plater-Zyberk at Arquitectonica in Miami to help plan the layout of Seaside, and to draw up the town's building code. Seaside's first houses went up in 1982. Since then, the architectural world has praised it as a community that blends function, beauty, and a definitive sense of place like no other.

The popular 1998 movie *The Truman Show* (starring Jim Carrey) brought even more national attention to Seaside. Production designers needed the perfect, idyllic small town as a backdrop. They considered building a movie-set town from scratch on Paramount's lot, until someone showed them a picture of Seaside.

Although more crowded now than Robert Davis likely envisioned, a visit to Seaside and a stay in one of the cottages still evokes a summer vacation from decades past. From wandering through the open-air beach shops, to getting a hotdog at one of the food trailers in front of the town center, to crossing the sand dunes onto one of the finest powder-sand beaches in Florida, Seaside is a perfect place to decompress.

It's also a terrific place to sample some fine Florida Panhandle cuisine.

The tiny walk-up Shrimp Shack sits just behind a sand dune on the beach side of County Road 30A. I always order a basket of steamed, peppered peel-and-eat Gulf pink shrimp (or royal reds), and a tall fresh-squeezed lemonade, then kick back on their beach-sand-on-the-floor screened porch, and feast while watching beachgoers come and go. They also have oysters, and buttered Florida lobster tail, with steamed corn on the cob on the side. Somehow it all tastes just a little bit better when you are close enough to the Gulf to smell the salt in the air and feel the sea breeze.

The Shrimp Shack, Seaside

Right next to the Shrimp Shack is Seaside's first (and by my per-
sonal estimation, one of Florida's best) restaurants, Bud & Alley's.
Back in 1987, Seaside had yet to be "discovered." Robert Davis had
only been building for about six years when surfing buddies Dave
Rauschkolb and Scott Witcoski approached him about putting a
restaurant on the beach side of County Road 30A. They decided
to name it after Robert and his wife Daryl's dachshund, Bud, and
Scott's cat, Alley. In 2006, Scott sold his interest back to Dave, but
Alley's silhouette still joins Bud's on the sign. Bud & Alley's serves
steaks worthy of the best classic steakhouse, and some fabulous fresh
seafood. Their crab cakes are spectacular, and probably the most
popular dish, but I am partial to their seared diver scallops served
over grits with roasted peppers and bacon.

Cottages on the beach, Seaside

Great Southern Café overlooks the town circle and does a praise-worthy job of representing what I have dubbed "Panhandle Cuisine." It blends coastal Florida seafood with good-old southern Georgia, Alabama, and spicy New Orleans cooking styles. What you get are dishes like crab cakes and fried green tomatoes with roasted red pepper rémoulade, and grits à ya ya—shrimp and grits with spinach, applewood-smoked bacon, and Gouda cheese grits. Try their seafood celebration—a platter with grilled fresh-catch fish, blackened shrimp, fried oysters, and the best part: smoked corn tartar sauce.

Natchez Pavilion, Seaside

If you are a folk/acoustic/singer-songwriter music fan, then Seaside offers something else special. Every January they host the 30A Songwriters Festival. Over the years it has spread to include additional locations all along County Road 30A, but the heart of the festival is still in Seaside. It has evolved into an event that attracts both local and nationally known performers, and attendees get to see and hear them close in a variety of intimate venues.

DON'T MISS
The view of the quartz sand beach and the emerald
Gulf from the top of one of the walk-over pavilions

Main Street, Rosemary Beach

ROSEMARY BEACH

Population not listed on census

*A*t the opposite (east) end of County Road 30A the town of Rosemary Beach (founded in 1995) accomplishes some of the same walking-friendly resort community goals as Seaside. But instead of replicating the Florida cracker cottage style, Rosemary Beach is designed to appear more like an old colonial-style Caribbean/West Indies town. However, for me, it also feels very much like the Cinque Terre coastal villages in Italy that I visited a few years ago.

Like Seaside, cottage rentals are most popular, but there are other options as well. The Rosemary Beach Inn (it was called The Pensione Inn when I stayed there in 2012) is an elegant, intimate four-story, red-stucco boutique inn (eleven rooms). It was designed by Miami architectural firm Trelles Cabarrocas and completed in 2001. A decade later it underwent a major interior remodel. The inn anchors the south end of Rosemary Beach's quaint Main Street across from Western Green Park and a boardwalk that crosses the steep dunes onto the beach.

Across the street The Pearl hotel also offers luxurious accommodations, but in a larger venue (fifty-five rooms), plus a spa and rooftop bar and restaurant.

For fine dining I like Restaurant Paradis. It is known for its cast iron seared filet mignon, but my favorite is the skin-on grilled snapper.

For a more casual (but still delicious) eatery try the Summer Kitchen Café, on the sidewalk in front of the Rosemary Beach Inn.

DON'T MISS
Dinner at Restaurant Paradis

Mexico Beach General Store

MEXICO BEACH

Population: 1,114

*M*exico Beach's 2010 census population was 1,114 but that number likely dropped dramatically after Hurricane Michael nearly leveled the town in October 2018. When I drove through Mexico Beach exactly one year later, I was horrified to see the totality of the damage. It looked like the aftermath of an atomic explosion. In 2020, they made substantial progress and were on the verge of a grand comeback. The progress is rapid, and rebuilding will continue through the next year, so I have listed the Mexico Beach Community Development Council's and the City of Mexico Beach's websites in the appendix to access the most up-to-the-minute reports.

The Grady Market and The Consulate Suites, Apalachicola

APALACHICOLA

Population: 2,354

*P*erhaps no other Florida town has a history so deeply rooted in the sea as Apalachicola. The Apalachicola River has always been the town's lifeblood. In the 1820s, a large cotton shipping port was found here. From the 1860s to 1880s, sponge harvesting was big here—until the industry moved to Tarpon Springs. In the late 1880s, cypress, oak, and pine milling and shipping revitalized the town. And then in the 1920s it became the center of Florida's booming seafood industry.

It has always been known as Florida's oyster capitol. Historically, the town claimed that up to 90 percent of Florida's oysters had come from Apalachicola Bay's fertile waters. The clear, clean fresh water flowing from the Apalachicola River, combining with the salty Gulf of Mexico, created a perfect brackish balance for breeding in the shallow waters of Apalachicola Bay. Apalachicola oysters had a well-deserved reputation for being just a little sweeter, a little tastier. Sadly, that has been interrupted today.

Soda fountain, Apalachicola

Since the early 2000s, Apalachicola's oyster population has been on the decline. In the Appalachian Mountains, snowmelt and rainwater drain and filter over waterfalls, down mountain brooks, and eventually converge with major rivers like the Chattahoochee—which feeds Lake Lanier, just north of Atlanta, Georgia. Lake Lanier is one of Atlanta's primary sources of water. Atlanta's exploding population has been syphoning off more and more of that water, which ultimately feeds the Apalachicola River, and the bay's perfect brackish balance has been upset and can't produce oysters as abundantly as it once did. Lawsuits are being vigorously fought, but it's a battle that has gone on for a long time, and now Apalachicolans have decided to put a temporary five-year moratorium on oyster harvesting in the bay so that the oyster beds can have a chance to recover.

Still, Apalachicola has worked hard to maintain its status as a work-ing town whose livelihood has, for centuries, been tied to the sea. To-day, shrimping surpasses oystering as Apalachicola's dominant seafood business. The town continues to embrace and promote its heritage, drawing visitors to its restaurants, shops, galleries, bed and breakfasts, and inns in downtown.

Shrimp boat, Apalachicola

Despite the oyster harvesting moratorium, Apalachicola is still one of the best seafood restaurant locations in Florida. Two of its restaurants—Apalachicola Seafood Grill and the Owl Café have been there for more than one hundred years. And fresh oysters are still on every restaurant's menu. They are brought in from other locations up and down the coast.

The Owl Café sits one block from Apalachicola's waterfront, within sight of the shrimp boats docked along the river. Brothers John and Constantine Nichols opened their restaurant and boarding house here in 1908, to serve dockworkers. Back then the specialty of the house was "whole loaf," a hollowed-out loaf of fresh-baked bread filled with oysters. Today, the Owl Café offers an assortment of entrees like black grouper fillet sautéed with artichoke hearts and roasted garlic, and shrimp, chicken, and sausage jambalaya.

Apalachicola Seafood Grill, the town's oldest restaurant, opened in 1903. A vintage sign out front advertises the "World's Largest Fried Fish Sandwich"—that would be their half-pound Alaskan haddock sandwich. A weekly features menu favors southern and New Orleans dishes. My Cajun red beans and rice with blackened fish, shrimp, scallops, andouille sausage, and cornbread matched the best I have had in the French Quarter or New Orleans.

You'll have to go down the riverfront road a few blocks to get "up the creek," but finding Up the Creek Raw Bar will be a welcome reward. Patrons have a serene view of the Apalachicola River from a second-floor screened porch at this unpretentious cafe. I love their peel-and-eat shrimp and their oysters Moscow (with caviar).

Tamara's Café is another favorite. Tamara Suarez, a former television producer from Caracas, Venezuela, came to Apalachicola in 1998 and opened Tamara's Café Floridita on Avenue E in Apalachicola to rave reviews. Ten years later Tamara's Café moved two blocks away to Market Street, and Tamara turned over the reins to her daughter Marisa Getter and son-in-law Danny Itzkovitz. Tamara's Café's menu mixes native Venezuelan recipes with Caribbean and Florida dishes. Their pecan crusted grouper with jalapeno sauce as well as their paella are popular regular items, but on my last visit I tried a special: pan-fried whole lionfish over black beans and rice with fried plantains. Lionfish is a nonnative, invasive species to Florida's reefs, aggressively attacking native fish. The state of Florida has been actively campaigning to encourage catching this colorful, but destructive fish. Lionfish is light, flaky, and very flavorful.

Proving its perennial heartiness, Apalachicola always finds a way to reinvent itself. One of the town's most significant transitions kicked off in 1983 when out of towner Michael Koun came for a visit, and then just decided to stay. The Gibson Inn had been boarded up for some time, when Michael, with help from his brother Neal, bought the hotel for $90,000. Over the next two years they spent more than $1 million meticulously rebuilding and restoring it to its original turn-of-the-century grandeur. The Gibson Inn became the centerpiece of Apalachicola's burgeoning Historic District. When the National Trust for Historic Preservation published its coffee table book, *America Restored*, the Gibson Inn was one of the two Florida buildings featured.

The three-story, Victorian-style hotel with verandas wrapping around three of its sides and a cupola-capped tin roof, is the first thing you see after crossing the Highway 98 bridge over the Apalachicola River. It was the Franklin Inn when James Fulton Buck opened it in

1907. The name changed when sisters Annie and Mary Ellen Gibson bought it in 1923. These were grand years at the inn, but the opulence of that era declined with the passing decades. The Koun's best architectural reference was a collection of old photos taken in 1910. The photographer had spent that year taking pictures of Apalachicola and the surrounding area. Ultimately, several of his pictures were hung on the walls in the Gibson Inn's dining room.

Four-poster beds and other period antiques decorate each of the Gibson Inn's thirty-one guest rooms. Wooden slat blinds shade the windows. It took genuine artisans to build the lobby staircase—from scratch, using just a single surviving newel post as their guide. Ornately crafted woodwork can be found throughout the inn. The downstairs lobby, restaurant, and bar are finished in cypress. Adirondack rockers sit on the wrap-around verandas. My favorite room, the bar, has a grand nautical feel about it, as if it belonged on the *Titanic*. Just two weeks after the Gibson reopened in November 1985, Hurricane Kate slammed Florida's Panhandle. Undaunted, the Kouns kept the bar open and threw a Key Largo-style hurricane party. Humphrey Bogart would have approved.

In 2018, Michael Koun decided it was finally time to retire. He sold the hotel to brother and sister Steven Etchen and Katharine Couillard. On my most recent visit to Apalachicola in late 2020, I checked on the Gibson Inn and found that the new owners were in the middle of significant renovations and said they were shooting for a full reopen by early 2021.

Two other historic Apalachicola lodgings that I can recommend are the Consulate Suites and the Coombs House Inn.

The red brick J. E. Grady and Company Building at 76 Water Street was built in 1900 to replace a wooden 1884 building destroyed by a waterfront fire earlier that year. John Grady operated his ship chandlery business downstairs and rented upstairs office space to the French Consulate. In 1998, following a three-year renovation, the Grady Market—a clothing, art, and antiques store, opened downstairs, and the Consulate Suites opened upstairs. I stayed for a weekend in their 1,300 square foot Consul Suite. It has two bedrooms, two baths, a full kitchen, and a sweeping balcony that overlooks the shrimp and oyster boats docked on the riverfront. It has eleven foot stamped-tin ceilings, wide-plank pine floors, and comfortable furnishings that made me feel very much at home.

Some of the palatial homes in the neighborhood on the west side of downtown belonged to wealthy turn of the century lumber barons. Apalachicola lumber baron James Coombs built his house in 1905. Much of the interior was constructed from the hearty black cypress from which Coombs made his fortune—including the paneled walls in the foyer, the floors, the massive ceiling trusses, and most notably the grand staircase. Interior decorator Lynn Wilson, known for her renovations on historic hotels like The Biltmore in Coral Gables and The Vinoy in St. Petersburg, bought (with husband Bill) the Coombs House from the Coombs family in 1992. She spent several years rebuilding and restoring it and has turned it into a Victorian showcase. Camillia Hall, a separate reception room with a large garden yard and a gazebo is available for weddings and other special events. In 1998, Lynn and Bill bought and restored the 1911 Marks House, one block east.

Apalachicola has enough galleries and shops to keep the most ardent antique and art aficionados busy browsing for a week. One that visitors should not miss is the Richard Bickel Photography Gallery. Richard Bickel's exceptional black-and-white photographs spectacularly depict lives connected to the sea, not just in Apalachicola but also around the world.

A remarkably interesting chapter in Apalachicola's history is chronicled at the John Gorrie Museum State Park on 6th Street. John Gorrie was a physician who came to Apalachicola in 1833. He became a driving force in the community and served as mayor, postmaster, and city treasurer, and he founded the Trinity Episcopal Church. His most significant contribution, however, was his invention of the ice-making machine.

Dr. Gorrie treated yellow fever victims during the epidemic of 1841. He was convinced that if he could find a way to cool his patients down, they would have a better chance of recovering. In 1842, he began working on a design for a device that would lower the temperature of the air in a room. By 1844, he had constructed a machine that cooled air by removing heat through the rapid expansion of gases (the same basic principle used in air conditioners and refrigerators today). An unexpected byproduct of the process was machine-made sheets of ice. In 1851, Dr. Gorrie received a US patent for his ice-making invention.

The museum chronicles John Gorrie's remarkable life and accomplishments. On display is a replica of his ice machine, built according to the plans in his patent. The sad ending to Dr. Gorrie's tale is that until his death in 1855, he worked hard to market the machine but was completely unsuccessful. He died never knowing the enormous impact his invention would have on the world.

DON'T MISS
The Richard Bickel Photography Gallery

St. George Island beach

ST. GEORGE ISLAND

Population: 734

*T*hirty-mile-long St. George Island serves as a natural protective barrier for Apalachicola Bay. Its sand dunes, stilt houses, dog-friendly beaches, and proximity to Apalachicola make it a popular vacation destination. Seclusion is the main attraction here. Most visitors rent one of the beach houses by the week or the month. Do not come here if you're looking for a lot of excitement or nightlife. This is more of a sit-in-a-beach-chair-and-read-a-paperback kind of place.

Although the atmosphere is laid-back, there are places to eat and shop on St. George. What was originally Eddy Teach's Raw Bar has changed hands and is now Paddy's Raw Bar. This is a classic open-air oyster and beer bar on St. George's bay side and it's usually the first place I head when I'm on the island. For more great fresh seafood and a Gulf-front view try the Blue Parrot Oceanfront Café. There is no shortage of shops on St. George but do not miss Island Dog Beach and

Paddy's Raw Bar

Surf Shop—a great spot for beach art and jewelry, plus apparel for beachgoers and their dogs.

There is a new landmark on St. George Island that replaces an old historic one. Little St. George Island, just west and separated from the main island by Government Cut Pass, had been home to one of three versions of the Cape St. George Lighthouse since 1833. The last one, built in 1852, suffered a century and a half of hurricane battering. In 1995, Hurricane Opal washed out a significant amount of its foundation, leaving the lighthouse precariously tilted to one side, subsequently deactivating it from service. In 2002, the base was rebuilt, and the tower righted, but it was not long before erosion put it in jeopardy again. In October 2005, it finally gave in and collapsed. A local group of diligent volunteers formed the St. George Lighthouse Association and took on a massive salvage project, saving more than twenty-two thousand of its bricks to be reused to build a new lighthouse. Using plans from the 1852 lighthouse found at the National Archives, the group built an identical one, largely from salvaged materials, on main St. George Island—where everyone could see it. The new lighthouse opened in December 2008. If you are in fairly good shape, hike the ninety-two

St. George Lighthouse

steps to the top for a spectacular view. Putting it on St. George Island was a stroke of genius. It looms on the horizon welcoming visitors as they cross the bridge, giving the island a magnificent icon.

DON'T MISS

The hike to the top of the St. George Lighthouse

Carrabelle Police Station

CARRABELLE

Population: 2,820

A half-hour east of Apalachicola, you will pass through the town of Carrabelle, at the mouth of the Carrabelle River. In the late 1800s, it was a lumber-shipping town with several large sawmills. Today, it is a sport and commercial fishing community that claims it had the "World's Smallest Police Station" in a phone booth in the middle of town, alongside Highway 98. Today, visitors can take pictures in front of a replica. In the early 1960, Carrabelle's police department consisted of one outdoor telephone box, but people kept using it for unofficial business. When an old phone booth became available from St. Joe Telephone Company in 1963, the town commandeered it for their police department.

Carrabelle Junction

For a good breakfast or lunch try the Carrabelle Junction coffee shop/diner right in the heart of downtown Carrabelle.

Sopchoppy Railroad Depot Museum

SOPCHOPPY

Population: 492

*I*t is hard to resist taking the detour up County Road 319, off Highway 98, just to pass through the town of Sopchoppy. It is an odd name that is likely a mispronunciation of two Creek Indian words that describe the river that flows past the town: "sokhe" and "chapke," meaning "twisted" and "long." Or, the Creek Indians might have been describing something else—worms. Worms have put Sopchoppy on the map. The variety that breeds in soil here is particularly fat and long—a fisherman's dream. The method used to bring them to the surface is called "gruntin'." The worm grunter's tools are a wooden stake and a flattened iron paddle. Something amazing happens when a grunter drives a stake into the ground and grinds the iron paddle against it: worms come wriggling out of the ground by the hundreds. The grunting noise that the grinding makes sends a vibration through the ground that makes the little slimy guys crazy. On the second weekend in April, Sop-

48

choppy holds its annual Worm Gruntin' Festival and Worm Grunter's Ball. There is lots of good food and live entertainment. A Worm Queen is chosen as well. The highlight, however, is the Worm Gruntin' Contest, which sees who can grunt up the most worms in fifteen minutes. In 1972, Charles Kuralt brought worm gruntin' to the attention of the outside world, much to the chagrin of locals. Following that publicity, the US Forest Service began requiring a permit and charging fees for gruntin'. In recent years, the Worm Gruntin' Festival has evolved into somewhat of a music festival, attracting top local and regional bands that play blue-grass, classic country, and something called swamp jazz.

Visitors that take that detour to Sopchoppy will feel like they have stepped back in time when they walk in to the Sopchoppy Grocery, an authentic country general store. At the other end of the building the tiny boutique Sand and Soul Designs has great hand-made jewelry and driftwood artwork.

Sopchoppy Grocery

Across the street the circa 1891 Sopchoppy Railroad Depot is now home to the Sopchoppy Depot Museum. This was originally a depot for the Carrabelle, Tallahassee and Georgia Railroad, which was subsequently acquired by the Georgia, Florida, and Alabama Railroad, and may be the only surviving depot for that rail line. It was restored by the city in 2010.

DON'T MISS
The Worm Gruntin' Festival if you
are there the second weekend in April

Swimming at Wakulla Springs Lodge at Edward Ball/Wakulla Springs State Park

WAKULLA SPRINGS

Population not listed on census

*W*akulla Springs claims the title of having the largest and deepest spring in the world. Its waters are so clear that the bottom—185 feet down—can usually be seen from the surface. Universal Studios chose Wakulla Springs as the filming location for its 1954 sci-fi/horror classic *The Creature from the Black Lagoon* because of its exceptionally clear waters.

It has also been the site of numerous significant archaeological excavations. Divers discovered a complete mastodon skeleton at the bottom of the spring in 1935. The mastodon now stands, reconstructed, in the Museum of Florida History in Tallahassee.

All manner of creatures thrive in Edward Ball Wakulla Springs State Park. Alligators, deer, raccoons, and even a few bears live there. But Wakulla Spring's most famous creature was Old Joe, an eleven-foot-long alligator. Old Joe was first spotted in the mid-1930s while the Wakulla Springs Lodge was being built. Over the decades he gained a reputation as a docile old gator that never bothered anyone. But in 1966 someone shot and killed him. Old Joe was estimated to be two hundred years old. Carl Buchheister, then president of the Audubon Society, offered a $5,000 reward for information that would lead to the arrest of the gunman, but none was ever found. Old Joe was stuffed and lives on in a glass case in the Wakulla Springs Lodge lobby. The plaque in front of the display reads, "Old Joe's first and only cage."

Edward Ball was the brother-in-law of Alfred I. DuPont. One of Ball's proudest achievements was the construction of the Wakulla Springs Lodge in 1937. He was also the executor and trustee of DuPont's sizable estate and trust. Ball built a banking, telephone, railroad, and paper and box manufacturing empire out of the trust—worth an estimated $33 million in 1935 when DuPont died. Ball had grown that into more than $2 billion by the time he passed away in 1981, at age ninety-three.

The twenty-seven-room lodge is essentially the same today as it was in the 1930s. Ball insisted that it always continue to reflect that era and that it never become so exclusive that it would not be affordable to "common folks."

Wakulla Springs Lodge reminds me of a palatial Spanish hacienda. The first thing that caught my eye when I walked into the lobby was the

Wakulla Springs Lodge

cypress ceiling beams with Aztec-style hand-painted designs on them. Blue and gold Spanish tiles frame the entranceway. The checkerboard floors are colored mauve and gray made from Tennessee marble tiles. A giant fireplace, made from native limestone and trimmed in marble, dominates the far wall. Just past Old Joe's case is the soda fountain shop. There is no bar in the Wakulla Springs Lodge. Instead, Ball, who was fond of ginger whips (ice cream, ginger ale, and whipped cream), had a sixty-foot-long solid marble soda fountain counter installed.

The lodge and grounds sit on the north bank of the springs. From the top of the twenty-foot-high diving platform above the springs, you can look down into the astonishingly clear water and see bream and bass schooling on the bottom. It is no wonder that Hollywood came to this location, not only to film *Creature from the Black Lagoon*, but also several *Tarzan* features, *Around the World Under the Sea*, and *Airport 77*.

DON'T MISS

Getting a ginger whip at the soda
fountain at the Wakulla Springs Lodge

Riverside Café, St. Marks

ST. MARKS

Population: 324

*D*rive twenty miles south on Highway 363 from Tallahassee, until it ends, and you will find yourself in St. Marks, which is at the confluence of the Wakulla and St. Marks rivers. Today, fishing, kayaking, bicycling, and eating oysters are the main reasons people come here, but St. Marks has a long, rich history.

In the 1600s, Spanish missionaries built the Mission San Marcos de Apalache. In 1680, Spanish troops built Fort San Marcos de Apalache, which throughout the next two hundred years was alternately rebuilt and occupied by Spanish, French, British, and eventually American troops. Remains of the fort can still be seen at its site just off State Road 363.

By the early 1800s, St. Marks had become an important shipping port. The Tallahassee Railroad Company built one of the state's first railroads, from Tallahassee to St. Marks, in 1837. Mules pulled the cars. Today, that route has been converted into the Tallahassee to St. Marks Historic Trail, a Rails-to-Trails project.

The St. Marks National Wildlife Refuge, just four miles east (go back up to Highway 98 then take State Road 59 south), is home to a wide variety of coastal woodlands wildlife—everything from anhingas to alligators. The St. Marks Lighthouse, at the south end of State Road 59 in the wildlife refuge, was built in 1829. This eighty-foot-tall stucco-over-brick structure had to be moved back from the encroaching sea in 1841. Confederate troops were stationed here during the Civil War.

Posey's Oyster Bar had been a St. Marks icon since 1929, and rightfully belongs in the Florida Oyster Bar Hall of Fame. Sadly in 2005, Hurricane Dennis flooded St. Marks and closed Posey's forever. Today, the Riverside Café picks up the mantle serving fresh oysters and seafood baskets. and lively local entertainment can be found there, right next door to the old Posey's location.

If burgers are your preference, go across the street to the Cooter Stew Café. By the way, they do not actually serve cooter (slang for turtle) stew, but they did assign turtle names to their various burgers.

If you intend to stay for more than a day try the Sweet Magnolia Inn, within walking distance of the riverfront. Sweet Magnolia has seven spacious and comfortable suites and is within easy walking distance to the riverfront.

Cooter Stew Café, St. Marks

The Suwannee River, White Springs

WHITE SPRINGS

Population: 766

*I*n 1935, the Florida state legislature chose Stephen Foster's melody "Old Folks at Home," better known as "Way Down Upon the Suwannee River," as the official state song. Ironically, Foster never once set foot in the state of Florida, much less on the banks of the Suwannee. (It is likely that, except for a single trip to New Orleans, Foster never ventured south of Cincinnati, Ohio.) In his original draft of the song, which was ultimately published in 1851, he wrote, "Way down upon the Pee Dee River," but it just did not ring true for him. (The Pee Dee River is in South Carolina, and he had never been there either.) With the aid of an atlas and the assistance of his brother, Morrison, Stephen tried inserting a variety of river names into his song, including Yazoo. None sounded right until he hit on Suwannee.

White Springs is home to the Stephen Foster Folk Culture Center and State Park, a 250-acre park and memorial to the songwriter found alongside the Suwannee River. It opened in 1950, ninety-nine years after "Way Down Upon the Suwannee River" was first published.

In the 1700s, White Springs was sacred ground to the local Indians. They felt that the spring, which spills into the Suwannee, had special curative powers. Indian warriors wounded in battle were not attacked when they came to the springs to recuperate. After settlers moved here in the early 1800s, word of the water's medicinal properties spread. Eventually, developers built hotels and a posh health resort and spa around the springs. President Teddy Roosevelt was a regular visitor.

Today, there are few remaining signs of White Springs' resort days. Of the original dozen hotels, the only one that remains is the 1903 Telford Hotel, a copper-roofed, three-story, brick and stone structure in the center of town. In its day, the Telford hosted Presidents Taft and Roosevelt, J. P. Morgan, John D. Rockefeller, George Firestone, and Thomas Edison. Sadly, today it is boarded up, although still standing.

Highway 136 crosses a deep gorge carved by the Suwannee River just before rolling into the tiny community of White Springs. It is a dramatic vantage point worth stopping to take in. Nearby American Canoe Adventures rents and sells kayaks and canoes and organizes trips on the Suwannee. Increasingly, year-round visitors are enjoying the beauty of the river from the vantage point of a canoe or kayak.

Just up the road is the entrance to the Stephen Foster Folk Culture Center and State Park. Your first stop should be the Stephen Foster Museum, housed in a large southern plantation house with six giant two-story white columns on its front porch. The north wing has a collection of old, unusual, and

Bell tower at Stephen Foster Folk Culture Center and State Park, White Springs

ornate pianos. One of the most interesting is an 1875 Steinway duplex scale piano with six tiered rows of keys. Another is a small upright Frederick Haupt/Leipzig that Stephen Foster had played regularly at the home of one of his neighbors in Pittsburgh. Morrison Foster's fold-out office desk and chair sit against one wall. A plaque describes the desk as the one that Morrison and Stephen sat at while studying the at-las for an appropriate river name for "Old Folks at Home." The center hall contains dioramas that portray scenes described in Foster's most popular songs. In the south wing there are more pianos and a ten-foot-tall Howard Chandler Christy painting of Stephen Foster from 1948.

The centerpiece of the park is the ninety-seven-bell carillon in the two-hundred-foot-tall brick bell tower built in 1958. The bells are of a tubular construction rather than of the more conventional cast type. The carillon plays a program of Stephen Foster tunes on an electronic music roll like a player piano's, and sometimes guest carillonneurs play. Across from the bell tower, in the Craft Square, artisans demonstrate their various centuries-old crafting skills like blacksmithing and wood carving.

The Stephen Foster Folk Culture Center and State Park holds special events throughout the year, but the biggest is the annual three-day Florida Folk Festival, held on the Friday, Saturday, and Sunday preceding Memorial Day. It is one of the oldest (since 1952) and most popular folk music and folk craft festivals in the country.

Near the park entrance, a wooden walkway leads to a scenic over-look on the banks of the Suwannee. The gorge is nearly one hundred feet deep. The river flows past at a fairly good clip. Limestone boulders hold up the bank on this side of the river, and tall cypress trees, thick with moss, lean out over the water.

The name Suwannee has two possible sources. In the 1700s, the river was called the Little San Juan, in acknowledgment of the San Juan De Guacara Mission located on its banks. Local dialect may have corrupted San Juan into San wanee. The more likely possibility is that the name is derived from the Creek Indian word suwani, which means "echo." This makes sense because the steep walls of the gorge formed by the river do create a good echo.

The Fairbanks House Bed & Breakfast, Fernandina Beach

FERNANDINA BEACH

Population: 13,169

*T*hirteen-mile-long Amelia Island anchors Florida's far northeast corner. To reach it from the south you need to cross the St. Johns River inlet via the ferry at Mayport. From the north it can be reached by bridge. The plush Ritz-Carlton Amelia Island Resort, where the world-renowned classic car Amelia Island Concours d'Elegance takes place each March, sits at the south end of the island. The historic town of Fernandina Beach occupies the north end.

Downtown Fernandina Beach received designation as a National Register of Historic Places Historic District in 1973, and that was expanded in 1987 to what today encompasses about fifty blocks. Beginning in 1977, Fernandina's main street from 8th Street down to Front Street underwent an extensive makeover. It was part of Atlantic Avenue at that time, but the city decided that along with its renovation, for the historic section they would revert to the street's original pre-turn of the century name, Centre Street. Now gas lamp-style streetlights stand over brick crosswalks at each intersection, and sidewalks wind around oak trees and benches, making it very pedestrian-friendly. Business owners followed suit and renovated their buildings to match the street's new look. Credit for this transformation goes to the Fernandina Restoration Foundation, spearheaded by native resident and attorney Buddy Jacobs. Other Florida small towns have done similar work in more recent years, but Fernandina was one of the first, and they continue with the process today.

Eight different country's flags have flown over Amelia Island. French Huguenot Jean Ribault was the first European to set foot on the island (which he named "Isle De Mai") in 1562. This did not sit well with the Spanish, since Juan Ponce De León had claimed all Florida for Spain when he landed near present-day St. Augustine in 1513. So, in 1565, the Spanish sent Pedro Menendez de Avile to kick the French out of Florida and off Isle De Mai, with great success. They renamed the island "Santa Maria."

Later, there were invasions from the British—the earliest around 1702, but the island remained a Spanish territory until the first Treaty of Paris ended the Seven Years' War in 1763, and Britain returned Cuba to Spain in exchange for all of Florida. British general James Oglethorpe gave Santa Maria its new name, "Amelia," after the daughter of King George II. But the British underestimated the unfriendliness of the Indians, how much swampland there was, and how many mosquitoes, snakes, and alligators there were in Florida, so twenty years later England traded Florida back to Spain. In 1812, a small group of US patriots who called themselves the "Patriots of Amelia Island," overthrew the Spanish on the island and raised their own flag for a very brief time. In the summer of 1817, Sir Gregor MacGregor seized control of Spain's recently completed island fortification, Fort San Carlos. MacGregor flew his "Green Cross" flag but withdrew a short time later. A few months after that, French pirate Luis Aury raided the island and raised the Mexican flag—unbeknownst to Mexico, by the way. By December of 1817, US troops had taken over the island and were holding it in trust for the Spanish. In 1819, Spain and the United States signed a treaty: the United States got Florida in exchange for taking over $5 million in debt that Spain owed the citizens of the United States. It took two years to iron out all the details, but in 1821 the United States officially acquired Florida and consequently Amelia Island from Spain. In April 1861, Confederate troops occupied Fort Clinch at the north end of the island, but federal troops regained it a year later.

It was the railroad that turned Fernandina into a thriving place in the mid- and late nineteenth century. Originally, the town was located about three-quarters of a mile north of its present location. In the 1850s, David Yulee promised its residents prosperity if they would agree to move the community south, closer to his railroad terminus and port on the Amelia River. They agreed, and Fernandina's golden era began. In a short time, luxury steamers from the north began bringing wealthy vacationers to Amelia Island. Luxury hotels were constructed, both in town and on the beach. Palatial Victorian mansions went up on the streets north and south of Centre Street. Fernandina's naturally deep harbor allowed large ships into its port, and the lumber, cotton, turpentine, phosphate, and naval stores shipping and rail transport industries boomed. The Spanish-American War in 1898 generated even more shipping and rail business. Not only had Yulee kept his promise, but the results of his efforts exceeded everyone's expectations. For nearly fifty years, the new Fernandina was both a world-renowned resort and a center of commerce.

During this time, Standard Oil mogul and railroad tycoon Henry Flagler set his sights on Florida. In the 1880s, he began building resort hotels along Florida's east coast. As they were completed, he would string them together with his railroad. But Flagler bypassed Amelia Island, choosing not to connect with Yulee's railroad line. As a result, by the early 1900s Fernandina's tourist trade had shifted south to St. Augustine (to Flagler's Ponce de Leon Hotel) and to West Palm Beach (to Flagler's Royal Poinciana Hotel). Fernandina's flourish fizzled almost as rapidly as it had begun. Had Flagler chosen to bring his rail line through Fernandina, Amelia Island may well have become a modern metropolis. The Victorian-era homes and Centre Street brick buildings would then, no doubt, have been replaced with larger and more contemporary structures. In a roundabout way we can probably thank Henry Flagler for his part in saving the historic Fernandina that exists today.

There is more history to be found at Fort Clinch State Park on the northern tip of the island. The road through the park turns north off Atlantic Boulevard, a few blocks in from the ocean, then winds through a tunnel of myrtle oaks. Thirty-foot-high sand dunes separate the road from the beach. Fort Clinch—named for General Duncan Lamont Clinch, who served during the Second Seminole War (1835–1842)—was built in 1847 (additional construction continued for several decades) by the United States to protect Cumberland Sound. No battles were fought here, but it was occupied by Confederate troops in 1861 and 1862 during the Civil War. Federal troops reoccupied it following General Robert E. Lee's order to withdraw. It was activated again during the Spanish-American War in 1898. Captain J. F. Honeycutt was given its command, but he found the fort half buried in sand and overgrown with cactus and weeds. Worse than that, the fort was infested with rattlesnakes. Honeycutt's crew spent most of their brief tenure restoring the facility to livable and usable condition. The state of Florida bought the fort in 1935 and began restoring it. Its last military occupation came during World War II, when the Coast Guard set up a station here.

Today, Fort Clinch appears as it did during the Civil War. Park rangers dress as Union soldiers and reenact the daily lives of soldiers garrisoned here in 1864. On one of my visits, I found a group of visitors in the infirmary (in the interior compound) who were listening to an actor portraying a Civil War medic describe his duties and his surgical tools: "These are my joint separators. It's much easier to do amputations with these than it is with a saw." I'm not sure I could have stomached medical attention during Civil War times.

The surrounding walls of the five-sided fort are four-and-a-half-foot-thick brick with tabby (concrete and shell) reinforcement. Ramps lead from inside the fort to the tops of the walls. Ten enormous cannons, placed atop the two walls that face the water, guard the sound. From here visitors have a terrific view across the sound, of shrimping fleets heading out to the Atlantic, and beyond that of Cumberland Island, Georgia.

Residential Fernandina is filled with grand nineteenth-century Victorian mansions—many restored, and some now elegant bed and breakfasts. Great examples can be seen on South 7th Street and on North 6th Street. The Bailey House (once a bed and breakfast, now a private residence) at the northeast corner of Ash and South 7th Street is a beautiful example of Queen Anne architecture. Its two octagonal turrets, one large and one small, extend to the third floor. Some of the windows are stained glass. Completed in 1895, it took steamship company agent Effingham Bailey three years to build. The house remained in the Bailey family until the early 1960s. The C. W. Lewis "Tabby" House, directly across from the Bailey House on South Seventh Street, was built in 1885. Tabby, a poured mixture of oyster shells and cement, was used to build the walls. The rough texture does not accept paint well, so it remains in its natural brownish-gray state.

The grandest of mansions in Fernandina Beach is the Fairbanks House, a colossal four-story Italianate estate. Considered by many to be the one of the finest and best-preserved examples of Italianate architecture in Florida, it has all the identifying characteristics of that nineteenth-century style: tall narrow windows—some with arches, decorative roof eaves and brackets, decorative porch columns, elaborately detailed molding and trim, ornate brick chimneys, and a fourth-floor tower.

The Fairbanks House was not for sale when Bill and Theresa Hamilton found it in 1997. They point out that the advantage of looking at bed and breakfast properties that are not currently for sale is that you're more apt to be looking at ones that are in tip-top shape. Nelson and Mary Smelker had owned and operated it as a bed and breakfast for about three years. Prior to that, it had been rented out as apartments.

"The Smelkers did an extraordinary job with this place," Theresa told me the first time I met her in 1998. "Mary Smelker did every bit of the decorating that you see. She made the bedspreads, the window treatments; she reupholstered the furniture with matching fabrics!" The Smelkers also did extensive remodeling and landscaping. They added a swimming pool, a parking area, additional bathrooms, plus they purchased three adjacent cottages and added them to the inn.

It met all of Bill and Theresa's criteria, and it was fully operational. "And we were charmed," adds Theresa, "by both the Fairbanks

House, and the town of Fernandina—a wonderful place, filled with genuinely friendly people. We fell in love with all of it."

The grounds take up half of the block between Beech and Cedar Streets. There are nine rooms in the main house—two are suites, plus the three cottages, for a total of eleven rooms. The Tower Suite (the only room on the third floor) has two bedrooms, a living room, and a kitchen. A ladder leads up into the fifteen-foot-high glass-enclosed fourth-floor tower. The house has ten fireplaces. The living room fireplace is framed by tiles that depict Shakespearean characters, and the dining room fireplace has Aesop's Fables characters on its tiles. The floors are heart of pine, and the grand staircase is built from Honduran mahogany.

Confederate Civil War major, former state senator, historian, educator, and one of the founders of the University of the South in Sewanee, Tennessee, George Rainsford Fairbanks was lured to Fernandina in 1879 by railroad magnate and then-senator David Yulee, to run Fernandina's *Florida Mirror* newspaper.

Fairbanks built his house in 1885—at the height of Fernandina's golden era. He commissioned the home's design to famous architect Robert Schuyler. It was the town's most extravagant residence. It had indoor plumbing, a telephone, a cistern for collecting rainwater, and a dumbwaiter for lifting firewood from the basement to the upper floors. Yes, the Fairbanks House has a basement—a Florida rarity.

Local lore claims that Fairbanks had built the house as a surprise for his wife. Reportedly, Mrs. Fairbanks was not pleasantly surprised. "Too ostentatious," she was rumored to have proclaimed—and the house became known as "Fairbanks' Folly." Theresa was not convinced that that is how it really happened. She explained to me, "Just look at the size of these closets—and the number. Look at the layout of the kitchen. A woman was involved in the design of this house, and I think it's likely that it was Mrs. Fairbanks."

When I visited in 2000, I stayed in one of the cottages—a quaint one-bedroom with a king size bed, a kitchenette, and a bathroom with both a shower and a Jacuzzi tub.

Breakfast at the Fairbanks House is a marvelous treat. We ate on the verandah, overlooking the pool—banana sorbet with kiwi fruit sauce and orange-pecan French toast.

I was delighted to be greeted by Theresa and Bill Hamilton once again when I returned to the Fairbanks House in 2019. This time I stayed in the third floor Tower Suite. It is the only room on the third floor. A ladder leads to the fourth floor glass-enclosed tower, which is furnished with an antique French game table and chairs. The view across the rooftops of Fernandina's Victorian Mary-Poppins-like neighborhood is breathtaking.

Five years before his death, George Fairbanks and his granddaughter watched from the tower as the southern horizon lit up from the blaze of the great 1901 fire that leveled downtown Jacksonville, more than forty miles away.

A couple blocks around the corner from the Fairbanks House sits mint-green Addison on Amelia Island Bed & Breakfast. It consists of three houses—one old and two new. The original house was built in 1876 for local merchant Frank Simmons. The other two structures were built in 1996 and are perfect architectural matches with the original house. All three surround a lush garden courtyard with brick walkways and a fountain centerpiece.

No two of the fourteen rooms are alike, but all are luxurious. Most have whirlpool baths, and some have canopied and four-poster beds. My room, number 12, overlooks the courtyard. It is spacious and comfortable and has the largest bathtub I have ever seen in a bed and breakfast.

Bob and Shannon Tidball had owned the Addison since 2007, and they were gracious hosts when I stayed there. I asked Bob about the Addison's distinctive mint-green exterior color. He told me that it is actually Sherwin-Williams "Greensleeves." "I keep dozens of cans of it," he said. Since the house is a historic structure, the color had to be approved by Fernandina's historical commission. Bob explained that keeping the historic house (and the new additions) painted and properly maintained was a perpetual process.

In 2017, Lisa and Ron West purchased the Addison and have continued the inn's tradition of elegant and relaxing lodging.

Purportedly, Fernandina's Florida House Inn was Florida's oldest continuously operating inn, at least until 2010 when it changed hands and was closed for a while for renovations. It was built in 1857 by David Yulee of the Florida Railroad Company. A few years later during the Civil War the town was occupied briefly by Union troops, and they used it as a barracks. After the war, the Florida House Inn was purchased by an army major who had been stationed at Fort Clinch (on the north tip of Amelia Island). Over the decades the inn's dignitary guest list would include various Carnegies, Rockefellers, and DuPonts, Henry Ford, and Jose Marti. Stan Laurel and Oliver Hardy stayed at the inn as well. Today, there are sixteen rooms, all furnished with period antiques, and the Florida House Inn has become a popular wedding venue.

Fronting Centre Street you will find the graceful Amelia Island Williams House. It was built in 1856 and is named for surveyor Marcellus Williams, who purchased it in 1859. The Williams family remained in the house for a century, except for one interruption. Union troops took over Fernandina for a while during the Civil War, so Williams moved his family to Central Florida during the occupation. The Union army used the house as an infirmary. Antebellum folk-Victorian best describes its style. Elaborate gingerbread on the porch columns (added to the house in 1880 and designed by Robert Schuyler—the same New York architect who designed the Fairbanks House) are its signature motif. An ornate wrought iron fence surrounds the property. In 1993, Dick Flitz and Chris Carter bought the house and turned it into a bed and breakfast. Current owners Bryon and Deborah McCutchen purchased it from them. There are five rooms in the main house and five more in the adjacent Hearthstone Cottage and Carriage House.

East of town, on the beach, the Elizabeth Pointe Lodge resembles a grand old Cape-Cod-style mansion, with its shingle sides and gambrel roof, but it was built in 1992. A stand of sea oats on a low bluff are all that separate it from the wide beach and the Atlantic Ocean. There are twenty rooms in the main lodge and five more in the adjacent Ocean House and Miller Cottage. The main lodge sits on stilts, so the lobby, breakfast room, and library/sitting room are on the second floor. The decor here is distinctly nautical/New England, particularly in the lobby, with its huge stone fireplace, wicker chairs with overstuffed cushions, and library shelves filled with books. Panoramic windows of-

Palace Saloon, Florida's oldest.

fer a spectacular sunset view. I stayed in the ocean-facing upstairs suite in their adjacent Ocean House, with its own patio and a boardwalk that leads through the sand dunes to the beach.

Another Fernandina "Florida's oldest" is the Palace Saloon, at the northwest corner of 2nd and Centre Streets. The Palace is likely Florida's oldest operating saloon. German immigrant Louis Hirth bought the building and opened the bar in 1903. It had been constructed in 1878 as a haberdashery. Even if you are a teetotaler, you should stop in and see this historic establishment. There were plenty of bars in Fernandina around the turn of the century, but the Palace was considered the "ship captain's bar"—a hangout for the elite. Push open the old-west-style swinging doors and you will step back in time. It is easy to picture Vanderbilts, Rockefellers, and DuPonts toasting their good fortune alongside sea captains and sailors on shore leave in here. The sixteen-foot-high ceilings are ornately formed from pressed tin—popular in nineteenth-century architecture but a lost art today. In 1905, Hirth added the forty-foot-long hand-carved mahogany bar with mahogany caryatids supporting the mirror behind the bar. In

1999, a fire burned much of the Palace's interior, but after a two-year restoration, it reopened in 2001. Thankfully, the mahogany bar and its original fixtures were saved.

Great restaurants abound in Fernandina. It is hard to pick a favorite, but I keep going back to Espana. Chef Roberto Pestana and his wife Marina came to Fernandina and opened España in 2004. Roberto had been operating the Pompano Beach restaurant that his Portuguese-born parents had opened two decades prior. España is very much a traditional Portuguese- (and Spanish-) style restaurant. Their extensive tapas menu features many seafood offerings, like *gambas al ajillo* (shrimp in garlic sauce), *almejas borrachas* (drunken clams) with onions and garlic in white wine sauce, and of course ceviche. Their authentic Portuguese and Spanish seafood entrees include, among others, *pargo olé*: spicy snapper with shrimp and roasted poblano and *mero a Lisboeta* (grouper Lisbon), topped with tomato, onion, capers, and olives, the dish that I feasted on the last time I was there. Their specialties, however, are *paella marinera* (seafood paella) with clams, shrimp, lobster, scallops, mussels, calamari, plus whatever the fresh fish of the day is; and *calderada de mariscos* (Portuguese fisherman stew). Both are prepared to order and serve four or more people.

Fernandina is one of Florida's best fresh seafood locations. The modern commercial shrimping industry had its beginnings here. Traditionally, shrimp had been caught using two boats and a seine net. But in 1913, Billy Corkum, a Gloucester, Massachusetts, fisherman, came to Fernandina and adapted an otter trawl net: a large bag-shaped net for shrimping that's towed behind a single boat. It dramatically improved efficiency and is the method almost all commercial shrimpers use today.

Two of my Fernandina seafood favorites are Timoti's Seafood Shak and The Crab Trap, both a block off Centre Street.

Local restaurateur and former city commissioner Tim Poynter opened Timoti's in 2012 and put local chef Brian McCarthy in charge of the kitchen. "Local" seems to be Timoti's theme. They get their seafood fresh from Fernandina's docks every morning. I am partial to their tuna poke and lobster roll.

The Crab Shack is in the historic Sydel Building, named for the two brothers who built it in 1877. It was one of the first brick buildings constructed in Fernandina after a fire swept through the town in 1876. Owner Richard Germano opened The Crab Shack in 1979, and still runs it today along with his daughter Holly. These people really know their crabs. Steamed Dungeness crab, stone crab claws, blue crabs—they have it all—and their fluffy hush puppies are terrific too.

If it is possible to pull off casual and elegant at the same time, Joe's 2nd Street Bistro does it. Joe's occupies a quaint 1903 Charleston single-style house with a courtyard alongside and a picket fence out front. Chef Ricky Pigg and his wife Mari bought it in 2012. Their seafood bouillabaisse, with lobster claw meat, shrimp, deep-water scallops, little neck clams, and fish, might be the best I have ever had.

DON'T MISS
The historic Palace Saloon

Historic Castillo de San Marcos National Monument, St. Augustine

ST. AUGUSTINE

Population: 15,415

I have tried to confine my list of small towns in this edition to those with populations of less than 15,000, but I had to make one exception. St. Augustine just squeaks over with 15,415, but I could not leave this town out.

Florida's northeast coast bills itself as the "First Coast," and for good reason. Although Christopher Columbus is routinely credited with "discovering" America, he never got any farther than the Bahamas and the Caribbean. Columbus never actually set foot on mainland America. It was another European explorer (who had sailed with Columbus on earlier expeditions), Spaniard Juan Ponce de Leon, who first landed on Florida's beaches on April 2, 1513. There is some argument about the exact location where de Leon landed. Depending on which historian you talk to, it was either a bit north of where St. Augustine is now, or just south of Daytona, at Ponce Inlet, or maybe just south of Cape Canaveral near Melbourne.

Ponce de Leon was ostensibly searching for gold and pearls, but he was also obsessed with finding something else: a special spring rumored to produce water with youth-giving properties. This spring, the "Fountain of Youth," was supposed to have been on the island of Bimini in the Bahamas (Bimini was the old name for Andros, not the Bimini we know today). After doing some exploring, he figured out that he had found a place too big to be an island, and promptly claimed possession of the new land in the name of King Ferdinand of Spain. It was Eastertime and the flowers and trees that he found there reminded him of Spain's "Pasque Florida," The Feast of Flowers, so he named it Florida.

When it comes to old and historic in Florida, one would be hard pressed to find more than in St. Augustine. Not only is this the oldest city in Florida, but also the oldest continuously occupied city in the United States. In 1565, King Philip II of Spain sent Pedro Menendez de Avile to run the French out of what is now northeastern Florida. Menendez and his troops first sighted the coast on August 28, The Feast Day of St. Augustine, and named the spot where they landed and settled eleven days later in that saint's honor. The settlement grew into a village, and eventually, a city.

Many of the historic markers seen on St. Augustine's buildings in-dicate construction just after the turn of the eighteenth century, which coincides with a rebuilding period following a 1702 battle that left most of the city in charred ruin. Historians believe that the oldest house, the Gonzalez-Alvarez House on St. Francis Street, was constructed some-time between then and 1727. The St. Augustine Historical Society has owned and operated the house since 1918. Today, it contains the Museum of St. Augustine History.

The city's more lavish development took place following the arrival of Henry Flagler in the mid-1880s. In 1888, he built the 450-room Ponce de Leon Hotel—a spectacular collection of Spanish Renaissance architecture buildings, with towers, arches, domes, balconies, and stained-glass windows. Today, the Ponce de Leon is the centerpiece of the nineteen-acre campus of Flagler College. The Lightner Museum, across King Street from Flagler College, was originally another Flagler hotel—The Alcazar. Publisher Otto Lightner bought it in 1946 and opened the museum in 1948 to display his collection of Victorian furnishings, sculpture, cut glass, and artwork.

At the top of St. Augustine's list of historic sites is the Castillo de San Marcos National Monument—the "Old Fort." It is the oldest European fortification remaining in the continental United States and stands guard over Matanzas Bay at the north end of the historic district. Earliest construction dates to 1672. The fort's thick coquina-and-oyster-shell block walls were designed to absorb cannonball strikes. Spain, Britain, the Confederate army, the Union army, and the United States have variously occupied it. The fort is open for tours year-round except on Christmas Day.

Today, St. Augustine is one of Florida's most popular destinations for vacationers and history buffs. Narrow avenues and alleyways interweave St. Augustine's historic district, bounded by the Matanzas River on the east and Flagler College on the west. The area was designated a National Landmark District by the National Park Service in 1970, and in 1983 more of the surrounding neighborhood was added as a National Register District. Many of the buildings have balconies, which hover over the streets. Horse-drawn carriages clip-clop along cobblestone roads. It has the quaint look and feel of an old English village—not surprising since some of the older structures were built during British occupation, from 1763 to 1784.

Plaza de la Constitución Park, between Cathedral Place and King Street, bisects the north and south segments of the historic district. St. George Street is cordoned off for pedestrians heading north. Here it's a mix of touristy and historic but venture a block to either side of St. George and you'll find quirky antique shops, cafes, and quaint bed and breakfasts, some occupying historic three-century-old buildings. There are some note-worthy eateries here. Catch 27, on narrow Charlotte Street, occupies one of those old houses. A chalkboard at the entrance will tell you what they have fresh that day. I can vouch for their spicy and creamy version of shrimp and grits. They put blackened shrimp in a creamy sherry sauce on a polenta cake in lieu of traditional grits, and it works well. They also have St. Augustine gumbo with clams, shrimp, sausage and Minorcan spices, shrimp and fish tacos, and blue crab cakes. At the Floridian, on Spanish Street, their menu is a tasty mix of southern coastal and New Orleans cuisine, like barbecue pulled pork and waffles, and shrimp and sausage manque choux (with creamed corn, poblano peppers, and cheese). Espresso devotees have three great choices, all up near the north end of St. George Street: Crucial Coffee, City Perks Coffee, and St. Augustine Coffee House.

Head south on St. George Street and it is equally as historic but less touristy. Walk a few blocks south into St. Augustine's historic Lincoln-ville residential district to find Preserved (now my very favorite St. Au-

gustine restaurant) in a circa 1840 Victorian house that was once home to Thomas Jefferson's granddaughter. I feasted on grilled maple leaf duck with collard greens and black-eyed peas. My dinner guest Nancy had the out-standing braised beef short ribs with roasted mushrooms and brussels sprouts. If you only have time to dine at one restaurant in St. Augustine, make it this one.

Meander south on Avile Street from King Street to find two more excellent,

Hypolito Street, St. Augustine

tucked-away cafes: La Herencia, a cozy, authentic Cuban café, and the equally authentic but Brazilian restaurant Café Sol Brasileirissimo, where I savored their *feijoado completa*, which is essentially everything in the kitchen—spicy beef, sausage, smoked pork, black beans, rice, shredded collards, with salsa and orange slices on top.

Also on Avile Street I found the offbeat and captivating Bouvier Maps & Prints. This is the most marvelous little shop, with old prints and lithographs, old maps, and rare books. History buffs and serious collectors of antique print works and documents will tumble down a deep rabbit hole in this place.

Not unexpectedly, St. Augustine is teeming with charming bed and breakfasts, and there is one grand historic hotel as well.

The quaint 1898 three-story Agustin Inn is situated off the beaten path on quiet cobblestone Cuna Street. Their tree-shaded courtyard is a perfect, peaceful spot to enjoy coffee and breakfast in the morning.

Bayfront Marin House Bed & Breakfast has a commanding view of Matanzas Bay. Minorcan colony refuge Francisco Marin built the original house on this location sometime in the 1780s. In the 1890s, it was extensively enlarged by owner Captain Henry Belknap. Following the turn of the century it continued to be added on to by various owners, and in 2003 it was completely restored and turned into a bed and breakfast.

Carriage Way Bed & Breakfast, along the carriage route at the corner of Cuna and Cordova Streets, was built in 1883 by carpenter Edward Masters, who moved to St. Augustine to work on Henry Flagler's Ponce de Leon Hotel.

The Casablanca Inn has an infamous history. Following the Prohibition Act of 1919, St. Augustine became a busy smuggling port. During the 1920s, the Casa Blanca was the circa 1914 Matanzas Hotel, and US treasury agents were regular patrons. The lady who operated the Matanzas Hotel at that time apparently had an arrangement with smugglers who were bringing their contraband into Matanzas Bay by night. If no agents were checked into the hotel, she would climb onto the roof-top widow's walk and wave a lantern as an "all clear" signal. Reportedly, after fourteen years of Prohibition, this innkeeper died quite wealthy. Legend claims that her ghost can be seen waving a lantern from the roof of what is now the Casablanca Inn.

Don Manuel Lorenzo Solana, a member of one of the oldest Spanish families in St. Augustine, built the home in 1763, which is now the Casa de Solona Bed & Breakfast. Away from the commercial district in St. Augustine's oldest residential section, it was built out of coquina stone, just like the fort Castillo de San Marco. He added on to it later, in the early 1800s. Solana was one of last remaining "Mounted Dragoons" of the Spanish army in St. Augustine following British occupation. Casa de Solona has ten sumptuously decorated (and rumored to be haunted) rooms.

The Casa de Suenos Bed & Breakfast occupies the former home of James Colee, a surveyor for Henry Flagler, who built this house in 1904 across the street from his family's stagecoach and carriage business. It was originally a simple clapboard cottage, but in the 1920s cigar manufacturer Patalina Carcaba purchased it and completely remodeled it into a Mediterranean/Spanish eclectic style with varied-height flat roofs, parapet walls, and tall arched windows—an architectural style that it retains today.

Carl Decker, a carpenter/builder who came to St. Augustine to take part in the Henry Flagler development boom, built the home that is now the Cedar House Inn in 1893 as his own, and then built four others in the surrounding neighborhood on speculation. Over the years it has been a private residence, rental property, and for a while in the 1970s a fraternity house for Flagler College.

Inn on Charlotte Street Bed & Breakfast is a two-story brick house built in 1918 by attorney Levi Nelson, who later became St. Augustine's mayor. The large front porch with a swing and wicker rocking chairs invite guests to sit and read or sip tea. All eight rooms are decorated with period antiques. The carriage house is like a secret hideaway, tucked away behind the main house—the Marjorie Rawlings Bungalow room sits downstairs, and Anna Marcotte's Hideaway is upstairs. I stayed in the upstairs Hideaway prior to the inn's 2003 renovation. I found the Inn on Charlotte Street charming then and it is even more so today.

The Kenwood Inn is a classic example of mid-nineteenth-century Victorian architecture, with a wide two-story veranda that wraps around three of its sides. Claw-foot bathtubs and four-poster beds—some with canopies—continue the Victorian theme in each of the rooms. The house was built in 1865 and opened as a boarding house in 1886, which might make it the oldest "still-operating" inn in St. Augustine. Located in the quiet southern end of the Historic District, it is only a block west of the waterfront, and a block north of St. Augustine's "oldest house."

The house that is now the Old Powder House Inn was built in 1899, and sits on property where, a century before that, soldiers had warehoused gun powder during the second Spanish occupation of St. Augustine.

Something different for historic St. Augustine, the Saragossa Inn Bed & Breakfast is a 1924 Sears Craftsman-style bungalow in the quiet northwest residential section of the Historic District was restored and converted into a bed and breakfast in 1990.

There is "old" in St. Augustine, and then there is "very old." The St. Francis Inn falls into the latter category. It was built in 1791 and is one of only a few original true Spanish colonial architecture buildings left in Florida. While it has not functioned continuously as an inn, this is likely the oldest building which is currently an inn in St. Augustine. Just eight years after Spain reacquired Florida from Great Britain, Spanish infantry sergeant Gaspar Garcia built his home in St. Augustine on land granted to him by the king of Spain. It was not unusual for Spain to grant property to soldiers as a reward for meritorious duty. Houses, during those tumultuous times, were built to withstand attack. Garcia built his from thick coquina limestone (similar to the walls of the nearby fort Castillo de San Marcos), and he built it flush against the corner formed by what are now St. Francis and St. George Streets. The only problem was that those two streets did not cross at a precise right angle. To make it fit, Garcia built his house in a slightly trapezoidal shape. As a result, there are no perfectly square or rectangular rooms in the inn. As old buildings go, the chronology of prior owners of what is now the St. Francis Inn is long. Many were military figures, like British marine colonel Thomas Dummett, who purchased it in 1838. The colonel's daughter, Anna Dummett, was the first to convert the home into an inn. Anna's brother-in-law—Confederate major William Hardee purchased it in 1855, and then sold it to John Wilson in 1888. It was Wilson who added the third floor and mansard roof to the main inn. He also built several surrounding buildings—one of which is the Wilson House across the street, which houses two suites for the St. Francis Inn. From 1894 on, the main house was variously rented as a residence, apartments, and operated as a hotel. It was owner Ralph Moody who gave it the name "St. Francis Inn" in 1948. *Ghosts of St. Augustine* author Dave Lapham reports that the St. Francis Inn has a ghost. As legend tells it, Major Hardee's son and Lilly, a slave, were madly in love—something that was considered taboo at that time. The young Hardee, distraught over their dilemma, committed suicide—but he is not the ghost. It is Lilly who has been seen walking the halls of the St. Francis Inn.

Victorian House Bed & Breakfast sits in the quieter (and older) historic neighborhood south of King Street. It was built in 1897 by

Alberto Rogero, whose ancestors were Minorcans that settled in St. Augustine a century earlier.

The circa 1880 Westcott House's location, at the south end of Avenida Menendez, was obviously chosen due to its terrific views of Matanzas Bay. Dr. John Westcott came to St. Augustine in the 1850s and soon became involved in its development, particularly where transport was concerned. One of his projects, the St. Johns Railroad, ran tracks from the San Sebastian River, which runs right through St. Augustine, to the town of Tocoi, to the west on the St. Johns River. He was also instrumental in promoting the Intracoastal Waterway, which runs through Matanzas Bay right in front of his house. Westcott House was restored and converted into a bed and breakfast in 1983. The view of the bay, from one of the big wicker chairs on the wrap-around porches, is unparalleled.

In 1888, Boston entrepreneur and architect Franklin Smith opened the Casa Monica Hotel on property that he had purchased from Henry Flagler. It was constructed at the same time and in the same architectural style (Spanish Renaissance with Moorish Revival elements) as Flagler's St. Augustine hotels: the Ponce de Leon Hotel—now Flagler College and the Alcazar Hotel—now the Lightner Museum.

Less than four months after it opened, Flagler bought the hotel from Smith and renamed it the Cordova. In 1902, Flagler built a bridge between the Cordova and his Alcazar Hotel, next door, to make them one hotel.

Eventually, the Cordova would fall victim to the Great Depression, and after it had been closed for three decades, St. Johns County bought the building in 1962 and, over the next two years, remodeled it into the St. Johns County Courthouse.

In 1997, Richard Kessler, Central Florida hotelier and former CEO of Days Inns of America, bought the courthouse and spent two years on a complete restoration, bringing it back to its original Flagler-era splendor. He reopened it in 1999 with its original name, the Casa Monica Hotel—named for Saint Monica, mother of Saint Augustine.

Casa Monica resembles a palace as much as a hotel. The exquisite restoration included rebuilding the original hotel's carriage entrance. The elegant lobby features a bronze fountain, antique chandeliers, and historic maps and original Jean Claude Roy artwork on the walls. The rooms have Spanish wrought iron frame beds and mahogany furnishings. Each of the Casa Monica's five towers is a multistory luxury suite. I have stayed there twice and always find it to be both exceedingly elegant and ideally situated for walking throughout the city.

There is more to see and do when you exit the Historic District of St. Augustine and cross Matanzas Bay on the Bridge of Lions.

Just across the bridge O'Steen's Restaurant, historic in its own way, has been serving good, fresh seafood for six decades. Railroad employee Robert "Chief" O'Steen and his wife Jennie opened their restaurant, across the bridge from old St. Augustine, in 1965 following a railroad strike. Long-time employee Lonnie Pomar, who started working there when he was just twelve years old, bought it from the O'Steens in 1983. The small sixteen-table and six-person counter restaurant and its menu have essentially not changed. O'Steen's does not take reservations or credit cards. Walk up to an outside window and put your name on the list and they will call you. This is a local's place. When I was there, I noticed lots of conversation between tables. Everybody knew everybody else. O'Steen's is known for good, fresh, simple food, in generous portions. They are most famous for their shrimp, fried in a cracker-meal batter spiced with locally-grown datil peppers, a St. Augustine Minorcan (Minorcans arrived here in the late 1700s) specialty. But instead of shrimp I had their fresh catch of the day: broiled flounder with hush puppies, green beans, and rice and gravy, and it hit the spot.

While on this side of the bridge, there are two more must-not-miss sites to see.

The 165-foot-tall St. Augustine Lighthouse was constructed between 1871 and 1874 and is still an active US Coast Guard navigation aid. The 219-step hike up a cast iron spiral staircase to the top can be exhausting, but the view is unbeatable. Downstairs, the 1876 lightkeeper's quarters have been converted into a museum. Ghost stories abound at the lighthouse. One tells of a lightkeeper named Andreau who fell to his death in the 1850s while painting the 1824 lighthouse that occupied this site prior to the current one. Occasional haunting "incidents" and "encounters" in both the lighthouse and the keeper's house are often attributed to Andreau.

Before the arrival of Disneyworld, Florida was dotted with roadside tourist attractions: marine aquariums with performing dolphin shows, mermaid inhabited springs, even Wild West towns with daily shoot-outs, but the most iconic were the alligator farms. The oldest of these is the St. Augustine Alligator Farm Zoological Park, which originally opened on South St. Augustine Beach in 1893. Two early Florida entrepreneurs, George Reddington and Felix Fire, had started collecting live alligators to show to tourists. They hit pay dirt when the South Beach Railway Company added the Anastasia Island Tram to shuttle vacationers between the city of St. Augustine and the beach. Reddington's and Fire's claim to fame was "World's Largest Alligator Farm." After a storm tore up the tram tracks in 1920, they moved the alligator farm inland and a bit further north, closer to town. New owners expanded the facility in the late 1930s and the alligator farm flourished. It is still a fascinating place to visit, both for its amazing collection of animals and for its historical significance. In 1989, the Association of Zoos and Aquariums extended their accreditation to the St. Augustine alligator farm, and over the years the University of Florida has conducted extensive wildlife research there.

St. Augustine Alligator Farm Zoological Park, St. Augustine

DON'T MISS
The historic Fort Castillo de San Marcos

Hodges Park, Keaton Beach

KEATON BEACH

Population not listed on census

*K*eaton Beach was included in the 1999 second volume of the first edition of *Visiting Small-Town Florida* because it was way off the beaten path. It had this terrific little hot dog stand that I dubbed, "The hot dog stand at the edge of the world," which overlooked the beach. It had been there since the 1970s and survived one of the most destructive storms (and it was not even a hurricane) to ever hit the central Gulf Coast. It is long gone now—not the victim of severe weather but of economics.

From *Visiting Small-Town Florida*, Volume 2:

> In the very early morning hours of March 13, 1993, the third most devastating storm ever to hit the continental United States made landfall on the north end of Florida's Big Bend area. Its strongest winds struck the tiny coastal communities of Dekle Beach and Keaton Beach; where ten people were killed, and 150 homes were severely

damaged or destroyed (only 2 houses in Dekle Beach were left un-scathed). The total loss for the entire state of Florida would end up at 26 lives and over $500 million in property damage. Over the next couple of days, the storm would continue across the state and all the way up the northeast coast, turning into a horrific blizzard. Because the storm hadn't formed as a traditional hurricane does, it wasn't given a name—despite record storm surges and winds well over one hundred miles per hour. Most simply remember it as the "No Name Storm of 1993."

Those who experienced it refer to it as "The Storm of the Century."

Keaton Beach occupies property originally owned by a business-man named Captain Brown who operated a sawmill and turpentine factory here back in the mid-1800s. Brown admired his bookkeeper, Sam Keaton, so much that he named the little community after him. Hodges Park on the tiny man-made beach, and access to good fishing in the Gulf, are the main draws today. A commemorative plaque at Hodges Park dedicates the park to the memory of those who died in the storm and to those who survived. Reading the plaque is sobering. It lists the names and ages of the Taylor County residents who died. Four were children. Repeated last names indicate that whole families were wiped out.

Roy's Restaurant, Steinhatchee

STEINHATCHEE

Population: 737

*I*t is pronounced "Steen-hat-chee," which in Creek loosely translates to "dead man's river," possibly a reference to the color of the water. Looking down into Steinhatchee River is like looking into an inky abyss. It is not pollution that makes the water so dark. It is tannic acid that naturally leaches into the river from cypress and pine trees growing along the shoreline. The village of Steinhatchee, at the mouth of the Steinhatchee River, has long been a popular launching point for fishing in the Gulf, but scalloping on the grass flats just out from the mouth of the river is its prime attraction.

The bite-sized and sweet-tasting scallop is relatively easy to spot, with its distinctive two-finned shell. Bay scallops usually reside in five to ten feet of water, nestled in grassy-bottom coastal areas. Mask, snorkel, fins, and a mesh collection bag are the only acceptable tools needed to gather them (scuba gear is strictly prohibited). Scallops come in two varieties: the smaller "bay" scallops and the larger, deep-water

Steinhatchee Landing, Steinhatchee

(sometimes called "diver") scallops. Bay scallops can be collected both recreationally and commercially, while deep-water scallops are almost exclusively the domain of commercial harvesters. Recreational scalloping has always been a favorite Florida pastime and no place is more popular for it than Steinhatchee. Florida scallopers must have a Florida saltwater fishing license and can only collect them within the boundaries of the Bay Scallop Harvest Zone—along the Gulf Coast "Big Bend" area from Mexico Beach (just west of Apalachicola) down to Aripeka (just north of Tarpon Springs). Scallop season runs from the last weekend in June through the last weekend in September.

Two miles upriver, up State Road 51, is the Steinhatchee Landing Resort, a nature-conscious village that wraps around a bend on the north bank of the Steinhatchee River. Florida cracker-style cottages and homes line Steinhatchee Landing's live oak–shaded lanes.

General Zachary Taylor had ordered the building of Fort Frank Brooke alongside the Steinhatchee River in 1838, during the height of the Second Seminole War. There is convincing historical evidence that it was built near, or possibly right on, the location of Steinhatchee Landing. In a *Gulf Coast Historical Review* article, historian Niles Schuh points out that reports and letters from army personnel who operated in this area during the Second Seminole War record that "the falls of Steinhatchee River are six miles above Fort Frank Brooke." If their mileage estimates were accurate, this description would place the fort at the same bend in the river where Steinhatchee Landing is now. From the bottom of the river at the bend, scuba divers frequently retrieve artifacts like utensils and buttons from military jackets.

Nearby Steinhatchee Falls can be reached by continuing northeast up State Road 51 about six miles to a dirt road on the right. Follow the dirt road for about a mile to the Steinhatchee River. The falls are just an elevation change that speeds up the current over some rocks and creates a set of rapids, a rare sight in Florida. The river narrows here. Hundreds of years ago, this was the only spot where Timucuan Indians, and later Seminoles, could traverse the river on foot.

You would expect good seafood in a place like Steinhatchee and it does not disappoint. Roy's Restaurant, overlooking the mouth of the Steinhatchee River, has been a Steinhatchee staple for half a century. They opened in 1969. Their menu includes many locally caught specialties like soft-shell crab, blue crab claws, and crabbed-stuffed flounder. I suggest their grilled seafood platter with shrimp, oysters, flounder, an in-shell deviled crab, and a generous heap of that Steinhatchee specialty: bay scallops.

DON'T MISS
Dining on fresh scallops at Roy's Restaurant

Consider the Lilies Thrift Shop, High Springs

HIGH SPRINGS

Population: 6,178

*I*n 1884, the Savannah, Florida, and Western Railroad extended its tracks from Live Oak south to Gainesville. It passed through a little community known as Santaffey, named after the Santa Fe River. The rail line put up a depot and a post office. Five years later, the townspeople changed the name to High Springs. (Apparently, there was once a spring on top of a hill in the middle of town.) The phosphate boom of the 1890s increased traffic, and a new rail, connecting High Springs with Tampa, opened in 1893. Two dozen trains passed through each day. In 1896, Henry Plant's Plant System Railroad Line—which later merged with the Atlantic Coast Line, built a roundhouse where railroad cars could be pulled off the tracks. They also built a steam engine repair and maintenance shop, a boilermaker shop, a carpentry shop, and an icehouse for produce in the freight cars. The town's population swelled to more than three thousand. High Springs had become a major railroad repair depot. Today, that origi-

Mural, downtown High Springs

nal depot has been restored and now contains various business offices, and for a while it was home to one of Florida's best railroad museums.

After World War II, railroad lines began converting from steam-driven engines to diesel, and High Springs' railroad business evaporated. Three decades later, the town was rediscovered as a recreational hub because of the surrounding springs and rivers. For canoeists, kayakers, tubers, scuba divers, and cave divers, it is the ideal bivouac. The Santa Fe River skirts the north edge of town. Poe Springs Park, Gilchrist Blue Springs State Park, and Ginnie Springs (private operated, not a state park) are just a few miles east. O'Leno State Park is just north of town on Highway 441. Ichetucknee Springs State Park is only fifteen miles northeast on Highway 27. Individual canoe, kayak, and inner tube rentals are available at Ginnie Springs Outdoors. But for a premium guided group trip I recommend Lars Anderson at Adventure Outpost (see appendix). I have paddled with Lars several times and he knows more about the history of Florida's rivers, and about the wildlife that lives in them, than anyone I have met. Adventure Outpost operates out of High Springs but Lars travels to most Central Florida rivers.

High Springs is also an interesting place to visit for nonaquatic types as well. Downtown High Springs' selection of antique shops draws day and weekend visitors from around the state. In the mid-1980s, downtown revitalization began with the restoration of the two-story brick Old Opera House building (originally built in 1895) on Main Street. Today, it is home to the Great Outdoors Restaurant. Its assorted menu ranges from salads and burgers to steaks and pasta dishes, and its Spring House Tavern has become the area's top live music venue. For great Tex-Mex try El Patio across the street. And if it is sweet baked goods you are craving, go to Spins: Sweet & Savory around the corner, plus they have lunch sandwiches as well.

High Springs has attracted antiques shoppers for decades and great shops line Main Street. The Bird Nest Vintage Market has an eclectic collection of vintage furniture, antiques, and collectables. Another intriguing spot is Consider the Lilies Thrift Shop, just around the corner. Consider the Lilies is a nonprofit, volunteer-run consignment store whose proceeds go to benefit local children's charities.

DON'T MISS
Consider the Lilies Thrift Shop

Shops on Cholokka Boulevard, Micanopy

MICANOPY

Population: 635

*T*he town of Micanopy was originally called Wanton's Trading Post when it was officially established in 1821. However, the Seminole Indian village of Cuscowilla existed here long before that. Spanish explorer Hernando de Soto had come across Timucuan Indians living near here back in 1539, and there is archaeological evidence that suggests that this area was populated prior to the Timucuans, perhaps as far back as ten thousand years ago. Naturalist William Bartram reported visiting the Seminoles' Cuscowilla in 1774. The town name changed to Micanopy in 1834, in honor of Seminole chief Micanopy. It is likely the oldest inland town in Florida.

Moss-draped branches of grand oak trees shade the sidewalks along the several-block-long main street, Cholokka Boulevard. "Downtown" Micanopy, with its 150-year-old store fronts, is a wondrous find for curio shoppers and antique collectors. If you have seen the 1991

Michael J. Fox/Julie Warner movie *Doc Hollywood*, then you will recognize Cholokka Boulevard. In the movie, Micanopy was the perfect double for the fictitious small southern town of Grady.

Micanopy dodged the modernization bullet back in the early 1960s when the Department of Transportation rerouted Highway 441 just to the east of town, rather than through it. When Interstate 75 was built a few years later, it, too, missed Micanopy by several miles to the west. As a result, Cholokka Boulevard, as well as the few residential blocks around it (all declared a National Register Historic District in 1983), all seem frozen in time.

Overnight visitors will find Micanopy's Herlong Mansion Bed & Breakfast everything a bed and breakfast should be: historic, elegant, inviting, and perhaps even haunted. This majestic red brick, Greek Revival-style southern plantation house features four massive Corinthian columns out front. The carefully renovated interior has the home's original leaded glass windows, twelve-foot-high ceilings, mahogany, maple, and oak floors, and quarter-sawn tiger oak paneling.

Zetty and Natalie Herlong moved to Natalie's family home in Micanopy in 1907, after their Alabama lumber business was destroyed in a fire. Natalie's parents, the Simontons, had built what was originally a two-story wood-frame farmhouse back in the 1840s. But the Herlongs wanted something a bit grander, so in 1909 they remodeled by constructing this brick mansion on top of and around the original farmhouse.

The Herlongs relaunched their lumber business in Micanopy and became prominent citrus farmers as well. When Natalie passed away in 1950, her six children inherited equal shares of the house, and an eighteen-year-long battle for sole ownership ensued. Eventually, her sister Inez was granted legal possession. On the very first day of her ownership, while cleaning in the second-floor bedroom that she and her sister Mae had shared during childhood, Inez collapsed, went into a diabetic coma, and died shortly thereafter.

Occasionally over the years, guests and staff have reported the sound of footsteps or doors opening and closing upstairs when no one is there, usually in or around Mae's room.

Herlong Mansion, Micanopy

The Herlong Mansion has changed hands several times over the last few decades but thankfully each owner has maintained its historic integrity and elegant ambiance. The Herlong Mansion Bed & Breakfast has eleven rooms or suites, plus a carriage house and a cozy cottage. Most are furnished with four-poster beds and period antique furniture; and some have their own fireplaces—there are ten throughout the house. This is one of the state's most popular bed and breakfast and they have become a much-sought-after wedding and special events venue as well. By the way, Micanopy is just twelve miles south of Gainesville, so they book out well in advance for University of Florida football game weekends.

There are two small cafés in town: Coffee n' Cream and Old Florida Café, right next door to each other—good places to grab a light breakfast or lunch. But if you are really hungry and favor barbecue, drive out past the edge of town to Highway 441 to the Pearl Country Store. Yes, it looks like (and is) a convenience store/gas station but don't let that fool you. The Pearl has some of the best barbecue ribs, chopped pork, southern-style vegetables, and home-made pie in Central Florida. David and Peggy Carr bought the convenience store in 2002 and then promptly reinvented it as a country general store and barbecue joint. David Carr is the son of Archie and Marjorie Carr, noted sea turtle conservationists and environmentalists. Peggy is a landscape architecture professor at the University of Florida. They both grew up in this area and know it well.

Browsing the shops in Micanopy can be an all-day venture, and there are a few where I always seem to spend a disproportionate amount of time. Micanopy Trading Outpost has a wonderful selection of antique tables and dressers, but I am most captivated by their collection of Florida Highwaymen prints and original paintings. In the 1950s, the Florida Highwaymen was a group of African American artists that traveled a circuit around Florida, setting up road-side showings of their stunningly beautiful scenic landscape paintings. The tiny Gallery Under the Oaks next door has more original paintings—some by local artists, plus prints, and stained glass and hand-crafted gifts. Across the street, Delectable Collectables carries some unusual decorative sculpted pieces, pottery, and jewelry. Dakota Mercantile has more jewelry, plus vintage holiday and garden items.

The Micanopy Historical Society Museum occupies the circa 1890 Thrasher Warehouse. J. E. Thrasher opened his general merchandise business in 1896 and stored his inventory in the warehouse. When his store burned down in 1911 Thrasher moved everything into the warehouse and continued to operate from there. It has been the home of the Micanopy Historical Society's Museum since 1983. Intricate displays tell the story of this area's history from Timucuan Indian occupation to William Bartram's visit in 1774 to the Seminole Indian Wars, to the Civil War, and up through recent times.

One of the most fascinating, and frankly creepiest, places in Micanopy is the Micanopy Historic Cemetery (placed on the National Register of Historic Places in 1983), on the northeast edge of town. Take Seminary Road east out of the center of town, to Smith Avenue, and look for the sign directing you toward to cemetery. Micanopy Cemetery was founded by local physician H. L. Montgomery in 1826.

The further you venture into the cemetery, the older and more towering the oak trees, and the older the headstones. It was back here where I found the Herlong Family plot. Their headstones are among the largest, a reflection of the family's past stature. Further toward the rear of the property the oaks seem to form a massive canopy of branches and Spanish moss overhead that turns the place dark, even in the middle of the afternoon. I cannot imagine what it might be like at night.

DON'T MISS
The Micanopy Historic Cemetery

Marjorie Kinnan Rawlings's house at Cross Creek

CROSS CREEK

Population not listed on census

*I*f you grew up in Florida and attended school here, chances are Marjorie Kinnan Rawlings's *The Yearling* was on your assigned reading list. I was in elementary school the first time I read *The Yearling* (and *The Secret River*), and Rawlings's descriptions of Cross Creek and of early twentieth-century rural life in Florida left an unforgettable impression on me.

Pulitzer Prize-winning author Marjorie Rawlings lived in Cross Creek and wrote books and short stories about living in rural north-central Florida in the 1930s and 1940s. The most famous were her fictional *The Yearling* and her autobiographical *Cross Creek*. Cross Creek is a quiet little place, situated between Orange and Lochloosa Lakes, about twenty-two miles south of Gainesville. Remarkably, even today this area is sparsely populated. Rawlings's circa 1890 home and the surrounding property are now the Marjorie Kinnan Rawlings State Historic Site. "The Creek," as the locals refer to it, is an actual creek that connects Lochloosa Lake on the east side and Orange Lake on the west side. Marjorie Rawlings herself describes it best:

> Cross Creek is a bend in a country road, by land, and the flowing of Lochloosa Lake into Orange Lake, by water. We are four miles west of the small village of Island Grove, nine miles east of a turpentine still, and on the other sides we do not count distance at all, for the two lakes and the broad marshes create an infinite space between us and the horizon.

Cross Creek was fresh in my mind the first time I visited the Marjorie Kinnan Rawlings State Historic Site back in 1996 to research my first edition of *Visiting Small-Town Florida*. I marveled at how closely, in real life, her home matched the one in my imagination. Even the floor plan had a haunting sense of familiarity to me. I felt as if I had visited this place in a dream and knew what to expect from room to room. Here was the front porch, where Marjorie sat countless hours at her typewriter and mixed the personalities she had come to know with the stories that she wove. *Jacob's Ladder*, *When the Whippoorwill—*, *Golden Apples*, *Cross Creek*, *The Sojourner*, and *The Yearling* all came to life in this very

Marjorie Kinnan Rawlings house at Cross Creek

space. There is the birdbath in front of the house where, in the summer, redbirds would scold her for not replenishing it with fresh, cool water. Here is the screen door that her pet raccoon, Racket, learned to open and close for himself. Here is the indoor bathroom, added five years after she moved in, between the previously separate south side and north side of the house, whose sloping floor "has proved no friend to the aged, the absent-minded and the inebriated," wrote Marjorie.

From the parking area it looks like any other state park facility. Rawlings's house is hidden from view by her orange grove, but things change when you walk through the rusty old gate. There is an eerie sense of stepping back in time. A dirt path leads through the small (still-producing) grove. Between the rows of trees, pine logs are stacked, ready to light in the event of a freeze, just as she described in her chapter on winter. Back then, a midnight sounding of the train whistle was their warning when the temperature dropped to freezing. Grove hands and neighbors alike would spend the night lighting and stoking the fires in a desperate attempt to keep the crop warm enough to make it through the chill. There is a chicken coop to the left (with chickens in it) and the barn, to the right, is filled with old farming implements. Just beyond the barn is the turn of the century Florida cracker-style house. I was struck with the distinct feeling that I had come to a place where I lived in a previous life—not reincarnation—just that her descriptions were so vividly imprinted in my mind. By all appearances, someone lives here. On the west side is a duck pen, with ducks waddling in and out through its open door. In the backyard is a simple vegetable garden, and behind that the outhouse.

It was Marjorie Rawlings's wish that, after her passing, her house be kept as it was when she lived there. The curators have done a marvelous job of honoring that request. She left it to the University of Florida Foundation, which maintained it from her death in 1953 until donating it to the Florida Department of Natural Resources in 1970. I've been back to the Marjorie Rawlings house countless times, and with each visit I still get that sense of wonder and feel her presence, just as I did the first time I visited.

Marjorie Rawlings died quite suddenly of a brain hemorrhage in 1953. She was only fifty-seven years old. Norton Baskin, Marjorie's second husband, had said that she had wanted to be buried at a small cemetery in Citra, just south of Island Grove. Apparently, through some miscommunication between Norton and the funeral home, she was inadvertently buried in the wrong cemetery—Antioch Cemetery, down a dirt road east of Island Grove. Rawlings's grave is a simple, flat marble slab with no headstone. No signs lead you to it. No fence surrounds it. Nothing distinguishes it from anyone else's grave. Her epitaph reads, "Marjorie Kinnan Rawlings, 1896–1953, Wife of Norton Baskin. Through her writing she endeared herself to the people of the world."

Although there is no actual town at Cross Creek, there is a popular restaurant. When Ben Wheeler opened The Yearling Restaurant in 1952 it was one the first genuine "Florida cracker cuisine" restaurants, serving such rural fare as frog legs, gator tail, catfish, fried quail, collard greens, and turtle. It closed in 1992, but then local Citra resident Robert Blaur bought it and reopened in 2002. Thankfully, Blaur decided to keep The Yearling's original ambiance, and most importantly its authentic cuisine, intact. Even the restaurant's original 1970s–1980s head chef Junior Jenkins came back. Nothing beats consuming a heaping plate of plump fried frog legs while listening to bonafide blues guitarist Willie Green belt out "Kansas City Here I Come." And the only place where you can enjoy both at the same time is at The Yearling. If you ever thought you wanted to try frog legs, The Yearling might be the best place to do it. These are the tastiest frog legs I have ever had—the size of chicken legs and just as meaty. By the way, the adage about "it tastes like chicken" is true with frog legs: similar flavor, but just a bit chewier.

DON'T MISS
Touring Marjorie Rawlings's house

Wood & Swink Store and Post Office, Evinston

EVINSTON

Population not listed on census

*J*ust cross Orange Lake from Cross Creek is the tiny community of Evinston (the "E" is pronounced as a short "I," "Ivinston"), home to the historic Wood & Swink Store and Post Office. Micanopy merchant S. H. Benjamin built the store in 1882 as a warehouse to store freight offloaded from the railroad. Two years later, the local postmaster purchased it and used it intermittently as a store and post office. In 1913, it became the permanent post office and today appears on the National Register of Historic Places. Fred Wood's book, *Evinston Home: God's Country*, was my source for some interesting local history.

In 1905, H. D. Wood and his brother-in-law, R. C. Evins, acquired the store following the hasty exit of the previous owner, John Hester. Apparently, while standing in the front door of his store, Hester shot and killed Watt Barron and wounded his father, J. F. Barron. One version of the story claims that the shooting resulted from an argument over who had the best looking field of watermelons. Regardless of the cause, Hester was out and the Wood family was in. (In-law Paul Swink was a partner for just a couple years in the 1930s, and his name was left on the sign.) The store remains in the Wood family today, owned by Fred (Jr.) and his wife Wilma Sue Wood (who was the postmaster until she retired in 2010). The store is a veritable time capsule, and likely Florida's oldest operating post office. Just inside the door stands a partition wall with a post office service window in the middle, surrounded by old-style post office boxes. Some of them date back to 1882. An ancient cash register sits atop the counter next to the PO boxes. Tables and countertops are filled with jars of various home-pickled vegetables, honey, and preserves. Farm implements hang on one wall. A glass case holds old tins of tobacco. Boxes of fresh vegetables line the floor next to a vintage Coca-Cola floor cooler filled with ice-cold sodas. Tea, spices, soaps, a few books, and a variety of sundries sit on the shelves behind the counter alongside old historic photos, a few paintings, and some pictures of Elvis Presley. Is this a general store? Is it a museum? The answer is yes, to both questions. A big, old wood-burning stove sits in the center of the store surrounded by rocking chairs. If only that stove could speak.

The first time I came to Evinston and the Wood & Swink Store, in 1996, Wilma Sue Wood introduced me to Jake and Pat Glisson, who lived a few blocks from the store. The Glisson's graciously invited me into their home, even though Jake was recuperating from bypass surgery. Pat had just made a batch of Christmas cookies and offered a plate before I had sat down. Jake Glisson was an accomplished artist and book author who grew up next door to Marjorie Rawlings. She wrote about the Glisson family in *Cross Creek*. A young Jake and Marjorie became close friends, even though Jake's dad and Marjorie did not always see eye to eye.

In Jake Glisson's autobiographical book, *The Creek*, he tells marvelous stories that illustrate what life was like for a kid growing up in Cross Creek. He witnessed firsthand many of the events about which Marjorie wrote, so some of his stories overlap with hers, but he tells them from his own viewpoint—sometimes to the consternation of Marjorie Rawlings scholars. He explained to me, "I thought that writers in a historical society would be interested in the license that Mrs. Rawlings used in writing, for instance, *Cross Creek*. Just that slight little deviation that can change the meaning, and in some cases was a little imaginary. I feel that it was part of her brilliance, that she did a little patchwork here and there, ever so delicately." Jake's love and respect for Marjorie Rawlings are apparent, particularly in his chapter "That Woman Next Door." Jake's point was that sometimes writers adjust things a little to make them fit, and Marjorie was no different in that respect. Rehearing those stories from a different viewpoint was one of the things that make his book so fascinating. Jake told me that writing *The Creek* was a return to his childhood: "The truth is, the day I finished the book I was a little depressed. Because in writing it, it was kind of like I went back there and did it all again. It was a fun experience."

Sadly, in April 2019, Jake Glisson passed away. He was ninety-two.

DON'T MISS
The Wood & Swink Store and Post Office

McIntosh Railway Depot, 1885

McINTOSH

Population: 496

*H*ighway 441 rolls across scenic pastureland between Micanopy and Ocala, and into the picturesque hamlet of McIntosh, on the west side of Orange Lake. Huge live oaks grace every yard, their Spanish moss-covered limbs spread out over the tops of homes and across streets. I have never seen so many grand oak trees in one place. Two of the grandest are on Avenue G in the front yard and backyard of what was once Margie Karow's Merrily Bed and Breakfast. W. E. Allen, McIntosh's first postmaster, built the house in 1888. Most of the other houses along McIntosh's avenues (B through H) are one-hundred-plus-year-old Victorians—some restored, some not. These were originally the homes of citrus and cotton farmers whose fields surrounded the town. After the big freezes of 1894 and 1895, the farmers switched to vegetables—crookneck squash, cabbage, lettuce. I am told that the old Gist House, at the corner of Avenue H and Fifth Street, was built with the revenues of a single season's crookneck squash crop.

Another farmer grew iceberg lettuce exclusively for the ocean liner *Queen Mary* and shipped it by train to New York. In 1983, a large segment of McIntosh, west from 4th Street to 10th Street, and south from Avenue D to Avenue H, was added to the National Register of Historic Places, with sixty-eight historic homes listed.

McIntosh's restored railroad depot, originally constructed in 1884 by the old Florida Southern Railroad, sits at the end of Avenue G. It was scheduled to be torn down in 1974, but thankfully, in 1973 a group of townsfolk who felt the depot was a valuable landmark formed the Friends of McIntosh to save it, and it is now home to McIntosh's Historical Museum. The museum hosts McIntosh's annual 1890s Festival, on either the third or fourth weekend in October (so as not to conflict with a University of Florida Gator game). It has become one of Florida's most popular small-town festivals, with tours of McIntosh's historic homes, storytelling, a parade, hundreds of arts, crafts, and antiques vendors, and live entertainment.

There is not much to eat in McIntosh, but just two miles up Highway 441 there is a particularly good Italian restaurant, Antonio's. Chef Antonio, native of the Isle of Ponza, near Naples, Italy, prepares authentic southern Italian fare like Genovese gnocchi and veal saltimbocca.

Sprague House Bed and Breakfast, Crescent City

CRESCENT CITY

Population: 1,535

*S*cenic US 17 rolls though fern-growing country north of Deland and brings you to Crescent City, which rests atop a bluff on the curved (hence "crescent") west bank of Crescent Lake.

The first families settled here in 1852, and a few more came in the late 1860s. In 1875, Charles Griffing bought most of the property and divided it into single-acre home lots and five-acre citrus groves. Griffing's wife, Jennie, changed the name of what was then Dunn's Lake to Crescent Lake because its shape reminded her of the crescent moon. The new town adopted the name of the lake.

US Route 17 becomes Summit Street when it passes through downtown Crescent City. Turn east onto Central Avenue and follow it four blocks downhill to Crescent Lake and you will find docks with covered boathouses lining the shore. This lake, like many others, once claimed to be "The Bass Capital of the World." However, Crescent City's big annual event is the Catfish Festival, held the first weekend in April.

The agenda includes bluegrass music, arts and crafts, a vintage car show, and a parade, but the highlight is the catfish skinning contest.

Next door to Crescent Lake's main boat dock is 3 Bananas, a classic rustic-atmosphere lakefront bar and grill. The menu features all the usual suspects: burgers, wings, and grilled chicken sandwiches; plus, one local favorite, their fried catfish sandwich. Walk around to 3 Bananas' waterfront backyard and check out their towering white cypress tree, which they claim to be more than six hundred years old.

There are some interesting turn of the century homes near and along the waterfront. One is The Sprague House Bed & Breakfast. Built in 1892 by a local citrus farmer, it was purchased in 1902 by Dr. Guilford Sprague, the town's mayor. Sprague's wife, Kate, ran the house as an inn. Famous former guests include William Jennings Bryant and President Theodore Roosevelt. Sprague House is a charming Victorian with two-story wraparound porches and stained glass windows. They offer four antique-furnished rooms.

3 Bananas Restaurant and Bar, Crescent City

Rosewood historical marker

ROSEWOOD

Population not listed on census

About ten minutes east of Cedar Key on Highway 24 you will come across a historical marker for Rosewood. Other than a few scattered bricks and boards in the woods close by, there are no structural remains of the original Rosewood community. But the marker, dedicated by Governor Jeb Bush in 1994, gives a brief description of the horrific tragedy that took place nearby in January 1923. The village of Rosewood, established in 1845, was originally populated by both Blacks and whites that worked mostly in red cedar harvesting and milling. By the 1890s, most of the red cedar was gone. The pencil mills in Cedar Key were closed, and Rosewood's population shrank. Most (but not all) of the families that remained were Black. They found work in the local turpentine industry. Some started their own businesses. They built a school, three churches, a train station, a general store, a Masonic lodge, and even had a community baseball team— the Rosewood Stars. It was a small, quiet, hard-working community.

On New Year's Day 1923, a white woman living in nearby Sumner claimed she had been assaulted by a Black man—a dubious claim according to historians. A search for the alleged assailant was joined by Klu Klux Klan members who had been at a march in Gainesville the day before, and it quickly escalated into a vigilante invasion of Rosewood. It was a bloody massacre. The village was destroyed and eight people—six Black and two white—were killed.

Historic Island Hotel, Cedar Key

CEDAR KEY

Population: 720

*L*ike so many of Florida's small towns it was the rail-road that brought commerce to Cedar Key. Florida's first cross-state railroad, David Yulee's Atlantic to Gulf/Florida Railroad Company Line ran from Fernandina to Cedar Key and was completed here in 1861. Cedar milling was this area's dominant industry from the 1870s through the mid-1890s. Pencil manufacturer A. W. Faber had a mill on Atsena Otie Key, half a mile offshore from Cedar Key. In 1896, a hurricane decimated the region. The pencil industry left, and Cedar Key regressed to a sleepy fishing village. Eighty years later it began to reinvent itself as an artist enclave. The town is called Cedar Key, but it is actually on Way Key—once a weigh station for sailing vessels to re-supply and drop ballast. And I guess it is fair to describe today's Cedar Key as way out there—geographically, artistically, and attitudinally.

The drive down Highway 24 from Otter Creek to Cedar Key is long and straight. If you're traveling it on the third weekend in October or the third weekend in April, you will likely run into a traffic jam miles before you reach town. Cedar Key's Seafood Festival and Old Florida Arts Festival are two of the oldest and most popular such events in the state. They are terrific festivals, but do not expect to see much of the town or to soak up its offbeat character. Any other time you will probably have the highway to yourself, and the most traffic you will encounter in town will be a bicycle or an occasional old pickup truck on 2nd Street. Cedar Key moves at an unhurried pace—dictated mostly by whim or the weather, hence its quirky charm.

The first time I visited Cedar Key (in the early 1990s) three of us flew up from Tampa in a friend's Cherokee 140. We followed the grassy coast north until the tiny island town magically appeared through the clouds out in the Gulf. We circled the town, made a low pass, and then dipped a wing twice. That was the signal to Edna Coulter, who back then drove the only taxicab in Cedar Key, to please meet us at the short airstrip on Piney Point—the next island over and give us a ride into town. Today, Cedar Key doesn't look much different than it did then.

Cedar Key's most famous landmark, the Island Hotel, stands near the east end of 2nd Street, Cedar Key's four-block-long main street. The building was originally Parsons and Hale's General Store when it was built in 1859. It survived hostile Union troop occupation during the Civil War, and its oak-beam frame and one-foot-thick tabby walls have stood up to floods, numerous hurricanes—including the devastating 1896 hurricane, and several fires—including one started by the hotel's owner during the Great Depression (the fire department was just across the street, and they saved it). Famous visitor John Muir described Parsons and Hale's General Store, in 1867, in his journal: "I stepped into a little store, which had a considerable trade in quinine, and alligator and rattlesnake skins."

In 1915, Simon Feinberg, a property investor, bought the building and remodeled it into the Bay Hotel. In the years that followed, the hotel changed names and owners frequently.

Today, the rustic ten-room Island Hotel looks just like it did in photographs from the 1940s. Everyone seems to agree that the hotel's heyday began in 1946, when Bessie and Loyal "Gibby" Gibbs bought the rundown inn (it had been a brothel for a number of years prior). They patched it up and renamed it the Island Hotel. Gibby ran the hotel's Neptune Lounge bar and Bessie ran the restaurant. Her culinary skills soon won them popularity and customers. Bessie is credited with inventing the hearts of palm salad. Today, the hotel's dining room is known for its native Florida seafood dishes—like their baked crab imperial and their garlic-and-butter clams Island Hotel over pasta. Another specialty is their soups—crab bisque is always on the menu, and if chilled melon is the soup du jour, do not miss it. But of course, they are most famous for serving Bessie's original recipe, hearts of palm salad.

It is worth mentioning that the Island Hotel is famously haunted (although I've stayed there numerous times and have yet to encounter any ghosts). Be sure to visit the tiny Neptune Lounge, one Florida's most quaint and classic bars. The painting of King Neptune, hanging behind the bar, was painted by Helen Tooker in 1948. That painting, like the hotel, seems to be blessed with multiple lives. It has survived gunshots and hurricanes—even flooding when a 1950 hurricane tore part of the Island Hotel's roof off.

Loyal Gibbs passed away in 1962. Bessie died (in a house fire) in 1975, but not before serving as a city commissioner, a city judge, and as mayor, and helping to found the Cedar Key Arts Festival.

Another popular restaurant, Tony's Seafood, occupies the circa 1880s Hale Building at the west end of 2nd Street. Eric Jungklaus opened Tony's Seafood (named for his brother, who helped him build the restaurant) in 2005. Eric's claim to fame is his award-winning clam chowder. It won the prestigious Newport, Rhode Island, Annual Great Chowder Cook-Off three years in a row. They finally asked him to retire from entry in the contest, so others would have a chance to win. With an emphasis on fresh and local seafood, Tony's serves some delectable dishes like grilled teriyaki shrimp, Tuscan shrimp Italiano, the local requisite steamed clams, and of course, award-winning clam chowder. Across the street from Tony's, the 1842 Daily Grind & Mercantile is a great spot for espresso and pastries. Another good breakfast and lunch place, 2nd Street Café, is two blocks up the street.

Bonish Studio and Bar, Cedar Key

Stroll along 2nd Street and you will find arts and craft shops and galleries. Artists have been finding Cedar Key's eclectic ambiance creatively conducive for decades, and many have made it their home. At Cedar Keyhole Artist Co-op and Gallery on 2nd Street local artists display and sell a wide variety of paintings, pottery, sculpture, and jewelry. Pat and Cindy Bonish run the Bonish Studio, simultaneously a photo gallery, a gift shop, and a cocktail bar. Pat is an accomplished landscape and model photographer, and their bar (in the gallery) has become a popular local's hangout.

Two blocks south of 2nd, Dock Street overlooks the Gulf. Here you will find tourist gift shops, more galleries, and several casual bar-and-grill eateries, in a collection of ramshackle, sea-weathered wood buildings that hang over the water. The eateries all have similar menus—fried fish, shrimp, and clams. Steamers Clam Bar & Grill is a popular place to sample local seafood. Their low country boil—with shrimp, crabs, mussels, corn, potatoes, and of course clams—is their signature menu item. Across the road, Big Deck Raw Bar is an open-air, walk-up joint that hangs precariously over the edge of the backwater. Do not be fooled by the unpretentious décor. I think Big Deck has the best grouper sandwich on the island. If it is a juicy burger you crave, cross the street to The Tipsy Cow Bar and Grill.

For lodging, in addition to the Island Hotel, there is the Cedar Key Bed & Breakfast which occupies the tin-roofed, two-story historic Wadley House. The Eagle Cedar Mill built it as an employee residence in 1880 at the height of Cedar Key's cedar industry boom. For a while, the daughter of David Yulee (Florida's first US senator and builder of the Atlantic to Gulf/Florida Railroad) operated a boarding house out of it. For lodging on Dock Street try the Harbour Master Suites. For a little more elbow room try one of these two waterfront condominium complexes: Island Place Cedar Keys or Old Fenimore Mill Condominiums.

Not many towns this small can boast two historical museums but Cedar key can. The Cedar Key Historical Society operates the Cedar Key Historical Museum in the 1871 Lutterloh Building at the corner of State Road 24 and 2nd Street. This is a terrific place to become immersed in Cedar Key's past. Exhibits include ancient artifacts and historic photos and documents. The other museum, the Cedar Key State Museum, is part of the state park system. It is just outside of town and includes the original homestead of local St. Clair Whitman.

One of Cedar Key's most interesting historical episodes involves John Muir, who is famous for chronicling his epic trek across the Sierra

Night Sky over Dock Street, Cedar Key

Nevada, prompting the creation of Yosemite National Park, and for creating the Sierra Club. But before he did all that Muir hiked from Indiana down to Fernandina Beach, and then down and across the state to Cedar Key, where he intended to hop a freighter to Key West and from there to Cuba. Instead, he stayed for several months while recuperating from malaria. Sawmill owner R. W. B. Hodgson and his wife, Sarah, took Muir in and nursed him back to health. You can read Muir's story about the trip in his *A Thousand-Mile Walk to the Gulf*. The Cedar Key Historical Museum is also an excellent resource on all things John Muir.

When Muir first arrived in October 1867, he crossed the marshy tidewater on a railroad trestle that terminated on the other side in the town of Cedar Key. Today, the Railroad Trestle Nature Trail, maintained by Florida's Nature Coast Conservancy, can be hiked from its north end (at Grove Street, three-quarters of a mile north of 2nd Street/center of Cedar Key) for about one-third of a mile until it ends at the water, where you can see the remaining trestle pilings from the original railroad bridge. Although a short hike, you might see some of this area's native wildlife: roseate spoonbills, ibises, and ospreys.

There is a burgeoning industry in Cedar Key. In 1994, Florida voters passed a constitutional amendment that limited the size of fishing nets to five hundred square feet, effectively instituting a commercial net-fishing ban, as of 1995. Multigeneration fishing families, put out of business by the new law, began to look for alternative ways to make their living in the industry they knew best—seafood. One result was the rise of aquaculture—seafood farming. The fertile shellfish grounds in the mud-bottom bay waters around Cedar Key made this an ideal location to begin clam farming.

One of Cedar Key's largest farmers is Southern Cross Sea Farms. On Friday afternoons they allow visitors to tour their facility. Coowner Jon Gill was our guide on my visit. Jon walked us through the operation's entire process. Southern Cross Sea Farms is vertically integrated. They spawn, hatch, raise, and grow their clams, then sell them fully grown, to wholesalers, markets, and some directly to retail restaurants. They also sell hatchlings, ready to be "planted," to other clam farmers.

The process begins in their spawning tanks where they circulate estuary water with phytoplankton "food." One clam can produce as many as two thousand eggs. The young seedling clams that result are then moved to the "nursery"—outdoor tanks where they can grow. The spawning and nursery phase takes about six months, after which the young clams are placed in large mesh bags and planted in the bay mudflats in two-acre plots leased from the state. They spend approximately a year-and-a-half maturing in the bay (with one interim transition to larger-hole mesh bags), and then are packaged and sold. Southern Cross overnight airships their clams all around the country.

Clam aquaculture is an ecologically-sound and environmentally-clean business. Since farmed clams grow in their natural habitat, are fed and raised only with natural processes and water from the bay, there is essentially no impact on the environment. In fact, clams are natural filterers and clean the water they live in. Today, Southern Cross is testing the waters with oyster farming.

DON'T MISS
The Neptune Lounge at The Island Hotel

Withlacoochee River in front of Blackwater Grill and Bar, Yankeetown

YANKEETOWN

Population: 529

*F*lorida's north-central Gulf Coast area, the Big Bend, now officially called the Nature Coast but sometimes unofficially referred to as the Cracker Coast, starts somewhere north of New Port Richey and curves around to somewhere east of Lighthouse Point, south of Tallahassee. What distinguishes it from the rest of Florida's coast is that there are, with just a couple small exceptions (see Keaton Beach chapter), no beaches here. The sea bottom, extending for miles out into the Gulf of Mexico, is seldom deeper than ten feet. Because of this shallow shelf there is little wave action to build up a beach. Without beaches, there are no high-rise condos and hotels, fewer T-shirt shops, and fewer Bermuda short-clad tourists. The Big Bend coastline is mostly grass flats and marsh—what quite a bit of Florida looked like a hundred years ago. Some of Florida's most scenic spring-fed rivers empty into the Gulf in this stretch, and some lightly populated fishing villages have grown up around these areas. Yankeetown is one of these.

It meanders snake-like alongside the Withlacoochee River for about six miles, a few miles inland from the Gulf.

Yankeetown experienced brief national fame twice during the 1960s. First, during the 1960 Nixon-Kennedy presidential campaign, the townsfolk held a debate and a straw election. The news wires picked up the story, and it was a national topic for several days. Nixon won in Yankeetown.

Yankeetown's second brush with fame came in the summer of 1961, when the Mirisch Company and United Artists came here to make a movie based on Richard Powell's novel *Pioneer, Go Home*. For the big screen, the title was changed to *Follow That Dream*. It starred Elvis Presley, who stayed in Yankeetown for two months. Elvis fans came from far and wide to see their idol making his ninth major motion picture. Extra traffic police had to be brought in to keep the crowds at bay. One of the main film's set locations was a bridge where County Road 40 crosses Bird Creek about a mile from where it dead ends into the Gulf. Locals have renamed County Road 40 from Highway 19 west the Follow That Dream Parkway.

See Yankeetown! signs, made from a single horizontal board with one end sawed to a point, could be found alongside many of North Florida's and Georgia's rutted roads in the 1920s and 1930s, long before See Rock City! became a common sight. They advertised a riverside retreat at Honey Bluff along the Withlacoochee River. The original name for the retreat was going to be Knotts, named after A. F. Knotts, a U.S. Steel Corporation attorney, former Indiana state representative, and former mayor of Hammond, Indiana. After his retirement, Knotts came to Florida in search of a place to build a camp for fishing and hunting, preferably on a navigable freshwater stream.

Knotts had handled all the land transactions when U.S. Steel built the town of Gary, Indiana, in 1905, so he was quite familiar with founding communities. Initially, he purchased some property on Crystal River but in 1920 found that he liked the Honey Bluff area on the Withlacoochee River better. He advertised the location to his friends back in Indiana, and some came and built shanties alongside the river. To get there they had to travel by rail to Dunnellon, then ride twenty-five miles to the coast with Hugh Coleman, the Star Route mail carrier. It was Coleman who started calling the place Yankeetown, since he was carrying so many Yankees to Knotts's fishing camp. The name stuck. A. F.'s nephew, Eugene Knotts, suggested they build a lodge on the river to be run by himself and his wife, Norma, to accommodate short-term visitors. This would become the Izaak Walton Lodge, named after seventeenth-century English author Sir Izaak Walton, who was best known for *The Compleat Angler*, his treatise on the art and virtues of fishing and in praise of a simpler and more leisurely lifestyle. The lodge opened in 1924.

In 1987, Wayne and Linda Harrington purchased and renovated the Izaak Walton Lodge and opened the Compleat Angler Restaurant. But on July 22, 1999, disaster struck when the wooden lodge caught fire. Except for parts of the kitchen, most of the building was destroyed. The Harringtons, ever determined, rebuilt and reopened fourteen months later. The new lodge, while not an exact replica, paid fine homage to the original.

The lodge and restaurant have changed hands several times since, and as of 2017 is home to the Blackwater Grill & Bar, an upscale prime steak and fresh seafood restaurant owned and run by former Flemings Steakhouse chef Chris Wakeman.

In addition, Yankeetown has a new casual waterfront eatery and bar, a breakfast, burgers, and wings joint called the Chik'n'Butt Café.

DON'T MISS
Dining at the Blackwater Grill and Bar

Dunnellon Oklawaha

DeLeon Springs

Crystal
River Inverness
Ozello
Homosassa
Weeki Wachee Floral City
Aripeka Pineola
Istachatta Webster
Trilby
Dade City

Cassadaga

Mt. Dora

Orlando

Groveland Christmas

Ozello

Tampa

Yeehaw Junction

Anna Maria
Holmes Beach Cortez

Sebring

Lake Placid

Arcadia

Lake
Okeechobee

CENTRAL REGION

De Leon Springs State Park

DE LEON SPRINGS

Population: 2,642

*A*n American Indian tribe, called the Mayacas by Spanish explorers (the first Europeans to encounter them in 1565), were the original inhabitants of the region around what is today named De Leon Springs. Archaeological evidence suggests that the Mayaca had likely been here for six thousand years and possibly as much as twelve thousand years. Ancient dugout canoes, five thousand to six thousand years old, recovered in the spring in 1985 and in 1990 are likely the oldest canoes ever found in the Western Hemisphere. In the early 1830s, a plantation here called Spring Garden was purchased by Colonel Orlando Rees who built a water-powered sugar mill next to the spring. The remains of the mill can be seen today in De Leon Springs State Park.

By the 1890s, tourists were coming to Florida in droves and businesses were looking for a hook to attract them. The story of Spanish explorer Juan Ponce de Leon's search for the Fountain of Youth was a popular one, and so Spring Garden became De Leon Springs.

Juan Ponce de Leon never actually came to this spring, but John James Audubon did. Audubon visited with Rees in 1831 on a bird-sighting expedition. They traveled up Spring Garden Creek to what is now Lake Woodruff National Wildlife Refuge.

In 1925, The Ponce de Leon Hotel, a small resort, opened next to the spring, and in subsequent decades a variety of tourist amenities would be added: alligator pits, exotic bird exhibits, a jungle boat cruise, and a waterskiing elephant show. In 1961, owners Peter and Marjorie Schwarze opened a restaurant overlooking the spring and adjacent to the sugar mill works. By the mid-1960s the attraction had lost its luster and it closed, however the Old Spanish Sugar Mill Restaurant survived.

In 1980, a local group organized and solicited the state of Florida and Volusia County to convert the site to a park. They were successful, and De Leon Springs State Park opened in 1982. Today, the seventy-two-degree spring is an extremely popular swimming and scuba diving

De Leon Springs State Park

spot. The park now has a museum, and the remains of the sugar mill's brickwork and machinery have been preserved. But the most popular draw to De Leon Springs State Park is still the Old Spanish Sugar Mill Restaurant where pancake lovers get to make their own at tables with built-in griddles. The wait staff bring spatulas and pitchers of pancake batter to the tables, along with an assortment of accompaniments: blueberries, bananas, pecans, and chocolate chips to mix in, and patrons become at-the-table breakfast chefs.

DON'T MISS

Making your own pancakes at the Old Spanish
Sugar Mill Restaurant at De Leon Springs State Park

Kayaking on the Rainbow River

DUNNELLON

Population: 1,840

*T*he quiet agricultural town of Dunnellon, at the confluence of the Withlacoochee and Rainbow rivers, found itself transformed into a mining boomtown overnight in 1889. That year, while digging a well in his backyard, Albertus Vogt discovered a vein of extraordinarily pure hard-rock phosphate. He took a sample to Ocala railroad man John F. Dunn, who promptly bought a half interest in the property owned by Albertus and his brother John. The Dunnellon Phosphate Company (named for Dunn's wife, Ellen) was born. One year later, the town of Dunnellon incorporated, and then almost overnight it experienced the same transformation that Wild West towns had gone through during the gold rush. Schemers and scam artists smelled quick money and moved in. Saloons and brothels went up by the dozens. Saturday night street gunfights were commonplace. It was a slice of the Wild West in the Deep South, but it would not last long.

The boom era, and the lawlessness that accompanied it, faded after the turn of the century. Then it disappeared completely when the European market for phosphate came to a halt with the onset of World War I. Dunnellon returned to its quiet-community status. Around 1930, F. E. Hemphill and Frank Greene began to develop an area about three miles north of town that included the Rainbow Springs basin (known then as Blue Springs). They built a lodge, pavilion, and dock for a glass-bottom boat. The springs changed hands several times over the next several decades. In the late 1960s, Holiday Inn and S&H Green Stamps jointly purchased the property and further developed it as a tourist theme park, complete with a monorail ride, glass-bottom boats, a paddle-wheel riverboat called the *Rainbow Queen*, and wild animal exhibits. But when Interstate 75 was built, it bypassed Dunnellon to the east by twenty-two miles. Tourist traffic dried up, and the Rainbow Springs attraction closed its doors in 1974.

The community of Dunnellon knew that it had something special with Rainbow Springs, however. It is a first-magnitude spring with the fourth highest volume in Florida and a year-round water temperature of seventy-three degrees. The crystal-clear Rainbow River teems with bass and bream, and river otters frolic on its shoreline. The spring is a wonderful natural resource that Dunnellon's residents could not stand to see go to waste. They wanted it to be accessible to the community, but they also wanted it to be preserved (and not as a theme park). Throughout the late 1980s, a group of volunteers from Dunnellon, Citrus Springs, and the Village of Rainbow Springs Garden Club worked diligently to restore the park, all at their own expense. Ultimately, they were able to convince the state of Florida to purchase the property in 1990 and turn it into a state park. In 1992, Rainbow Springs State Park opened on weekends only, with major financial and volunteer help from the community. In March 1995, it celebrated its grand opening as a full-time state park—one of the state's most scenic. The monorail, riverboat, and glass-bottom boats are long gone, but what's left is the natural beauty that has always been here.

KP Hole County Park, just south of Rainbow Springs State Park, is a good spot to kayak, canoe, and inner tube. All are available to rent, or you can bring your own. For a premium guided group kayak trip.

Swampy's Bar and Grill, Dunnellon

I recommend Lars Anderson at Adventure Outpost (see appendix). I have paddled with Lars several times, including on the Rainbow River, and he knows more about the history of Florida's rivers, and about the wildlife that live in them, than anyone I have met. Adventure Outpost operates out of High Springs but Lars travels to most all of the Central Florida rivers.

Two good (bathing suit-casual) riverfront restaurants are The Blue Gator Tiki Bar and Swampy's Bar and Grill. The Blue Gator, on the Withlacoochee River, serves an assortment of seafood baskets: grouper fingers, oysters, scallops, frog legs, and peel-and-eat shrimp, generously seasoned and delicious. Swampy's, right before the takeout point on the Rainbow River, leans toward New Orleans fare: etouffee, jambalaya, red beans and sausage, and blackened red fish topped with shrimp and andouille sausage.

DON'T MISS

The Rainbow Springs State Park. If you have time, rent a kayak and paddle on the beautiful Rainbow River.

Gator Joe's Beach Bar and Grill, Ocklawaha

OCKLAWAHA

Population not listed on census

*T*he tranquil community of Ocklawaha wraps around the north shore of Lake Weir, about twenty miles southeast of Ocala. In the summertime, Lake Weir is a popular waterskiing and fishing spot. Cabins and docks line the shore, and Gator Joe's Beach Bar and Grill, occupying an old 1926 stilt building, sits on the lake's edge.

Waterskiing, fishing, and eating some good grub are usually about as exciting as things get around here. But eighty years ago, less than one-quarter of a mile down the beach from Gator Joe's, the reign of one of history's most infamous bank robbery and kidnapping gangs ended in a bloody gun battle with the FBI. In the predawn hours of January 16, 1935, FBI agents caught up with the notorious Ma Barker Gang and engaged in a six-hour shootout that left Ma and son Fred dead.

Ocklawaha is a place far enough off the beaten path that if you were so inclined, you could hide away here for some time without being found. Arizona Clark "Ma" Barker, also known as Kate, must

GATOR JOE'S FOOT

JOE WAS A 15 FT. 7 IN. ALLIGATOR THAT LIVED ON LAKE WEIR IN THE EARLY 1900's. HE CAUGHT HIS FAME FROM THE MA BARKER GANG, WHO TRIED TO KILL HIM ON SEVERAL OCCASIONS; BUT JOE ULTIMATELY GOT THEM INSTEAD. HIS LOCAL LEGEND LED THE F.B.I. TO THE BARKER HIDEOUT ON JANUARY 16, 1935 AND AFTER A 4-HOUR GUN BATTLE THE GANG ALL LAY DEAD. IN 1952 JOE CROSSED PATHS WITH A LOCAL GATOR HUNTER NAMED VIC SKIDMORE   IN JOE'S FOOT HAS HAD MANY HOMES   UT FLORIDA AND EVEN IN KENTUCKY. IT WAS   O US FROM ONE F VIC's FRIEND MR. JIM TOWNSLEE.

Gator Joe's Beach Bar and Grill, Ocklawaha

have had that same impression when she came here in November 1934 and rented a two-story wood-frame house on the shore of Lake Weir under the alias Mrs. T. C. Blackburn. Ma and Fred Barker, "the Blackburns," were considered friendly by the locals. They were regulars and big tippers at the bar. But before long, boredom got the best of Fred, and he began shooting at ducks on Lake Weir with his machine gun, which that did not set well with the locals. When Fred let it be known that he wanted to hunt down "Old Joe," a legendary (and considered by most harmless) old alligator that lived in the lake (not to be confused with Wakulla Springs' Old Joe), the locals were enraged, and word of his intentions spread. Fred's description matched one on the FBI's most wanted list.

The Barker boys—Herman, Lloyd, Arthur (who was called "Doc"), and Fred—had always been bad eggs. As kids, they were bullies and thieves in their hometown of Webb City, Missouri, and later in Tulsa, Oklahoma. They spent most of their formative years in scrapes with the law. Ma, who as a child had seen in person and idolized Jesse James, not only tolerated these activities but encouraged them. She ultimately organized the Barkers into a criminal gang.

In 1922, police officers caught Lloyd during a post office hold up and sent him to Leavenworth. In 1927, the oldest brother, Herman, shot himself rather than be captured following a gun battle with police in Wichita, Kansas. Undaunted, the Barker gang continued its crime spree. The gang was joined by Alvin "Old Creepy" Karpis (nicknamed because of his menacing expression), a former Kansas State Penitentiary inmate and associate of Fred's. For a while, bank robberies were their specialty, and they always left a trail of dead bodies behind—policemen, innocent bystanders, and sometimes fellow criminals. Then the Barkers figured out that there was more money in kidnapping than bank robbing when they abducted William Hamm Jr. of the Hamm Brewing Company in St. Paul, Minnesota. They collected $100,000 ransom for his release in June 1933. In January 1934, Fred and Old Creepy kidnapped wealthy St. Paul banker Edward Bremer. Bremer's family paid $200,000, and he was returned unharmed.

By now the Barker gang was at the top of the FBI's Most Wanted list. They were on the run. They even went so far as to have a doctor accomplice try to surgically alter their faces and scrape their fingers so their prints would be unrecognizable. The gang split and went in different directions to try to foil the FBI. That may have been the beginning of their downfall.

In January 1935 in Chicago, FBI agent Melvin Purvis caught Doc and sent him to Alcatraz. In Doc's apartment, agents found a map of Florida with a circle drawn around Ocala and Lake Weir. Ultimately, however, it was Fred Barker's propensity for cruelty to animals that pinpointed their location for the FBI.

One hour before dawn, on the morning of January 16, 1935, fourteen agents quietly surrounded the house. Chief Agent E. J. Connelly announced, "We're from the Department of Justice. Come out one at a time." Ma Barker yelled in response, "All right, Freddie! Go ahead!" and the Barkers opened fire. Suddenly, residents of the sleepy town bolted upright in their beds, startled from their slumber by the rapid and continuous blasting of machine guns. FBI agents fired more than

1,500 rounds into the house for nearly an hour, and then continued to shoot through the windows intermittently for five more hours. When they finally went inside, they found Ma and Fred dead on the floor of the bullet-riddled upstairs bedroom. They also found an arsenal of rifles, machine guns, pistols, and ammunition. Ma was clutching her machine gun in her hands.

A year later, J. Edgar Hoover caught up with Alvin Karpis in New Orleans. Karpis spent thirty-two years in prison. Ten years after his release, he died of a drug overdose. Lloyd Barker served a twenty-five-year sentence and then was shot by his wife two years after his release. In 1939, Doc Barker attempted to escape from Alcatraz. He made it over the walls and was standing on the shore of the island when guards fatally shot him.

For many years, the privately-owned "Ma Barker House" sat overlooking Lake Weir, only rarely allowing visitors. Then, in 2016, the house (but not the property it was on) was donated to Marion County, placed on a barge, and floated across the lake to its new home at the Carney Island Recreation & Conservation Area. The house is maintained by the county and guided tours are available.

Gator Joe's Beach Bar and Grill is a great lakefront joint for Florida cracker cuisine like frog legs, catfish sandwiches, and gator tail. Gator Joe's pays tribute, not to the Barkers, but to lovable Old Joe himself (his actual paw hangs on the wall), although Gator Tail does feature prominently on the menu.

DON'T MISS
Seeing Old Joe's paw on display at Gator Joe's Beach Bar and Grill

Cassadaga Spiritualist Camp Bookstore

CASSADAGA

Population not listed on census

A century-and-half ago, self-proclaimed spiritualist George Colby had become financially destitute and was in poor health. Colby claimed, during a séance, that an Indian spirit guide named Seneca had instructed him to take a journey south, despite his situation. Seneca advised him to build a community where other spiritualists could learn, live, and teach. First, he must go by way of Wisconsin. In Wisconsin, Colby met T. D. Giddings. In another séance, Seneca directed the two of them specifically to go to Florida. Colby and Giddings's family settled on a lake in wild Central Florida that Colby claimed he had envisioned in the séance. In 1880, he built a home and filed for homestead on seventy-four acres. Homestead was granted four years later, but Colby did not stay. He set out across the country to lecture and hold séances. It was not until 1894 that a group from New York approached Colby about organizing the Southern Cassadaga Spiritualist Camp Meeting Association. In January 1895, he deeded thirty-five acres of his property to the association, and the community of Cassadaga was born. They held their first camp meeting the following month in Colby's home.

Cassadaga must have been at least somewhat financially successful for Colby and Giddings, although that was not its purpose. George Colby was able to live there for most of the balance of his life as the town's main spiritual advisor. Early writings about nearby Lake Helen describe T. D. Giddings's house as prominent and the first to have "real glass windows."

Originally, Cassadaga was just a winter retreat for psychics from up north. As more people arrived around the turn of the century, the association began leasing plots of land to them to build their own homes on. Today, this arrangement still exists with most of the homeowners today. Most of the town's residents are still spiritualists, mediums, or psychics. Cassadaga's current fifty-seven acres have been designated a Historic District on the National Register of Historic Places.

The association defines a spiritualist as "one who believes, as the basis of his or her religion, in the communication of this with the spirit

Cassadaga Cottage

world by means of mediumship, and who endeavors to mold his or her character and conduct in accordance with the highest teachings derived from such communion." Mediums, of course, are those who communicate with the spirit world.

The two-story Cassadaga Hotel was built in 1928 and is the town's centerpiece. It sits on the site of a previous building that had been there since just before the turn of the century but burned down in 1926. A few of the Cassadaga Hotel rooms are reserved for psychic reading sessions, which the hotel schedules, but the remainder are available for lodging. Naturally, it is haunted. Purportedly, an Irish singer named Arthur, who had lived there in the 1930s, passed away in his room. Arthur, a cigar smoker, appears to be a benevolent presence, and patrons report the smell of cigar smoke and occasional friendly taps on the shoulder. Sinatra's Ristorante, located in the hotel, specializes in Italian dishes like osso bucco and eggplant rollatini.

The 1905 Andrew Jackson Davis Building, across the street from the Cassadaga Hotel, was originally built as a lecture hall that doubled as an event venue. It is named for one of the early pioneers of the spiritualist movement. Today, it is still a center of activity, housing the Cassadaga Spiritualist Camp Bookstore. The store is a well-stocked source for books on metaphysics, spiritualism, and Cassadaga history, and is a good place to find New Age items like crystals, candles, and incense. It is also a one-stop sign up spot for psychic readings, past life regressions, and ghost tours.

It is worthwhile to take a walk down the narrow streets of Cassadaga. Start by picking up a self-guided walk brochure at the Cassadaga Spiritualist Camp Bookstore. Along the way you will see brightly painted gingerbread cottages, and some that seem a bit creepy, obscured by overgrown vines and overhanging Spanish moss. Most have a "Medium" or "Spiritual Guidance" shingle hanging out front. There are several small parks and gardens worth stopping at: Seneca Park, Medicine Wheel Park, and Horseshoe Park with its Fairy Trail.

DON'T MISS

The self-guided walking tour, starting at the
Cassadaga Spiritualist Camp Bookstore

Old Courthouse Heritage Museum, Inverness

INVERNESS

Population: 7,414

*I*nverness was originally named Tompkinsville, after two brothers and post–Civil War Confederate soldiers, who settled here in 1868. Records show that the name changed to Inverness in 1889. Local legend claims that an emigrant Scotsman (whose name no one can recall) became homesick while standing on the banks of Lake Tsala Apopka (adjacent to Tompkinsville/Inverness). It reminded him of the lake country near his home in Inverness, Scotland. At least one report claims that the Scotsman was one of the many phosphate-boom speculators who swarmed to north-central Florida in the late 1880s and early 1890s and offered to donate $2,000 toward the construction of a new courthouse if the name of the town was changed.

In 1887, the newly formed Citrus County had designated the nearby town of Mannfield as the temporary county seat. Four years later, a county election decided that Inverness would become the permanent county seat—much to the disappointment of the residents of

Mannfield and to the consternation of Senator Austin S. Mann, who developed Mannfield. W. C. Zimmerman, clerk of the circuit court at that time, refused to vacate the old Mannfield office, and refused to deliver the county records to the new location. He sat at his desk while the entire office was removed around him and loaded onto a wagon. Finally, the sheriff and a contingent of deputies loaded Zimmerman, still in his chair, onto the wagon along with his desk and boxes of records and transported everything to the new offices in Inverness. Accounts I have read say that Zimmerman continued to record minutes throughout the trip. Inverness went on to become a center of commerce while Mannfield became a ghost town. Zimmerman later became the Citrus County superintendent of schools.

At first, Inverness townsfolk feared that the widening of US Highway 41 in 1993, and the consequential bypass of their downtown Main Street, would be the equivalent of cutting off the blood supply to a limb. Happily, the opposite happened. Thanks to a committee of local businesspeople, instead of succumbing to a withering death, downtown Inverness got an injection of new life. Its one-block-long Main Street— the historic Citrus County Courthouse marking its east end and the twenty-foot-tall Bank of Inverness clock at its west end, is now a vibrant district with restaurants, galleries, and shops.

Today, gas lantern-style streetlights blend well with Main Street's restored buildings and storefronts. The brick three-story neoclassical-revival Masonic Lodge Building at the corner of Main and Pine Streets was considered a skyscraper when it was constructed (for $17,285) in 1910. The Masons leased the first floor to retail shops and the second floor to a dance and theater production group and used the third floor as their lodge. Today, the restored building once again has retail shops downstairs. The Citrus County Board of County Commissioners, a real estate office, and a law firm occupy the upper floors.

The old yellow brick 1912 Citrus County Courthouse, which replaced the original 1892 wood structure, has been immaculately restored under the supervision of the Citrus County Historical Society. The process, completed in October 2000, took eight years and $2.5 million. It is now home to the Old Courthouse Heritage Museum. Downstairs rooms that previously housed the offices of tax collectors, judges, and clerks of the court are now galleries portraying local history, exhibits of pre- and early-history artifacts, and one room is now the museum store. The most impressive room, however, is the old courtroom, which occupies the entire second floor. Architects used old photographs to accurately reconstruct details throughout the building, but for the courtroom they watched old reels of the 1961 Elvis Presley movie *Follow That Dream*. The closing scene for the movie was filmed in the second floor courtroom and was the best historical record of what the room looked like then. (Much of the movie was also filmed in Yankeetown. For more information, see the Yankeetown chapter.)

Many of Inverness' other buildings and houses from its prosperous turn of the century era are still in use. Some have been restored. One of the most impeccable restorations is Citrus High School, now the administration building for Citrus Memorial Hospital. This red brick two-story building, with a bell tower over its entrance, was originally built in 1911 and restored in 1992.

Another interesting historic home is the 1900 Hicks House at the corner of Tompkins Street and Osceola Avenue. Robert Hicks designed and built this unusual octagonal-shaped house to withstand hurricanes. It is still in the Hicks family today and may be the oldest home in Inverness.

Perhaps Inverness' most recognizable historic building is the Crown Hotel. This grand three-story wooden hotel building had much more humble beginnings. The Crown began life as a general store when Alf, one of the Tompkins brothers, gave his brother-in-law, Francis Dampier, property on which to build a store. Dampier built the store on one side of the street and his home on the other side. Sometime around 1900, Dampier moved his store from Bay Street to Main Street, and in 1907 he turned it into a boarding house called the Orange Hotel. Ten years after that, he sold it to a New York hotel syndicate, which moved it again in 1926, this time around the corner to Seminole Avenue, its present location.

In conjunction with the move, the New York group performed what must have been an amazing feat of construction in its day: they built an entirely new bottom floor, then hoisted the original two-story building up into the air and placed it on top of the new first floor to make a three-story hotel, which they named the Colonial.

Old Main Street, Inverness

The Colonial was a popular place for several decades, but by the 1970s it had fallen into serious disrepair. It had become condemned when, in 1979, British company Epicure Holdings purchased it and spent $2 million renovating it into the decidedly British Crown Hotel. At one time, the hotel even had its own authentic 1909 double-decker bus, purchased at an auction in London. It was an Inverness landmark that sat parked in front of the Crown for many years. The hotel was sold to Nigel and Jill Sumner in 1990, and then sold again in 2001 when it was converted into an assisted living facility, The Crown Court, which it remains today.

Bicycle touring has become extremely popular in and around Inverness. The forty-six-mile-long Withlacoochee State Trail, which runs roughly from Trilby in the south to Dunnellon in the north, was one of Florida's first "Rails to Trails" projects and is its longest paved rail-trail. The state bought the rail right-of-way, which was no longer in use, and converted it into a state park trail. It comes to its approximate two-thirds point in Inverness and passes through just a couple of blocks north of downtown.

There is plenty of good food, either on Main Street or within walking distance of it: Stumpknocker's for seafood, frog legs, and gator tail; Coach's Pub & Eatery for burgers and wings; there's outstanding pizza at Angelo's Pizzeria; and Cattle Dog Coffee Roasters is the best espresso spot downtown.

DON'T MISS
The Old Courthouse Heritage Museum (Elvis Presley was here!)

Lakeside Inn, Mount Dora

MOUNT DORA

Population: 14,516

Charming and picturesque in an almost New England fashion, Mount Dora is only thirty miles northwest of Orlando, but a century away in time. It could easily be Florida's version of Bedford Falls, particularly at Christmastime. Victorian homes, a postcard turn of the century main street, antique shops, superb restaurants, and inviting lodgings make Mount Dora one of Florida's most-visited small towns. It has become famous for festivals: an art festival in February, an antique boat festival and regatta in March, a seafood festival in September, and its annual bicycle festival in October, among others. But its most festive time is Christmas, with city-wide lighting and decorating, tours of historic homes, and a lighted parade.

Mount Dora can trace its history to the late 1800s when a local postmaster, Ross Tremain, provisionally named the small community of homesteaders Royellou—a combination of the names of his three children. After a few years, the name changed to Mount Dora,

135

after Dora Ann Drawdy, one of the earliest area homesteaders, back in the 1840s.

The town began to develop in earnest when James Alexander, John MacDonald, and J. P. Donnelly opened a ten-room inn overlooking Lake Dora in 1883. They named it the Alexander House, but subsequent owners would rename it the Lake House, and later the Lakeside Inn—which remains today. One historical highlight of note is that in the winter of 1930, Calvin Coolidge came to the inn for an extended sabbatical with his wife following his just-completed term as president. During their stay, he dedicated the newly completed Gables and Terrace Wings. James Barggren and Richard Dempsey bought the Lakeside Inn in 1992 and restored it to its 1920s–1930s heyday style. With the main building and two wings, the inn now has eighty-eight rooms, a lounge, a restaurant, tennis courts, a pool, and a dock on the lake. Perhaps the most enjoyable activity though, is sitting in one of the rocking chairs on the main lodge's expansive veranda, sipping iced tea and soaking up the view across placid Lake Dora.

Mount Dora offers additional intimate lodging as well. The Adora Inn Bed & Breakfast is just a one-block walk from downtown and occupies a beautiful artfully-restored three-story 1916 bungalow, with an interior that cleverly blends traditional arts and crafts with 1950s modern style. Arthur Natale and John Cataldo teamed up in 2005 to open The Adora. Both have extensive culinary backgrounds: Arthur honed his skills at restaurants in SoHo, New York, and John is a Culinary Institute of America graduate.

One of the most historic and ornate houses in Mount Dora is the Donnelly House at the uphill end of Donnelly Street between Fifth and Sixth Avenues. The Masonic Lodge currently owns it, so entry is limited to special events, but the outside is a grand example of Queen Anne Victorian style. In Donnelly's day—the late 1800s to early 1900s—it was referred to as the "gingerbread house." Donnelly had homesteaded 160 acres adjacent to property owned by Annie Stone, one of the earliest homesteaders. In 1881, the two married and began the development of what is now downtown Mount Dora. They built their gingerbread house in 1893. Donnelly, one of Mount Dora's most

Donnelly Street, Mount Dora

prominent citizens, went on to be the town's first mayor in 1910. In 1924, he sold the large tract of land across the street from his house to the city for a park named in honor of his wife.

Mount Dora has long been a popular destination with antique shoppers but is also known for its unusual shops. Pet lovers love to visit Piglet's Pantry Dog Bakery, where they bake "to-slobber-for" doggie treats and carry a great selection of gifts and toys for both dogs and cats, as well as their owners.

There is no shortage of great food in Mount Dora. The Goblin Market Restaurant is a hidden culinary jewel, nestled in a pedestrian alley. It may sound odd to get excited about soup, but theirs is amazing. Try their Irish whiskey onion soup or the crab bisque. Then choose from delectable entrees like New Zealand rack of lamb encrusted with fennel, mustard seed, and roasted garlic, topped with a brandy mint demi-glace; or wasabi-crusted salmon with a honey butter and soy glaze. At the Windsor Rose English Tea Room, they serve "spot on" traditional British fare, like cottage pie, and bangers and mash. At Pisces Rising diners have a terrific view of scenic Lake Dora. The menu mixes Caribbean/Cuban with dishes such as Cuban

Goblin Market, Mount Dora

yellowtail snapper; Spanish with seafood paella; Cajun with jambalaya; and Florida cracker with shrimp and grits.

Mount Dora is easily explored on foot, but if your legs get tired you can rent a Segway at Segway of Central Florida, right in downtown.

DON'T MISS
Lunch at The Goblin Market Restaurant

Ferris Groves Store, Floral City

FLORAL CITY, PINEOLA, ISTACHATTA

**Population: Floral City 5,308;
Pineola not listed on census; Istachatta 194**

*A*ll who drive down Orange Avenue in Floral City for the first time have to stop and marvel at the grand oaks that reach clear across the road to intertwine with one another. Over the past 130 years, those trees have grown tall and wide, crossing over the top of the road and forming one-quarter mile-long tunnel known as the "Avenue of Oaks."

Aroostook Avenue, with its own rows of oak trees, forks diagonally northeast from Orange Avenue and dead-ends at the shore of Lake Tsala Apopka. This was a busy steamboat port from which oranges, lumber, and the occasional passenger would ship out via the newly completed (in 1884) Orange State Canal down the Withlacoochee River to the railhead at Lake Panasoffkee. Aroostook Avenue was Floral City's original Main Street until the big freeze of 1894–1895 killed the area's citrus industry and ended the steamboat business. Fortunately for the town, right around the same time, phosphate was discovered nearby. Mines opened, and Floral City had a new industry.

The picturesque town of Floral City, established in 1884, has an impressive collection of historic homes and buildings. Some are restored but most are simply well preserved. Many were built during the phosphate boom (1890s–1910s) when Floral City's population swelled briefly to more than ten thousand with the influx of transient mine workers. At least one house predates that era: The Formy-Duval House, at 7801 Old Floral City Road (which runs north and south a couple of blocks east of Highway 41), was built in 1865. It is the oldest house still standing in the area. John Paul Formy-Duval was a cotton, sugarcane, and citrus farmer who owned vast tracts of land surrounding the southern end of Lake Tsala Apopka. Some of his land, 342 acres, would eventually become the town of Floral City.

Avenue of the Oaks, Floral City

The 1894 D. A. Tooke House, at 8560 Orange Avenue, and the 1910 J. T. Love House, next door at 8580 Orange Avenue, are two good examples of Queen Anne Victorian architectural style. Both are large one-story homes with twin steep-roofed gables. The simple wood frame Floral City Methodist Church, at 8508 Marvin Street (a block north of Orange Avenue), has been in continuous use since its construction in 1884. The cracker Victorian-style W. C.

Zimmerman House, at 8441 East Orange Avenue, was built in 1890. (See Inverness chapter about W. C. Zimmerman.) The cedar shingle-sided Soloman Moon House, at 8860 East Orange Avenue, was built in 1893. The 1904 William H. Dunn House, at 8050 South Bedford Road (on the west side of Highway 41 and several blocks south of Orange Avenue), is the boyhood home of well-known Florida historian Hampton Dunn.

The two-story 1889 Commercial Hotel (also called the Magnolia Hotel) at 8375 East Orange Avenue, with its full-width front porch, leaded stained glass windows, and triple-gabled roof, was originally the home of James Baker, son-in-law of town developer John Paul Formy-Duval. The house was relocated from its original location two blocks away in 1895 and converted into an elegant hotel. It is now a private residence.

Floral City's largest business is citrus grower Ferris Groves. Doc Ferris started his orange grove business in 1927 when he took over property on Duval Island (in Lake Tsala Apopka) on which his father had originally intended to build a golf course. Ferris reintroduced citrus to the area after its forty-year absence. In 1940, Ferris built a packing plant and a roadside fruit stand on Highway 41 just north of Orange Avenue. In 1955, he built a permanent fruit store and gift shop that still operates today. It is reminiscent of the many tourist shops that sprang up in the 1950s and 1960s along Florida thoroughfares. After another hard freeze in the mid-1980s, the folks at Ferris Groves changed their focus to strawberries, for which they are famous today. The store is generally closed during the summer season, so check before visiting.

The Withlacoochee State Trail (described in the Inverness chapter) passes through Floral City, so this is a popular spot for cyclists, and for touring motorcyclists. The Shamrock Inn (the trail passes right beside it) is a good spot to grab breakfast, lunch, or dinner, seven days a week. Try the corned beef sandwich.

Floral City has a curious list of residents who were relatives of famous people. Doc Ferris was the grandnephew of George Washington Gale Ferris, who invented the Ferris wheel and introduced it at the 1893 Chicago World's Fair. One of Floral City's early (1880s) orange grove farmers, Jacob Clemens, was the cousin of Samuel Clemens (Mark Twain).

Floral City resident Robert Dillinger (by all accounts, a mild-mannered fellow) was cousin to notorious 1930's gangster John Dillinger.

Floral City's best known native was Hampton Dunn, a longtime Tampa resident. When Mr. Dunn passed away in February 2002, Florida lost one of its finest historians (and one of my favorite Florida history resources). No one could bring Florida's past to life like Hampton Dunn.

History has always been important to folks in Floral City, and in 2009 the Heritage Hall Museum and Country Store opened in the old fire station building on Orange Avenue. The museum displays historic photographs and maps as well as dioramas that chronicle the history of Floral City and the surrounding region.

While this book is about small towns, occasionally the roads that run between them merit mentioning, which is the case with Istachatta Road (CR 39) heading south out of Floral City. It is one of my favorite top-down roadster roads, winding over scenic rolling hills, through oak hammocks, and past horse farms and pastureland for seven miles. It parallels and crisscrosses the Withlacoochee State Trail. Near its south end, it eases into quiet Pineola with its handful of residences and an old cemetery next to the New Hope United Methodist Church, one of the oldest churches in this area. Church founders built the original New Hope Church out of logs on this site in 1830, and then replaced

New Hope Church Cemetery, Pineola

it with a wood frame structure following a fire in 1886. In 1940, the congregation built the current church, reusing much of the lumber from the 1886 building. Some of their hand-hewn pews are from the original 1830 church. New Hope's annual October Homecoming draws a good-sized crowd of past parishioners from around the state.

Just past Pineola is Istachatta. The name has been variously interpreted as Creek Indian for "red man" and "man's river crossing." There was a ferry crossing here on the Withlacoochee River in the 1800s that was replaced by an iron bridge in 1910 (which is no longer there). Istachatta has a tiny post office across from what had been the Istachatta General Store—once a popular stop for bicyclists on the Withlacoochee Trail, which passes right next to it. But the store closed in the early 2000s. In 2010, Janie Schneck (the mother of Back Street Boys Nick Carter) bought and remodeled it into The Blue Canoe Café. Unfortunately, that, too, closed a year later, and the store remains abandoned.

Istachatta General Store, 1998 and 2020

DON'T MISS
A drive up Orange Avenue, the Avenue of the Oaks

Three Sisters Springs Park, Crystal River

CRYSTAL RIVER

Population: 3,186

Crystal River's most famous and favorite resident is the affable manatee. Somehow, sailors of yore mistook these blunt-nosed teddy bears-of-the-sea for mermaids. Actually, they are more closely related to elephants. Twelve months on a small ship without women could convince you otherwise though, I guess. Although they seem to be in perpetual slow-motion, manatees do keep busy. They are voracious herbivores. Adults can easily consume 150 pounds of mostly floating vegetation each day. These docile, one thousand-pound beauties really have only one enemy, and it is us. Boat strikes kill fifty to a hundred a year, and dozens more die from getting caught in flood gates, canal locks, or entangled in debris, like discarded fishing line and rope.

Manatees are protected by three laws: the Marine Mammal Protection Act of 1972, the Endangered Species Act of 1973, and the Florida Manatee Sanctuary Act of 1978. Happily, their population

144

has been growing in recent years. Come winter, manatees leave the cooling coastal waters for the relative warmth of rivers and springs. Three Sisters Spring, on Crystal River, has long been one of their favorite hangouts. In recent years record numbers have been coming to Three Sisters, so much so that wildlife officials often close the spring to swimmers, but you can still see them outside the spring in the river. There are some common-sense rules for swimming with manatees: no scuba gear; snorkel gear only; do not crowd them; don't chase them; don't move aggressively around them; avoid physical contact; and give them space. Most manatees seem at ease with just a few people swimming with them, and some are even gregarious, swimming right up to you. But it becomes a problem when lots of people crowd into their refuge, sometimes diverting them from the warmer springs. Educating the public about manatees has been tremendously successful in the effort to protect them, but the double-edged sword is that it has also generated more interest in seeing them in person in recent years—a lot more interest. Because of this, Save the Manatee has petitioned the US Fish and Wildlife Service to make several of the springs in Crystal River/Kings Bay (including Three Sisters Spring) permanent manatee sanctuaries, and to implement a "no-touch" policy. I've snorkeled with manatees twice in Crystal River and feel privileged to have been able to do so. The primal human-animal bond that you feel is extraordinary. And I know I have a better appreciation for them, having done it. But I have probably communed with the manatees at Crystal River for the last time. Since my last visit new strict seasonal, water temperature, and number of swimmers' limitations have been put into place, and this a good thing. (See the link to Fish and Wildlife Service Crystal River manatee rules in the appendix.)

There is a far less intrusive way to see them: the fifty-seven acre Three Sisters Springs Park, has a boardwalk that circumnavigates Three Sisters Spring from which you can look straight down into the glass-clear water and see the manatees, surprisingly well. The park is a smaller parcel within the Crystal River National Wildlife Refuge. In 2010, the City of Crystal River, in conjunction with the Southwest Florida Water Management District and the US Fish and Wildlife Service formed the Three Sisters Springs Park. Visitors begin at the park's

Cattle Dog Coffee Roasters, Crystal River

service center, just up Highway 19, where you can catch a shuttle for a short ride directly into the park.

There is another adventure for visitors in Crystal River—a must see for Indiana Jones types—the Crystal River Archaeological Park. This sixty-one-acre park is the site of a pre-Columbian, American Indian settlement that dates back some 2,500 years, and that may have been occupied continuously for 1,600 years. There are six burial, midden, and temple mounds here. Plus, two rock stele—monuments with ancient carvings—one with a crudely carved human face and torso. The stones were found in 1964 and are thought to have been erected around 440 AD. Archaeological evidence suggest that ancient native people traveled to this complex to bury their dead and conduct trade, some from other settlements as far away as (what is now) Ohio. Avid (although technically an amateur) archaeologist Clarence B. Moore was the first to excavate at the Crystal River site, in 1903. Today, it is a National Historic Landmark.

For lodging, Plantation on Crystal River has long been a popular place that is right on King's Bay. It has a spa, boat docks, rental kayaks, canoes, and john boats, and a good restaurant and tiki bar.

Another waterfront dining spot to consider is Charlie's Fish House. Charlie and Marion Kofmehl opened their original seafood market and restaurant here in 1960, and in the early 1970s sons Jimmy and Phil took over. In 1990, they built the current restaurant and consolidated the market under the same roof. Charlie's menu includes items like crabmeat stuffed turbot and Atlantic salmon Oscar with lump crab, asparagus, and béarnaise sauce.

I also found a terrific coffee and pastry shop, Cattle Dog Coffee Roasters (named as a nod to owner Stephen Dorst's blue heeler cattle dog Barney) where they pull expert espressos and roast their own beans.

Heritage Village, Crystal River's walking-friendly art gallery venue is across the street from Cattle Dog Coffee Roasters. Two that impressed me are the Franklin Anderson Gallery of Arts and the Coastal Art Gallery. Both feature some spectacular local artist's works: paintings, glass and wood sculpture, and pottery—including a fine collection of folk art face jugs at the Franklin Anderson Gallery.

Franklin Anderson Gallery, Crystal River

DON'T MISS
Seeing the Manatees at Three Sisters Springs Park

Peck's Old Port Cove Restaurant, Ozello

OZELLO

Population not listed on census

*A*bout halfway between Crystal River and Homosassa, Citrus County Road 494, also called Ozello Trail, winds west for about nine miles through swampy forest and palmetto scrub. Intermittently, as you near the coast, the road opens to saw grass savannas dotted with cedar bay heads. The community of Ozello is technically on an island, separated from the mainland by tributaries of the St. Martin River, Salt Creek, and Greenleaf Bay. Hundreds of water passageways crosshatch this region. Airboats are the transport of choice here. Until 1955, Ozello Trail was an oyster shell path with palmetto logs bridging the swampy sections. It frequently flooded, but this was no deterrent to the residents, who were accustomed to getting around by boat. From 1880 until 1943, Ozella's children daily paddled rowboats and canoes to their one-room schoolhouse on one of the many tiny hammocks in the bay just south of Ozello. They called it the Isle of Knowledge. The

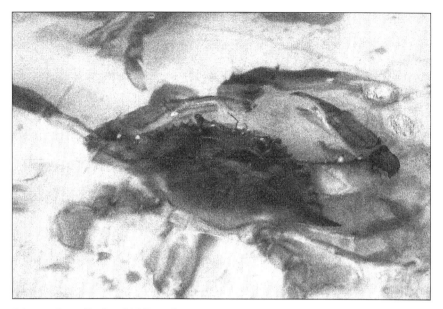

Blue crabs at Peck's Old Port Cove Restaurant, Ozello

island is still there (south off the end of John Brown Road), but unfortunately the schoolhouse is gone.

Ozello Trail ends at the edge of the open Gulf of Mexico and at Peck's Old Port Cove Seafood Restaurant and Blue Crab Farm. Calvin Peck began harvesting blue crabs in specially constructed tanks behind his restaurant in 1982. Around back, you can survey the operation. Hundreds of blue crabs fill fourteen tanks. I've eaten at Peck's many times, usually when I crave a heaping bowl of their steaming garlic crabs. They'll give you a bib, and you'll need it, but you're going to get splattered with crab shell, butter, and garlic anyway. Granted, the ratio of crab-meat-acquired to work-cracking-to-get-it is low, but it is so worth it.

DON'T MISS
Enjoying a heaping plate of blue crab claws at Peck's

Shelly's Seafood & Fish Market, Homosassa

HOMOSASSA

Population: 13,477

*T*he Homosassa River, one of the busiest on Florida's Gulf Coast, has long been popular for boating, and for access to fishing and scalloping in the Gulf. There is always a line on weekends at the public boat ramp next to Macrae's Marina. Once you do get on the water it is worth turning upriver a few hundred yards from Macrae's to see Monkey Island. It is a tiny island in the middle of the river, with its own (decorative) lighthouse and a tree house with ropes draped across the trees. This is home for a couple dozen monkeys, purportedly descendants of test monkeys from a 1950s polio vaccine lab. They have a reputation for mischief and are known to snatch food from passing boats, so don't get too close.

No surprise—there's good seafood to be found in Homosassa. The first time I drove by The Freezer I did not have a reason to stop because I thought it was a wholesale seafood warehouse, and it is. But if you walk up their loading ramp and through the freezer curtain, you

Underwater observatory at Homosassa Springs Wildlife State Park, Homosassa

suddenly find yourself in one of this area's worst-kept secrets. The Freezer Tiki Bar backs up to a creek that veers off the Homosassa River, and patrons often arrive by boat. There is a thatch roof over the tables but it's all open-air. It is cash only, and the only nonseafood item on the menu is hotdogs. Everything is fresh: steamed peel-and-eat shrimp, steamed blue crabs, stone crab claws (when they're in season, mid-October to mid-May), and their specialty: smoked mullet.

Shelly's Seafood & Fish Market, just around the bend from The Freezer, is another terrific fresh seafood spot for take-out or to take home and cook it yourself.

Two other good seafood restaurants, on the opposite bank of the river, are Seagrass Waterfront Restaurant and Crumps' Landing. Both serve great fresh-off-the-boat seafood, with a riverfront view.

For an interesting twenty-minute break on your way to the river, stop at the Yulee Sugar Mill Ruins. This was once part of a sugar plantation owned by Florida senator and railroad builder David Levy Yulee. Much of the steam-driven mill, which operated from 1851 to 1864, remains. The operation supplied sugar to troops during the Civil War.

Homosassa Springs Wildlife State Park, Homosassa

You could easily spend an entire day at the Ellie Schiller Homosassa Springs Wildlife State Park. This location had been a tourist stop since the early 1900s, but in 1964 the Norris Development Company purchased it and opened Homosassa Springs Nature's Own Attraction. The big draw was an underwater viewing observatory dubbed "Natures Fishbowl" where you could see bass and brim swimming right in front of your eyes. It was a place that fascinated me as an elementary school kid in the late 1960s. Today, paved wildlife observation trails and elevated boardwalks wind through the park. One segment is part of the Great Florida Birding Trail. And the Nature's Fishbowl is still there.

DON'T MISS
Smoked fish for lunch at The Freezer Tiki Bar

Bald eagles over Chassahowitzka

CHASSAHOWITZKA

Population not listed on census

*A*long this coast it is often difficult to tell where the saw grass ends and the Gulf begins. This is what much of Florida's Gulf Coast looked like a hundred years ago. You can see quite a bit of wilderness here. And if you are lucky you might see something else, but don't get too close. DOT signs warn drivers to watch for bears crossing. This is one of the few remaining habitats for Florida black bears. Just north of the Hernando-Citrus county line, Miss Maggie Road/ Highway 480 turns west off US 19 and winds down to Chassahowitzka (Timucuan Indian for "pumpkin place"). It ends at the Chassahowitzka River Campground and Recreational Area, the best place to rent canoes or kayaks to explore the Chassahowitzka National Wildlife Refuge. The refuge encompasses more than thirty thousand acres of brackish marsh and salt bays, stretching from Raccoon Point north to the mouth of the Homosassa River. It is home to several hundred species of birds, including a variety of herons, pelicans, ducks, ospreys, and even bald eagles. Manatees, green sea turtles, deer, and a small population of black bears live here as well.

Overnighters should consider the Chassahowitzka Hotel. David and Kim Strickland opened the current version in 2000, but it was David's grandparents, Ben and Eliza Smith, who built the original on this same site in 1910. In August 2020, the hotel sold and now has new owners.

Kayaking Weeki Wachee River

WEEKI WACHEE SPRINGS

Population: 13

When I was a kid in the 1960s, my family visited Weeki Wachee Springs many times. This was Florida's premiere tourist park, pre-Disney, and it had an underwater mermaid show as the main attraction. In 1946, an entrepreneur named Newton Perry, a former US Navy scuba diver (what they called "frogmen" back then), went looking for a site to open a tourist attraction when he came across Weeki Wachee Spring. It had been a dump site—filled with garbage, old appliances, and junked cars. But Perry saw potential and got the spring cleared out. His seemingly outlandish idea was to rig compressors to pump air through hoses routed under water so that girls dressed as mermaids could breathe through them while performing underwater shows. He built an eighteen-seat underwater theater with large glass windows, and on October 13, 1947, the attraction opened. By the mid-1950s, Weeki Wachee was one of Florida's most popular tourist stops. That got the attention of the American Broadcasting Company (ABC) who bought it in 1959. ABC expanded, enlarging the theater to four hundred seats and adding more elaborate shows. It was a huge success through the 1960s and into the 1970s. But by the mid-1970s, Disney World was drawing all the tourist trade away from Florida roadside attractions, and Weeki Wachee Springs gradually faded. Buccaneer Bay, a water slide park, opened adjacent to the spring in 1982, and that helped prop it up, but what really saved it was when the state of Florida converted it to a state park in 2008. Today, it operates as a quasi-theme park/state park and is busier than ever. Summer visitors pack the swimming areas and most importantly, the mermaid shows are still on year-round.

For those more interested in Weeki Wachee's natural side, the Weeki Wachee River, which flows from the spring and winds twelve miles to the Gulf, is a spectacularly scenic kayak trip. Kayaks and stand-up paddle boards are available for rent at the park.

Just up Highway 50 from Weeki Wachee Springs State Park is one of my favorite hole-in-the-wall seafood shacks, BeckyJack's. Becky De La Rosa opened the Food Shack (it was just Becky's then) back in the 1970s. Then in 2009, Kimberly Curtis and her husband, Joe Foster, bought it and put "Jack" in the name: homage to their friend and restaurant mentor Jack Newkirk, who owned Newk's Sports Bar in

BeckyJack's Food Shack

Tampa. BeckyJack's is a tiny place but filled to the brim with character (and with characters). There's a 1960s theme going on here, with wait staff clad in tie-dyed psychedelic T-shirts and a background soundtrack playing The Doors, Herman's Hermits, and the Beatles. The menu features a variety of fish sandwiches. The fish can vary with whatever they get fresh that day, but they serve it grilled, blackened, or "crunchy," which means fried in their proprietary Corn Flake and almond batter. They also make it as a Reuben. I've had the fish tacos, the crunchy fish sandwich, and last time in I had the blackened mahi sandwich, which was outstanding. There is sad news unfortunately: Kimberley passed away in 2015. But BeckyJack's was as busy as always on my most recent visit and Kimberley's exuberance and spirit still permeates the place.

DON'T MISS
BeckyJack's Food Shack

Historic Aripeka Post Office

ARIPEKA

Population: 142

US Highway 19, from Clearwater north to Hudson, is one of this area's most heavily trafficked roads. But five miles further north, turn west down Pasco County Road 595/Aripeka Road and the scenery changes dramatically. Pastureland replaces parking lots and then gives way to piney woods and brackish swamps as you approach the small coastal port community of Aripeka. It was called Gulf Key when it was first settled in 1886. Back then, visitors rode the Governor Stafford passenger steamer here for fishing and recreation. They stayed at the Osawaw Inn (now gone), built by the Aripeka Sawmill Company. Gulf Key adopted its new name from the company. Aripeka is most likely a slight variation on Arpeika, a Miccosukee-Seminole chief who also went by the unlikely name of Sam Jones. In 1830, just prior to the Second Seminole War, former governor/then-president Andrew Jackson mandated that all Seminole Indians be removed from Florida and sent to reservations out West. Chief Arpeika was one of eight tribe leaders who

Sign at Norfleet Fish Camp Bait and Tackle

refused to relocate his people. Instead, they fled south to the Everglades and established Sam Jones Old Town near present-day Fort Lauderdale. An alternate claim is that Aripeka is a mispronunciation of another Seminole leader's name, Apayaka.

Thankfully, Aripeka's rate of growth has been nominal over the past century. It is still a quiet fishing enclave. A few stilt fishing shacks appear alongside the road as it slows at a sharp S-turn, before bridging the south fork and then the north fork of Hammock Creek. The small Norfleet Fish Camp Bait and Tackle general store sits between the bridges and backs up to Hammock Creek. It's been here since the 1930s and today is run by second-generation owner Carl Norfleet. The faded wooden sign on the front depicts a palm tree, beach, and sunset paradise. It reads "Aripeka, Fla. 5.9 miles from Heaven." Inside, fishing lures, leaders, rod-and-reels, bait buckets, and long-billed hats hang on racks and occupy shelves alongside groceries. On one of my visits, I asked Carl Norfleet, "What is it that's five point nine miles away?" He replied, "Five point nine miles to the best fishing spot in the Gulf, but I'm not saying in which direction." This is the heart of Aripeka. No motels, no restaurants, just a quiet place to cast a net or drop a line and soak up the idyllic scenery. From here west, Hammock Creek spills out across a saw grass delta and into the Gulf of Mexico. If Heaven is 5.9 miles out there somewhere, then Aripeka must be the Pearly Gates.

Sumter County Farmer's Market, Webster

WEBSTER

Population: 1,151

*E*very Monday, the Sumter County Farmer's Market in Webster hosts Florida's largest and probably oldest flea market. Sumter County has always had an agriculture-based economy. Citrus was big here prior to the Great Freeze of 1894. After that, peppers, cucumbers, cabbage, lettuce, beans, and other vegetables became the staple crops. In the early 1900s, Webster was known as the "Cucumber Capital." In 1937, a group of local farmers formed a co-op and, without state funding or financial help from the county, built a market in the middle of Webster from which to auction their produce. The farmers built the facility themselves, harvesting cypress trees from nearby swamplands and using mules to drag out the lumber. The farmer's market was then and remains today a not-for-profit operation. It is still owned and operated by local agricultural businesspeople.

Over the decades, the market evolved along with changes in local farming trends. A cattle auction (now the second largest in Florida) replaced the vegetable auction, and people began to sell other items out of the empty produce stalls. These days the cattle auction takes place on Tuesdays, and the flea market on Mondays—fifty-two weeks a year, unless Christmas comes on a Monday.

The forty-acre facility can seem overwhelming to first-time visitors. A dozen roofed, open-air walkways with hundreds of vendor stalls, plus several more enclosed buildings and open paved lots, house more than 1,500 vendors, who contract for their spaces on an annual basis. Except for occasional intermittent cancellations, there are no vacancies. Each space has been booked for years. This is a busy place with a carnival-like atmosphere. The market opens at 6:30 AM and closes at 4:00 PM, and there is a crowd here most of the day. A sign at the entrance reads, "No trespassing, except on Mondays."

They sell everything here, some of it new but most of it used. One person's discards are another's treasure—antiques, computer equipment, hunting knives, power tools, parakeets, flowers, jewelry, watches, musical instruments, golf clubs, grandfather clocks, comic books, old records, Barbie dolls (and all accessories), Matchbox cars, sports trading cards, coins, and stamps. If someone collects it, there is a vendor for it here. There are clothes and whole bolts of fabric, bicycles and baby carriages, Nintendo games and stuffed teddy bears.

One of the most popular sections features rows of stalls filled with fresh fruits and vegetables: peaches, plums, pears, peppers, squash, nectarines, tomatoes, onions. A wonderful fresh aroma floats up and down these aisles. Speaking of food, they do not want you to go hungry, so concessionaires sell the usual assortment of corn dogs, curly fries, and Italian sausage sandwiches as well as tantalizing sweets like caramelized cinnamon-roasted pecans.

Little Brown Church of the South, Trilby

TRILBY

Population: 354

*A*bout seven miles north of Dade City there is a state road sign that reads "Trilacoochee." I wonder if the state was trying to save money by combining "Trilby" and "Lacoochee" into one name on one sign? Granted, these two tiny communities are right next to each other, but they are separate. Just west of Highway 301 lies tiny Trilby, at the crossing of Highway 98 and CR 575, where you will find the historic "Little Brown Church of the South"—officially the Trilby Methodist Church. Charter church members and the Reverend T. H. Sistrunk built this wood frame, tin roof structure, with its tall steeple rising above the entranceway, in 1897–1898. Ninety years later it underwent remodeling, but most of it—including the steeple outside, and the pulpit inside—is original. Next door, a historical marker explains that the 1870s settlement of McLeod changed its name to Macon in 1885 when the first post office opened. In 1896, the name changed again, this time to Trilby, after George du Maurier's popular novel of

162

Trilby Post Office Building, Trilby

the same name. Town officials also named several of the streets and the town's Svengali Square after characters from the novel.

At one time, Trilby had a bank, a school, a railway station, two hotels, a sawmill, a grist mill, a grocery store, a dry goods store, a drug-and-sundries store with a soda fountain, and a tuberculosis hospital. In the 1920s, it was a busy little town. That all changed in one afternoon in May 1925. Townspeople first spotted smoke coming from the second floor of the dry goods store around 1:00 PM. They quickly started a bucket brigade, taking water from the water tower at the south end of town. Dade City's fire truck rushed to the scene, but during the time it took to drive the eight miles, flames had consumed all the buildings on the west side of the railroad tracks. By 5:00 PM, firefighters had contained the blaze, but most of downtown Trilby was gone. Some was rebuilt, but the town never fully recovered from that tragic afternoon. Thankfully, one of the buildings left standing was the Little Brown Church of the South.

Classic Car Cruise-in, Dade City

DADE CITY

Population: 7,338

*T*wenty-five miles north of Tampa, the terrain turns hilly and scenic as Highway 301 rolls into Dade City. The name comes from Fort Dade, which was just west of here post-Civil War, and refers to US Army major Francis Dade who, along with his troops, camped nearby in December 1835, just days before meeting their demise at the Dade Massacre (near Bushnell), which sparked the beginning of the Second Seminole War.

History and heritage play an important role in this close-knit community. Most of the buildings downtown have been renovated rather than just torn down. The stately classical revival style 1909 county courthouse (this is the county seat for Pasco County), in the town square, underwent a $2.3 million, four-year restoration that was completed in 1999, and in 2006 it was added to the National Register of Historic Places.

History buffs will find the Pioneer Florida Museum & Village, on the north side of town, a fascinating place to visit—visitors feel like they have stepped back in time. When it opened in 1961, the Pioneer Florida Museum displayed pioneer-era (1800s to early 1900s) farm implements and equipment that had been donated to the Pasco County Fair. Since then, the museum has expanded considerably, acquiring five pioneer-era buildings that were relocated to the museum grounds: the 1878 Enterprise Methodist Church; a shoe repair shop built in 1913; the 1896 Trilby, Florida, train depot; a bright-red one-room schoolhouse from Lacoochee, Florida, built in 1926; and an 1860s farmhouse that belonged to John Overstreet, who built it from native heart pine, cut with a steam-operated band saw and hand tools on his eighty acre homestead farm near here. As was customary in those days, the kitchen was a separate building behind the house and connected by a covered walkway. That way if a fire started in the kitchen, it was less likely to burn down the whole house.

On display in the museum's main building are many locally found pioneer artifacts, plus some older items. One display case features an impressive collection of archaic arrowheads, some dating back to 3000–5000 BC.

With Dade City's interest in history, it is no surprise to find a lot of antique shops here. Most are within walking distance of the main downtown intersection of 7th Street (Highway 301) and Meridian Avenue. One that I particularly like is Sugarcreek Too Antiques—a curious little shop filled with vintage items, including vintage clothing and hats, and antique seasonal decorations.

Dade City has also evolved into somewhat of an epicurean destination. Phil Williams and Skip Mize opened Lunch on Limoges in 1979 inside the boutique and home décor store in the center of downtown Dade City, which has been in Phil's family since 1908. Lunch tables blend right into the colorful shop and lend a festive atmosphere. The black-and-white checkerboard floor and tall ceilings echo the busy sounds of the open kitchen, which Skip built himself. They serve what I can best describe as southern-gourmet fare. The chalkboard menu changes daily, plus there are a few regular items. One of their most popular is the very

Lunch on Limoges, Dade City

tasty pecan grouper. But their biggest draw must be the mouth-watering assortment of daily fresh-baked cakes and towering pies.

Kafe Kokopelli occupies a renovated 1916 building that was originally a Ford Motor Company dealership and service center that dates to when Ford still made the Model T. In 1996, Gail Greenfelder rescued the old building and opened Kafe Kokopelli, which was later, in 2013, purchased by chef Steven Queen. The menu might be best described as upscale Americana. I suggest starting with their skillet cornbread with maple-thyme butter, which comes in the cast iron skillet that it is baked in. Two favorite entree items are the stuffed (with mozzarella) meatloaf and the cajun pasta alfredo with blackened shrimp, chicken, and andouille sausage.

Another upscale spot, Green Door on 8th, combines a classic steak house—black angus ribeye, New York strip, and rack of lamb, with a New Orleans bistro—jambalaya, crawfish etouffee, and shrimp and grits.

Olga's Bakery, Dade City

Some other favorite eateries of mine: For classic old-country Italian, try Francesco's. Owner and Chef Francesco Locasto brought his recipes from his native Italy. For Mexican food you cannot beat Coyote Rojo, which opened 2016. Do not let the exterior fool you—they are in what used to be the front lobby for a 1950s mom-and-pop motel, and it is easy to drive right by and not notice them. But this is an outstanding and authentic Mexican restaurant. And for sweet treats, Olga's Bakery has been Dade City's best place for dynamite donuts, pastries, and turnovers since 1972.

Probably my favorite Dade City restaurant is also the least fancy. Stephanie Reaves and her husband Herold opened tiny cafeteria-style Steph's Southern Soul Restaurant in 2013. Stephanie, a former chef at Buddy Freddy's in Plant City, makes the absolute best fried chicken (restaurant or home cooked) I have ever eaten. Her meatloaf, pork chops, and chicken and dumplings are also outstanding. Pair them with collard greens, okra and tomato, broccoli casserole, squash casserole, or sweet potato soufflé and you have a plate of the best comfort/soul food that you will find anywhere. And do not forget dessert: Steph's red velvet cake, key lime cake, or peanut butter pie are my top choices.

Dade City enjoys its festivities. Every year they celebrate their favorite fruit: the kumquat, at the Kumquat Festival. The diminutive egg-shaped, tart-tasting kumquat can be eaten whole (skin and all), made into jams, marmalades, relishes, sauces, and even wine. But the festival favorite is kumquat pie: a tangy, creamy concoction usually served in an Oreo or graham cracker crust. The festival has grown to more than forty thousand attendees and takes up all downtown Dade City, and includes live music, a vintage car show, and arts and crafts booths. Traditionally, the event is held on the last Saturday in January.

DON'T MISS
Lunch at Lunch on Limoges

Richloam General Store

RICHLOAM

Population not listed on census

T he Green Swamp, roughly halfway between Orlando and the Gulf Coast, inhabits 560,000 acres of primordial swamp wetlands and flatlands. It is the headwater source for four major Central Florida rivers: the Peace, Withlacoochee, Ocklawaha, and Hillsborough rivers. Endangered Florida panthers and black bear have been sited here. Some even claim to have spotted the occasional skunk ape.

In 1921, the Atlantic Coast Railroad decided to relocate their Riverland, Florida, depot to the tiny community of Richloam, in the northwest corner of the Green Swamp. Subsequently, Postmaster Sidney Brinson decided to build a post office and general store there in 1922. In 1928, after being robbed, the store was burned to the ground, but undeterred, Brinson rebuilt and reopened just a month later. But in 1936 the postal service cancelled its official postal facility status and Brinson opted to close the store and instead rent it out as a residence. Over time, ownership passed down to various members of the Brinson family. It had sat vacant for decades when Eric Burkes, Brinson's grandnephew, began renovating the building, and then reopened the store in 2016. This is the only remaining building from the original community of Richloam. The store was added to the National Register of Historic Places in 2017.

Most days you will find Eric or his mother, Daisy, behind the counter. The original PO boxes can still be seen against one wall. The Richloam General Store shelves are stocked with a variety of smoked meats, along with their own brand of jams, jellies, pancake mix, barbecue sauce, local honey, pickled vegetables, salsas, and relishes. I am partial to their chowchow—a relish known in the south that's made from cabbage, onions, bell peppers, and jalapenos. You can also purchase ice cold sodas, candy from countertop jars, cast iron cookware, and some old fashion toys.

Just up and across the road an abandoned circa 1940s fire tower (not only used for monitoring fires, but also mustard gas tests that took place here during World War II) looks over property once owned by the Schroder Land and Timber Company, where aforementioned Postmaster Sidney Brinson was also the foreman. There is trailhead parking here for the Withlacoochee State Forest Richloam hiking trails that connect with the Florida National Scenic Trail, which bisects the Green Swamp.

To get here, take Highway 50 from Dade City, and watch closely for the Richloam Clay Sink Road sign directing you south. The store is about three-quarters of a mile down the road.

James Barbecue, Groveland

GROVELAND/ JAMES BARBECUE

Population not listed on census

*I*t is no secret that I am a barbecue nut, and on a per-petual quest to seek out outstanding barbecue joints. I have found lots of "pretty good" barbecue joints, but only a few "outstanding" ones. If I am willing to drive more than an hour to get to one then it must be outstanding, and that is the case for James Barbecue in Groveland. I have made the hour-and-a-half drive from Tampa numerous times. Groveland is about halfway between Orlando and Brooksville, and about a fifty-minute drive from either. Owners Gregory and Johnette James opened James Barbecue in 2016. Their motto, "You don't need teeth to eat James' ribs!," proudly appears on the sign and menu. It's an accurate statement. The meat on their slow-smoked ribs falls off the bone, and their pulled pork is just as tender, juicy, and tasty. Trust me: it's worth the drive.

Jungle Adventures, Christmas

CHRISTMAS

Population: 1,921

*O*n the counter at the post office in Christmas, Florida, there is a green ink pad and a box filled with rubber stamps to commemorate an assortment of holidays and special occasions. Patrons are encouraged to adorn their envelopes with the stamps.

The first time I visited I asked a counter worker (her name was Rose) if things got hectic here right before Christmas. "Hectic? Yes, but it is a wonderful time. The only people who come all the way to Christmas, Florida, just to mail their cards and packages are people who really love other people. Why else would they go through that much trouble just to have Christmas on their postmark?"

Not only do people come by in person but starting in November of each year the Christmas post office begins receiving boxes of letters and packages to mail out with the Christmas postmark. This small post office becomes a busy clearinghouse for parcels coming in from around

Christmas, Florida, Post Office

the world, and then going back out around the world, often right back to where they came from.

The Christmas postmark looks pretty much like any other: an oval with "Christmas, Florida" across the top, the date in the middle, and the 32709 zip code across the bottom. Each year, this little post office stamps and mails out more than three hundred thousand Christmas cards, quite a bit for an office that serves an area with a population of fewer than two thousand. "It starts to get crazy the day after Thanksgiving, but we love it," says Rose.

The current Christmas post office was built in 1987. Paintings on the wall depict the 1918 and 1937 post office buildings. The first post office was established in 1892 in the home of Postmaster Samuel Hurlbut. His son, Van, delivered the mail twice a week on foot to as far away as Chuluota, twelve miles to the north.

Christmas was originally Fort Christmas. In only two days, US Army troops, under the command of General Abraham Eustis, built

Fort Christmas

the eighty-foot-by-eighty-foot log fort with two blockhouses. They began construction on December 25, 1837—hence the name. One of many forts built during the Second Seminole War (1835–1842), Fort Christmas no longer stands, but there is an impressive re-creation built in 1977 at the twenty-five-acre Fort Christmas Historical Park on Fort Christmas Road, two miles north of SR 50. The park also has a collection of pioneer homes, a one-room schoolhouse, and a sugarcane mill.

If you are going to drive all the way to Christmas to mail those Christmas cards you might as well continue up the road four more miles and visit Jungle Adventures. Look for the two hundred-foot-long "Swampy the Alligator" out front. It is a somewhat kitschy throwback to Florida's 1950s–1960s roadside tourist attractions, and in fact this one dates back to that era. It is predominantly an alligator park, but they have other wildlife too, and many are rescues: turtles, snakes, possums, skunks, peacocks, even a few coyotes, bears, and an endangered panther.

Molly Goodhead's Raw Bar, Ozona

OZONA

Population not listed on census

*T*he first homesteaders began arriving in what is now Ozona in the mid-1870s. In 1882, they platted the community and gave it a name: Yellow Bluff. A post office opened four years later. Shortly thereafter, Florida's yellow fever epidemic broke out and residents of Yellow Bluff needed to change the name to something that sounded healthier. They came up with Ozona. Over the decades, Palm Harbor has grown up around Ozona, but the little village still manages to hang on to its quiet, quirky charm. Some outsiders get an introduction to Ozona via the Pinellas Trail (a rails-to-trails bicycle path) that opened here in 1990, but most come for a pair of really good restaurants: Molly Goodhead's and Ozona Pig.

Laurel Flowers opened Molly Goodhead's Raw Bar & Restaurant in 1985 in a circa 1919 house that belonged to the Stansells, a multi-generation pioneering family from this area. The catchy name (Molly Goodhead is their mermaid mascot) brings customers into this Key

West-like casual eatery, but it's the good food and fun atmosphere that brings them back. The menu runs the full seafood gamut and includes oysters—raw or steamed—steamed clams, steamed mussels, steamed peel-and-eat shrimp, calamari, gator tail, and all kinds of fresh caught fish. Molly's grouper sandwich—fried, blackened, or chargrilled—is one of best around.

Chris and Bobbie Painter opened Ozona Pig, across the street from Molly Goodhead's, in 2004. Their slow hickory-smoked ribs, pulled pork, and beef brisket are excellent, but my favorite is their Brunswick stew—as close to the authentic coastal-Georgia version as I have found anywhere.

Next door to Ozona Pig is an interesting shop called Antiques and Uniques, that has a treasure trove of vintage collectibles: 1950s–1960s memorabilia, old record albums, plus some colorful Florida-themed interior decorations. It is a great place to wander through and you'll probably run across something you can't live without!

Antiques and Uniques, Ozona

DON'T MISS
A stroll through Antiques and Uniques

Rod and Reel Pier and Café, Anna Maria

ANNA MARIA, HOLMES BEACH

Population: Anna Maria 1,762; Holmes Beach 4,305

*T*he towns of Anna Maria and Holmes Beach, on seven-and-a-half-mile-long Anna Maria Island, have been favorite close-by getaways for west coast Floridians since the early 1900s. Much of the island's charm perseveres because Anna Maria residents have managed to fend off the invasion of high-rise condos and towering hotels that crowd Florida's shoreline elsewhere. It is a tough battle. Developers want to take advantage of the attraction, but a local construction code that limits building height to thirty-seven feet does its best to keep them in check. So, Anna Maria Island can hang on to that easy-paced, beach town flavor, so reminiscent of Florida's west coast beach towns in the 1950s–1960s.

Most people assume that the name Anna Maria has a Spanish origin, and that is a reasonable assumption since Spanish explorers, including Ponce de Leon and Hernando de Soto, sailed this coast in the early 1500s. Old Spanish maps that predate Florida's inclusion in the United States show the island as Ana Maria Cay. Another contingent, however, claims that the name is Scottish and should be pronounced Anna Mar-EYE-a. Many of the island's longtime residents pronounce the name with the long "i."

George Emerson Bean stopped on uninhabited Anna Maria Island sometime in the early 1890s while sailing from his home in Connecticut down to the Gulf. He fell in love with it and vowed to return with his family. In 1893, he filed for homestead on 160 acres on the north end of the island. With the help of his sons, he built its first residence near where the Rod & Reel Pier is now. Bean died in 1898, but his sons and their families continued to live and build on Anna Maria.

John Roser was a German baker who invented the recipe for the filling of Fig Newtons. He had sold his recipe to Nabisco and moved to St. Petersburg to retire when he met George Bean Jr. In 1911, they teamed up to form the Anna Maria Beach Company and began the first commercial development of the island. That same year, the city pier was built to serve as a dock for day excursion boats from Tampa. It was not until 1921 that the Cortez Bridge opened, connecting Bradenton Beach at the south end of the island to the mainland. In 1913, John Roser built Anna Maria's first church as a memorial to his wife, Caroline. Each Saturday, a pastor from a different church on the mainland came to the nondenominational Roser Memorial Community Church by boat, gave Sunday services, and then returned on Monday. The church is at the northeast end of Pine Avenue and is still active today.

Anna Maria's main road, Gulf Drive, runs up the center of the island. For most of the Gulf side, in lieu of a beach road, a succession of two-block-long avenues with tree names like Palm, Willow, Cedar, Oak, and Maple dead-end at the beach. Pine Avenue—the exception—runs all the way east to the bay.

There are lots of terrific places to dine on Anna Maria Island, some upscale but most beach casual. The Rod & Reel Pier and Café, just around the northern point of Anna Maria Island is a place with great sentimental value to me. It's where I often ate lunch with my good friend and golfing buddy, Andy Duncan, who passed away in 2014. The Rod & Reel is a microcosm of everything that is both charming and sublimely quirky about coastal Florida in general and Anna Maria in particular. It occupies a two-story shack that sits on the end of the wooden pier built in 1947. There is a bait-and-tackle shop downstairs and a tiny short-order diner upstairs. Waves passing under the pier cause the wooden structure to creak and sway gently back and forth. Looking northwest, diners have a view of Passage Key and Egmont Key and the Gulf of Mexico beyond. To the northeast you can see the Sunshine Skyway Bridge crossing the entrance to Tampa Bay. The Rod & Reel has one of the better grouper sandwiches on Florida's west coast, but it is *the* best place to eat one. Pelicans perch on the railings, patiently awaiting a fisherman's tossed treat. Manatees, dolphin, and stingrays routinely glide by beneath the pier. A raucous thunderstorm can blow up without a warning, and then disappear just as quickly. If you are lucky you might get to see a waterspout. And, if you catch something off the pier that is plate-worthy, you can probably talk the kitchen into cooking it for you.

Beer-and-burger joint Duffy's Tavern, in a screen-windowed shack on the north end of the island, has been an Anna Maria icon since Duffy Whiteman opened it in 1958. Pat Guyer bought Duffy's in 1971. Although a popular local's spot, customers come from as far away as Tampa and Lakeland just for lunch. In 2003, Pat and her five daughters (who all work there) moved Duffy's to its current location on Gulf Drive. Same great atmosphere, cold beer, and great food, but now with air conditioning! I always get the same thing: a cheeseburger and a bowl of their killer chili. Pat Guyer, an Anna Maria icon herself, became regularly active in Anna Maria Island politics. She sat on the city council for many years and was elected mayor of Holmes Beach in 1990. Sadly, in 2010, Pat Guyer passed away, and I think it is accurate to say the town lost its matriarch. The Guyer daughters (all with names that start with "P") still run the place and continue the Duffy's tradition.

One of Anna Maria Island's most ardent cheerleaders is Ed Chiles (son of Governor Lawton Chiles). In 1979, Ed bought a small beachfront diner, which had been converted out of old army barracks in 1946 and built it into one of west coast Florida's most popular seafood

Sandbar Restaurant, Anna Maria

restaurants. In the years since, he is added two more nearby: The Beach House in Bradenton Beach and Mar Vista on Longboat Key. The Sandbar's regular menu includes enticing items like pan seared crab encrusted sea scallops; shrimp Florentine with spinach, tomatoes, and white wine lemon-butter sauce over pasta; and a good peel-and-eat Bud and Bay shrimp (boiled in Budweiser and Old Bay seasoning) appetizer. When the weather is nice The Sandbar will set up tables on the sand, for true "beachfront dining."

Restaurateurs Sean and Susan Murphy came to Holmes Beach and opened Beach Bistro in 1985. The Murphys arrived by way of New Orleans, where Sean worked at Arnaud's. Beach Bistro is a tiny place right on the beach, much understated from the outside, but elegant on the inside. With limited seating, a reservation is a must. Sean's savory Bistro bouillabaisse is exceptional. A couple decades later the Murphys decided to open a second restaurant, Eat Here, which takes a more casual approach to ambiance. Their menu mixes some casual items like burgers, with more Beach Bistro-like seafood dishes. They have applied the same perfectionist attention to quality and preparation, and the food rivals their own Beach Bistro, and I do not feel out of place dining there in shorts.

Eat Here, Anna Maria

Anna Maria Islanders Jason and Leah Suzor opened their Water-front Restaurant in 1994 in a circa 1922 beach house with a wrap-around porch. It sits just across the road from Anna Maria's City Pier (not to be confused with the Rod & Reel Pier), with a view across the mouth of Tampa Bay. Their mostly-seafood menu includes an assort-ment of outstanding appetizers. I like their salmon smoked over apple-wood (they smoke it in-house). And Waterfront has the best grouper tacos on the island.

Waterfront Restaurant, Anna Maria

Great food, great beaches, great fishing, and a disdain for intrusive commercial over development combine to make Anna Maria as close to a perfect Florida beach town as I can find.

DON'T MISS
Getting a grouper sandwich at The Rod & Reel Pier

Dock at Star Fish Company Market and Restaurant, Cortez

CORTEZ

Population: 4,436

*C*ortez may be the last of something once commonplace in yesterday's Florida: a coastal commercial fishing village. Everything in Cortez is somehow related to seafood, fishing, or boats. Simple clapboard cottages, many dating back to the 1920s, make up the quiet neighborhood surrounding the boat docks and fish warehouses that line the shoreline along Anna Maria Sound. In the mid-1800s, it was known as Hunter's Point, but locals called it "the Kitchen" because of the abundance of seafood caught in these waters. Cortez occupies the western tip of a point of land that juts out into the sound and can be reached from Bradenton Beach via Highway 684/ Cortez Road Bridge. Signs along Cortez Road advertise smoked mullet, fresh shrimp, outboard motor repair, bait, and fishing charters. In 1888, a post office was established here, and the name Cortez was submitted, likely a reference to Spanish explorer Hernando Cortes, who conquered Mexico and the Aztecs for Spain in 1519. However, there is no indication that Cortes ever explored Florida.

The town grew into a small but busy fishing community, with mullet netting, processing, and shipping the primary industries. Much of Cortez's history is divided between "before 1921" and "after 1921," when a hurricane blew in from the Gulf without warning. A storm surge destroyed the docks and sank whole fleets of fishing boats. A large passenger steamship, the *Mistletoe*, went down in the storm. Residents crowded into the town's brick schoolhouse for shelter while their homes washed away. The only building left standing on Cortez's waterfront was the Albion Inn hotel.

There are two exceptional seafood joints here, and third generation Cortez seafood business owner Karen Bell is at the helm of both. Star Fish Company is one of those Cortez commercial seafood businesses that started back in the early 1920s. In the 1960s, they added a small retail market. Then in 1996 Karen Bell bought the business and decided to put some picnic tables on the dock out back and sell fish sandwiches. Essentially, Karen has been in the business her entire life. Her grandfather Aaron Bell started the A. B. Bell Fish Company (next door) in 1940, and she runs that now too. Star Fish Company Restaurant is still just picnic tables on the dock behind the market, except there are more of them. It's cash-only, and whatever you order will be served in a cardboard box. The food—grouper, oysters, shrimp, mullet, pompano, crab cakes, shrimp or oyster po'boys, and conch fritters—is fantastic. In 2013, Karen, along with business partners Bobby and Gwen Woodson, opened a second Cortez restaurant: Tide Tables (at Channel Marker 48), next to the Cortez Bridge, just a few blocks away from Star Fish Company. It's the same great fresh seafood (a little more extensive menu), and the same great old-Florida fishing village atmosphere as Star Fish, but with a little extra elbow room.

Another authentic old-Cortez spot worth checking out is bait shop bar and grill Annie's Bait & Tackle, across the road from Tide Tables. It is also a good place to line up a fishing charter.

Cortez has always appreciated the importance of its heritage and connection to the sea. In 2007, the Florida Maritime Museum opened in Cortez's historic 1912 schoolhouse. The museum is a joint project undertaken by the Florida Institute of Saltwater Heritage, the Cortez Village Historical Society, and Manatee County. Exhibits include tools, equipment, and historic photographs from Cortez, as well as from other historic fishing villages along Florida's Gulf Coast.

Out on Cortez Road there is another must-visit place that almost qualifies as a museum. At Jan Holman's warehouse-size Sea Hagg nautical/antique/curio shop, you could spend days rummaging through the shelves of salvaged seagoing hardware—ship's wheels, portholes, propellers, and compasses, plus larger-than-life sculptures, local artist paintings, bizarre Neptunian home decorations, even a genuine diving bell. I think even Jacques Cousteau would be impressed.

DON'T MISS
A visit to the Sea Hagg nautical and antiques shop

The Desert Inn, 2020 and 1996,
Yeehaw Junction

YEEHAW JUNCTION

Population: 320

A legendary piece of quirky Florida history is gone. At 3:00 AM, three days before Christmas 2019, the driver of a semitrailer hauling orange juice while heading north on US 441, crashed head-on into the Desert Inn at Yeehaw Junction. He told state troopers that it was dark and did not realize he had crossed the west shoulder and left the road. He was ticketed for careless driving, and troopers say he was not driving impaired. I will speculate though: sounds like he was asleep at the wheel. Most of the front of the inn (the location of its restaurant) was destroyed. The roof collapsed as well from the impact. Fortunately, no one was there at the time, and the driver was not injured. The Desert Inn has been closed since 2018.

The Osceola County Historical Society (its offices are in Kissimmee) owns the Desert Inn, and it does have a rich and colorful history. As of this writing the Historical Society is still evaluating what to do with the property.

No book about small towns in Florida would be complete without mentioning Yeehaw Junction. The unusual name gets everyone's attention. Some say it is the more socially acceptable version of its original name, Jackass (the four-legged, floppy-eared variety) Crossing. Jackasses hauled lumber to railroad loading depots in the early 1900s, and this was a major crossing on their route. Yeehaw mimics the sound a jackass makes. Others contend that the name is a variation on the Creek Indian word yaha, meaning "wolf."

Truck drivers and traveling salesmen in the 1940s and 1950s knew Yeehaw Junction as the intersection of two of Florida's major thoroughfares, Highway 441 and State Road 60. The Desert Inn (it was originally called Wilson's Corner in the early 1930s) at the intersection's northwest corner was their standard stop for fuel, food, and a night's rest. According to some, they might also have found a night's illicit entertainment. George and Stephanie Zicheck bought the old inn in 1986 from the estate of Fred and Julia Cheverette, who had owned it for forty years. The Zichecks's daughter, Beverly, began operating it the following year.

"My parents had homes in Tampa and West Palm Beach, and Yeehaw Junction is midway between the two, so we passed by here a lot," Beverly explained to me when I first visited in 1996. "They bought the inn in 1986. When I first started operating it in February 1987, everyone who came through the door would tell me, 'Please leave it like it's always been. Do not change anything.'" A 1950s Desert Inn postcard, which hung on the wall, was proof positive that the place looked exactly as it did back then. And the historic marker out front confirmed that Beverly intended to keep it that way. "When they passed the new commercial driver's license laws, business took a dive because the truckers couldn't buy beer and liquor at the package store anymore," she explained. "I needed something to revitalize interest in the place, and that's when I decided to start working on getting the Desert Inn included on the National Register of Historic Places. I can assure you that that is not something that happens easily. It was a lot of work."

During the first six months of her endeavor, she waded through Tallahassee's bureaucratic pea soup. First, they sent her the wrong forms. Then they sent someone down to Yeehaw to help her, but that person was promptly transferred to another department. Finally, out of frustration, Beverly called Florida state representative Bud Bronson. Within a week she received all the correct paperwork. Then she began the task of piecing together the Desert Inn's history. Through her contacts with several historical societies, she met Lucille Wright Sturgis, a writer who had done National Register projects before. Beverly and Lucille dug through libraries and court records and interviewed people who had lived and worked in this area as far back as the 1920s. The Desert Inn was finally placed on the National Register in January 1994.

The dining room and bar end of the inn sat close to the apex of the intersection of Highways 441 and 60. The sound of air brakes and rumbling diesels was a constant background noise. Inside, the dozen or so tables and booths were arranged around the u-shaped bar. An old Wurlitzer jukebox played mostly country classics—George Jones, Elvis Presley. Beverly had collected some strange Florida memorabilia: plaques with clever sayings, stuffed jackalopes, rattlesnake skins, and other oddball knickknacks, many with a "jackass" motif. They were all hanging on the walls or displayed on shelves or on the bar. Two lifelike wooden Indians permanently occupy one corner table.

Although Yeehaw Junction might not have been a place where you would spend an entire vacation, you could stop by at the Desert Inn if you are passing through—grab a burger, have a bowl of chili, enjoy looking at the quirky decor. In 2008, Beverly considered putting the inn up for sale but ended up keeping it and leasing it out instead. Eventually, it did change hands and the new operators did their best to keep the place going, but in August 2018 it finally closed.

The Osceola County Historical Society reports that their structural engineers are still trying to determine if anything can be rebuilt there, but it does not look good. Fortunately, a few weeks prior to the accident valuable artifacts from inside the Desert Inn had been removed and put into the Historical Society's archival storage, as part of their earlier restoration efforts, so some pieces of Desert Inn and Yeehaw Junction history still live on.

Sebring International Raceway

SEBRING

Population: 10,600

The name "Sebring" is legendary in the auto racing world. Even if you are not a racing fan, it is likely that you are familiar with the 12 Hours of Sebring, North America's oldest sports car endurance race. In the 1970s, I attended the race (an event that many back then dubbed "Florida's Woodstock") half a dozen times. It would have a pivotal influence on my life. In 1987, I acquired my SCCA (Sports Car Club of America) license and would go on to race for thirty years. My racing partner, Doug Davidson, and I participated mostly in endurance races, which could last anywhere from ninety minutes to twenty-four hours, and required multiple pit stops, refueling, and driver changes. In our three decades of racing, we brought home sixteen first-place trophies. Thirteen were from races at Sebring, what we considered our "home" track.

Following the end of World War II, quite a few military air bases became inactive, and sport car racing enthusiasts figured out that these were practically ready-made racetracks. That was the case in 1949 with Hendricks Field at Sebring, when aeronautical engineer, entrepreneur, and racing enthusiast Alec Ulmann got the idea of using some of the runways as straights and connecting some of the twisting access roads in-between to make a racetrack. The first race was a six-hour endurance race on New Year's Eve, 1950. The first twelve-hour race took place in March 1952. Originally, the track was exceptionally long—5.2 miles. In 1983, it was reconfigured and shortened to 3.7 miles. The front and back straightaways are still the original airport runway paving, and famously bumpy and jarring to drive. I can attest to that. Exiting turn 17 leading onto the front straight is a teeth-rattler!

The town of Sebring embraced racing from the start. Racing schools, race car shops, and other ancillary racing businesses have made Sebring their home. There is some sort of race, school, or race car test going on at the track every week of the year and it keeps the town busy. Down-town Sebring runs along the east side of Lake Jackson. The center of downtown is a circular park with roads radiating from it, appropriately

Circle Park Drive

enough like spokes in a wheel. There are some notable eateries here. Sebring Soda & Ice Cream Works, in the historic 1922 J. B. Brown Building on "the circle," is a terrific ice cream shop that reminds me of an old-fashion soda fountain, and I am most intrigued by their selection of vintage glass-bottle sodas. One block up the road is Dee's Place, a classic diner renowned for its big, hearty breakfasts that include omelets and waffles, and for their baked goods such as muffins and cinnamon rolls. It's a great spot to "fuel up" first thing in the morning. Dimitri's is a Greek and pizza restaurant located behind the old Kenilworth Hotel (now closed), and their Back Alley Bar and Grill next door is popular with racers on their way back from the track.

On race weekends I usually stayed at Inn on the Lakes, a wonderfully comfortable upscale hotel with one of the best restaurants in Sebring, Chicanes, that serves excellent cedar plank salmon and Danish baby back bibs.

DON'T MISS
Getting ice cream at Sebring Soda & Ice Cream Works

Mural at Lake Placid

LAKE PLACID

Population: 2,479

Ninety-five percent of all caladium plants sold commercially around the world are grown at farms around the outskirts of the town of Lake Placid. A temperate climate and an abundance of boggy muck-soil near the lakes make this area ideal for growing caladiums, though they are not native to Florida. Caladiums originated in the Amazon basin and were brought to the United States for the Chicago World's Fair in 1893. They were first grown commercially in Apopka in the 1920s. Occasional winter freezing temperatures forced the industry to move further south in the 1930s, eventually finding the perfect home in Lake Placid and Highlands County. August and September mark the peak of the caladium season. Every year the town hosts the Lake Placid Caladium Festival, a grand two-day event that features musical performances, arts and crafts displays, a classic car show, and of course lots of beautiful caladiums.

In addition to caladium fame, Lake Placid is also one of the most famous mural cities in the country. In 1992, a group of local artists and art-patrons came up with the idea of making Lake Placid a mural town. Forty-seven larger-than-life murals grace the walls of buildings throughout downtown Lake Placid.

Lake Placid's first mural, Tom Freeman's *Tea at Southwinds*, on the side of the Caladium Arts and Crafts Co-op building, was dedicated in May 1993. It depicts three elegantly dressed ladies in the 1940s enjoying an outdoor patio at the former Lakeside Inn. They represent the three ladies who founded the Caladium Arts and Crafts Co-op: Harriet Porter, Sue Ellen Robinson, and Carol Mills. The co-op (at Interlake Boulevard and Pine Street) is a ten-thousand-square-foot store, gallery, and showcase for the work of its two-hundred-plus members, all Highlands County artists and craftspeople.

Ordinarily, I would not put a grocery store on my list of things to see, but the Lake Placid Winn Dixie on Highway 27 is different. On its outside south wall is a mural of epic proportions. At 35 feet high and 175 feet long, it is a panoramic depiction called *Cracker Trail Cattle Drive*. Artist Keith Goodson has painted a hauntingly realistic scene that shows Florida "cracker" cowboys of yesteryear moving their herd across the southern plains of the state. The term "cracker" comes from the cracking of the whips used to maneuver the herds of cattle. It stuck as a nickname for Florida cowboys. Some of the cows almost seem to follow you from one end of the mural to the other. Listen carefully and you will hear the cracking whips and mooing cows of a Florida cattle drive. Music is piped through speakers on the roof to add another dimension to the mural experience. The Lake Placid Mural Society calls it "moosic."

Highway 27 glides across the Highlands County hills south of Sebring eventually leading you to Lake Placid. From the road you can see for miles in any direction. Elevated vistas like these are not a common sight in Florida. But here, broad, rolling hills alternate with lakes in the low spots. Like a small mountain range, the Lake Wales Ridge runs parallel to Highway 27 about twelve miles to the east. I think I know why Melvil Dewey fell in love with this area the first time he saw it.

In 1927, seventy-six-year-old Dr. Melvil Dewey—the same Dewey who invented the Dewey decimal library cataloging system, came to

Florida in search of a southern version of his hometown, Lake Placid, New York. What Dewey envisioned was a resort that would mirror the Lake Placid Club but with a milder climate in winter. He knew he had found what he was looking for when he first laid eyes on the small agricultural community of Lake Stearns. Dewey wasted no time in making arrangements with local landowners. In 1928, Lake Stearns incorporated under its new name, Lake Placid. The names of two of the surrounding lakes were also changed: Lake Childs be-

came Lake Placid and Lake Stearns became Lake June-in-Winter (the lake in New York is simply Lake June). Sadly, Dewey was not able to enjoy his newfound paradise for very long. Although Florida provided a welcome respite from his chronic bronchitis, Melvil Dewey passed away three years after moving here. But with plans already underway, his widow, Emily, continued to develop his dream. The Great Depression stunted progress in the early and mid-1930s, but ultimately Lake Placid grew into the attractive community that it is today. It is still growing, not so much in size but in character.

Looming over the horizon is the 270-foot-high Placid Tower. When it was built in 1960, it was the tallest concrete masonry structure in the world. Nearly five thousand tons of concrete and steel reinforc-

Lake Placid Tower

ing went into its construction. The view from the open-air eagle's nest is spectacular, but unfortunately the tower has been closed since 2007. The Chamber of Commerce reports that there have been potential buyers that would reopen it, no deals have yet to be struck.

Lake Placid's city limits extend only around the uptown area, which technically makes the city of Lake Placid only 1.25 miles square. Lakes border it on two sides. Lake June-in-Winter wraps around the west side of uptown, with Lake Placid further to the south.

Just beyond Lake Placid's caladium fields is twenty-seven-thousand-acre Lake Istokpoga, famous worldwide for record-size largemouth bass. Avid bass fishermen from around the country make the pilgrimage here for tournaments, or just a shot at landing a record lunker.

Lake Placid has not only gained a reputation as an arts community and as the Caladium Capital of the World, but also as the home of Toby's Clown School and Museum, where more than a thousand graduates have gone on to become professional clowns and quite a few found work over the years in Ringling Bros. and Barnum & Bailey Circus, based in Sarasota.

For sustenance in Lake Placid I have a couple suggestions. Glenda Jean's Country Kitchen serves a wide assortment of hefty burgers, plus some good southern comfort food, like country-fried steak, meatloaf, and buttermilk fried chicken. At Morty & Edna's Craft Kitchen try the homemade biscuits with gravy or their frittata of the day for breakfast, or the "Notorious" BLT made with Canadian bacon for lunch.

DON'T MISS
Taking the murals walking tour,
starting at the Caladium Arts and Crafts Co-op

Wheeler's Goody Café, Arcadia

ARCADIA

Population: 8,314

*V*isitors to Arcadia might note that a disproportionate number of downtown buildings have "Built in 1906" noted on them. On Thanksgiving night 1905, downtown Arcadia suffered a devastating fire. Apparently, it began in a livery stable, but the cause was never determined. High winds rapidly spread the flames. The townspeople fought valiantly to extinguish it, but at that time Arcadia had no public water system or firefighting equipment. By dawn all but three buildings had been consumed. Miraculously, no one died.

Two days later, Arcadia's business leaders passed the city's first building codes, which stated that all reconstruction had to be done with brick or concrete. Not long after, they built a city water supply and organized a fire department. Arcadia rose, like the proverbial phoenix from the ashes, to become a thriving south-central Florida community.

Arcadia is in cattle country and for more than ninety years it has been nationally famous for its annual All-Florida Championship Rodeo. First held in 1928 as fundraising event for the local American Legion chapter, it is Florida's longest running and largest rodeo event.

In more recent decades, Arcadia has become popular for another kind of wrangling—for antiques. Four blocks along Oak Street (the town's main street) there are a dozen antique shops, plus more at the historic Arcadia Opera House, which contains an antique mall.

The Mediterranean-style opera house, built in 1906, occupies an entire city block at the corner of Oak Street and Polk Avenue in the center of downtown. In the 1910s, Arcadians strolled up its steps on Saturday evenings to watch plays and traveling vaudeville shows. When silent movies emerged in the 1920s, it became the movie theater. Today, the stage and dressing rooms have been converted into a museum. A 1902 Deere and Webbe (forerunner of the John Deere Company) horse buggy and an Indian dugout canoe of undetermined age—discovered at the bottom of the Peace River—dominate the stage. Props, costumes, handbills, and newspaper clippings from early Arcadia Opera House days hang on the walls. The signatures of performers along with the names of their performances are still visible where they were scrawled on the dressing room walls, as was the custom with traveling shows in the 1900s and 1910s. Old movie projectors, film reels, theater seats, and silent movie equipment preserved from the 1920s and 1930s are also on display.

Rodeos and antique shopping aside, I really need only one reason to come to Arcadia: the vanilla peanut butter pie at Wheeler's Goody Café. Wheeler's began as Fiegel's Goody Café in 1929, when fifty cents would buy a good hot lunch. Alene Davis was a waitress at Fiegel's in the 1930s. She married the owner, C. B. Fiegel, and they ran the café together until he died in 1951. When Alene remarried, to Walter Wheeler, she changed the name to Wheeler's Goody Café. Wheeler's has changed hands a couple times over the years, but even with different owners it's still consistently serves the best southern home-cooked grub within a hundred miles and the best homemade pies on the planet. I ate lunch there in 2020 and am pleased to report that the fried catfish, collard greens, and two slices of vanilla peanut butter pie were as delectable as always.

DON'T MISS
Having homemade pie at Wheeler's Goody Café

Jensen Beach

Lake Okeechobee

Boca Grande
Bokeelia
Pineland
Matlacha
Captiva
St. James City
Sanibel

Clewiston

Briny Breezes

Everglades City
Ochopee
Goodland
Chokoloskee

Miami

Card Sound

No Name Key

Islamorada

Big Pine Key

Key West

SOUTH REGION

Bunk House Coffee Bar, Jensen Beach

JENSEN BEACH

Population: 13,477

To me, it almost seems like twenty-four-mile-long Hutchinson Island is politely thumbing its nose at their overdeveloped, traffic-jammed neighbors to the south. Maybe it's the lack of proximity to a large metropolitan city; maybe it's just the laidback surfer culture. Surfing is a big deal here. The underwater topography just offshore from Hutchinson generates an ideal reef break, one favorable to long rolling swells. Winter is best, but surfers hit the waves along this coast year-round. Jensen Beach, which anchors Hutchinson Island's south end, has long been a surfing town. The good-vibe attitude is every-where—you almost feel like you are in a Bruce Brown movie (if you do not know who Bruce Brown is google *Endless Summer*). Surf shops, with boards, accessories, and of course surf wear, are abundant. So are tiki bar restaurants. There are just enough people here that there is always something fun going on, but not so many that Hutchinson Islanders have to put up with daily traffic gridlock (like cities to their south do)—in other words, Jensen Beach is just right.

The Jensen Beach Causeway (Northeast Causeway Boulevard) links the southern end of Hutchinson Island with the mainland, crossing the Indian River/Intercoastal Waterway into "Downtown" Jensen Beach. In addition to a few tourist shops there are several good dining spots. They are all very casual—this is a beach town after all. Conchy Joe's Seafood Restaurant & Bar opened 1979. It serves good fresh seafood, has a lively bar—usually with live entertainment—and a terrific Indian River-front view. The Hoffmann, next door, enjoys the same view but in a smaller setting. It's also a bar and grill but specializes in authentic German fare: bratwurst, schnitzel, and tasty potato pancakes. Crawdaddy's, on downtown Jensen Beach's one-block-long main street, leans toward New Orleans/Creole dishes: jambalaya, blackened fish,

Conchy Joes, Jensen Beach

and of course crawfish. For coffee lovers who love a friendly local coffeehouse atmosphere, the Bunk House Coffee Bar is the place to spend your mornings. Owner and head barista Kelly Adams is always behind the counter pulling perfect shots of espresso, but the real boss is Lil, her lovable red border collie and official greeter. Bunk House is all-vegan, so no dairy products are served, but Kelly makes the almond, coconut, soy, and rice creamers work. Cross the Jensen Beach Causeway back onto Hutchinson Island to reach Kyle G's Prime Seafood & Steaks, perched on a bluff overlooking the Atlantic. Owner Kyle Greene started in the restaurant business as a dish washer when he was fifteen years old and worked his way up through a variety of upscale steak and seafood restaurants. He has applied all that acquired knowledge to building Jensen Beach's top restaurant, serving superb seafood dishes like roasted black grouper Oscar, citrus blackened tuna, lobster carbonara, plus steaks, and be sure to get the Maine lobster mac and cheese as a side.

Technically, the very southern tip of Hutchinson Island is considered Stuart Beach, but it is close enough that I am including some must-visit places here.

The first is Gilbert's Bar House of Refuge. In the late 1800s, much of Florida's Atlantic coastline, particularly the southern half, was sparsely populated. Shipwrecks and other sea vessel calamities were commonplace, so between 1876 and 1885 a US government federal agency called the United States Life-Saving Service constructed ten House of Refuge stations along Florida's beaches. Nine were on the Atlantic coast, the furthest north just south of St. Augustine and furthest south near Miami. One other "House" was constructed on Santa Rosa Island, on the Gulf of Mexico near Pensacola. Only one House of Refuge remains today: Gilbert's Bar House of Refuge, at the south end of Hutchinson Island. It was commissioned in 1875, with construction completed in 1876, on one of Florida's rare rocky shorlines (compacted shell) bluffs (hence the "Bar"). It was operated by the US Coast Guard through World War II and later in 1955 acquired by the Martin County Historical Society to be turned into a maritime museum. The historical society petitioned to have the location added to the US National Register of Historic Places in 1974, and it underwent an ex-

Elliott Museum, Jensen Beach

tensive renovation the following year. The museum offers both guided and self-guided tours and features exhibits of lifesaving equipment, along with displays that tell the history of local shipwreck rescues.

Just north of Gilbert's Bar House of Refuge you will find the Florida Oceanographic Center and the Elliott Museum. The Florida Oceanographic Center opened in 1964 as a nonprofit organization to study and help preserve Florida's coastal ecosystems. It conducts daily education programs (you will see lots of school class field trips) but anyone can visit. Its 750,000-gallon lagoon is populated with sharks, sea turtles, rays, and all manner of Florida sea life. Across the road at the Elliott Museum (managed by the Historical Society of Martin County, same as Gilbert's Bar House of Refuge) it houses an outstanding collection of vintage automobiles, airplanes, boats, and bicycles, plus a variety of historical displays about early inventions. Founder Harmon Elliott opened it in 1961 to honor his father, Sterling Elliott, a prolific inventor with more than 125 patents to his name.

DON'T MISS
A visit to the Elliott Museum

Port Boca Grande Lighthouse

BOCA GRANDE

Population not listed on census

*S*ix-mile-long Gasparilla Island and the village of Boca Grande are only accessible by a six-dollar-per-car toll bridge at its north end, or by boat or seaplane. That relative isolation has allowed it to hang on to its tranquil, tropical, laid-back atmosphere. There are no stoplights, and the only structure more than three stories tall is a steel-girder 1927 lighthouse tower (still functioning) on the southern beach. Tin-roofed bungalows nestled among ghostly banyan trees make up the surrounding neighborhood, which was originally developed in the 1890s by Albert Gilchrist, who would later become Florida's twentieth governor. For the better part of a century, generations of Florida families have been coming to Boca Grande for the relaxed island vibe, pristine beaches, and world-famous tarpon fishing.

Through most of the 1800s, Gasparilla Island's few inhabitants were transient—some Cuban mullet fishermen and a few rumrunners. But in 1885, phosphate was discovered midstate. Mining companies began

Gasparilla Island Lighthouse

transporting it by barge down the Peace River and out to Charlotte Harbor. Suddenly, Gasparilla Island, at the mouth of Charlotte Harbor, had become an important piece of property. The town of Boca Grande (Spanish for "big mouth," referring to Boca Grande Pass at the mouth of Charlotte Harbor) sprung up at the island's southern end to accommodate workers unloading phosphate from river barges and reloading it onto ships sailing abroad. In 1907, the Charlotte Harbor and Northern Railroad line replaced the river barges.

The name Gasparilla Island conjures up the image of a clandestine pirate's hideaway, and there is some history to back that up. Real pirates like Henri Caesar and Brewster "Bru" Baker did sail the southwestern coast of Florida and probably visited Gasparilla Island in the 1700s.

However, this area's most famous pirate, Jose Gaspar, was almost certainly a myth created out of tall tales told by an old Cuban fisherman, Juan "Panther Key John" Gomez, in the late 1800s. In 1918, the Charlotte Harbor and Northern Railroad released a publication, *The Gasparilla Story*, which pieced together some of Gomez's anecdotes. It also contained sales advertisements for railroad-owned property in Boca Grande, the terminus of the railway on Gasparilla Island. Those early property sales efforts turned out to be lackluster, but the romanticized fable of Jose Gaspar became accepted as genuine. The truth is that Gasparilla Island was likely named after a group of Spanish priests who ran a mission in Charlotte Harbor. Old charts, predating Gaspar's presumed lifetime by two hundred years, show Gasparilla Pass as Friar Gaspar Pass.

With a year-round (unofficial) population of less than a thousand, Boca Grande is uncrowded and unhurried. Residents get around in electric golf carts. There is even a golf cart path running the length of the northern half of the island, which leads south to "Downtown" Boca Grande where you will find an assortment of specialty shops, boutiques, galleries, and some outstanding restaurants. Its centerpiece is the restored 1911 Railroad Depot Building on Fourth Street at Park Avenue, where folks line up for homemade ice cream at The Loose Caboose.

It is no surprise that fresh seafood is a specialty at Boca Grande restaurants. "Fresh catch" here really does mean that it was caught that morning. One of the most notable places for fresh fish is Temptations, on Park Avenue. Temptations' interior is like a time capsule from 1947, the year they opened. It is the type of place where Humphrey Bogart might have hung out. Have whatever the "fresh catch" is with one of their outstanding sauces, like Thai sweet chili. The tiny "Temp" Bar, next door, is the place to hear big-fish stories, just be mindful of their "Please No Profanity" sign behind the bar.

Miller's Marina has been a Boca Grande icon for decades. While the marina itself is gone, the boat docks remain, and it makes a classic waterfront setting for Miller's Dockside and its upstairs cousin the Eagle Grille Restaurant. Miller's Dockside serves tasty appetizers like tuna nachos, calamari fritto, peel-and-eat shrimp, and steamed mussels in onion garlic butter, plus entrées like blackened grouper and Gasparilla shrimp and grits. The upstairs Eagle Grill offers more of the same with a few upscale additions, like seared Thai scallops in nori-soy-sake butter.

Another long-time Boca Grande landmark restaurant, the Pink Elephant, is now operated by the Gasparilla Inn (across the street). Seared crab cakes, chargrilled lamb chops, and almond-crusted cedar plank salmon are just a few of their excellent entrées. The Pink Elephant's desserts are deservedly famous—particularly their key lime pie, which is as rich and dense as a New York cheesecake. The Gasparilla Inn also operates The Inn Bakery (and Coffee Shop), the best place for big, fluffy donuts, stuffed croissants, and espresso drinks.

There is only one beachside Boca Grande restaurant, South Beach Bar & Grille, on the south end of the island. I think it contends for Boca

Grande's best casual seafood joint, and a great place to catch a sunset and a cocktail.

Most visitors to Boca Grande rent or own vacation homes, but there are three notable lodgings, and all are within walking distance of downtown.

The (aforementioned) Gasparilla Inn, originally the Hotel Boca Grande when it was built in 1911, is a palatial and historic hotel. In 1930, industrialist and developer Barron G. Collier bought it and added a solarium and columns to the front entrance. Today, it is an opulent resort in the tradition of Collier's era with a golf course, tennis courts, swimming pools, and a full-service spa. The main hotel has 154 rooms. Nineteen additional quadruplex cottages (which can be opened to accommodate families or groups) occupy several blocks in the surrounding neighborhood. Citrus trees, Australian pines, and towering palms grow throughout the grounds.

The Gasparilla Inn also operates The Innlet, a two-story Boca-Grande-Bayou-side motel a half mile north, with its own full-service marina. The Outlet Restaurant tucked away at one end is Boca Grande's best-kept secret breakfast spot.

For a place that feels like a friend's home, one block from the middle of town on 4th Street, The Anchor Inn offers just four rooms—two suites and two studios, all with kitchenettes, in a house built in 1925.

Besides fishing and walking the shell-strewn beaches, visitors to Boca Grande pass the time browsing the shops. Fugate's, Boca Grande's beach supplies, beach wear, gifts, and sundries store at 4th Street and Park Avenue, opened in 1916. It is the oldest continuously operated business on the island and is still run by the Fugate family. It reminds me of the beach sundry shops that I recall from summer visits to Indian Rocks Beach in the 1960s. At Boca Grande Outfitters, a block south of Fugates, you will find the best selection of fishing gear, sports, and outdoor wear.

Boca Grande has some wildlife too—at least of the feathery or green-and-scaly kind. The island is home to a variety of seabirds—pelicans, herons, and egrets. A few decades back someone let a pair of pet iguanas loose. Today, their many descendants are frequently spotted sunning on the seawalls.

Port Boca Grande Outfitters

South of town you will find Boca Grande's two lighthouses: The Gasparilla Island Lighthouse, a 105-foot-tall, steel-girder structure built in 1927, stands alongside the public beach on Gulf Boulevard. The other, at the southern tip of the island, serves as a channel marker for Boca Grande Pass. Built in 1890, it is thought to be the oldest building on Gasparilla Island. It fell into disrepair in the 1960s, was restored, and then recommissioned in 1986, and is now part of the Gasparilla Island State Park. The Port Boca Grande Lighthouse Museum opened there in 1999.

For another look at Boca Grande history visit Whidden's Marina, bayside on 1st Street. This two-story tin-roof marina was listed on the National Register of Historic Places in 2000 and remains virtually unchanged since Sam Whidden built it in 1926. It is a functioning museum—still operating as a marina, and still run by the Whidden family. They have dedicated one section of the building to their maritime museum that chronicles the history of Boca Grande from the 1920s to present.

For decades, treasure hunters have sifted the sands of Gasparilla Island, and the barrier islands around it, in search of buried pirate treasure, but little of value has been found. It turns out, the mythical pirate's island and its village of Boca Grande are the real treasure.

DON'T MISS

Shopping at Fugate's beach shop

Clewiston Inn

CLEWISTON

Population: 8,020

*T*he Clewiston Inn is the oldest hotel on Lake Okeechobee. Originally built in 1926, the inn was destroyed by a fire in 1937. The U.S. Sugar Company, whose headquarters have been in Clewiston since 1931, rebuilt the inn in 1938 to accommodate and entertain visiting executives and dignitaries. Four two-story columns support a traditional southern gable that protrudes over the inn's entrance. Neatly pruned palm trees line the circular drive where it sweeps underneath the gable. This is a Rhett-and-Scarlett kind of place. Bird's-eye cypress paneling covers the lobby walls all the way up to its open-beam ceiling. The terra cotta tile floor is waxed to a glossy shine. A wide staircase with brass railings leads to the second floor. The rooms are comfortable and decorated in a simple yet elegant 1940s style. When you check in, you will receive a bag of sugar cookies.

The sugar cookies are nice but the real reason I came to the inn was because I had heard about the stunning J. Clinton Shepherd oil-on-canvas mural that wraps around all four walls in the inn's Everglades Lounge. Shepherd lived at the inn for the better part of 1945. Every day he took treks into the Everglades to sketch Florida's native wild animals and plants. When he felt that he had accumulated enough material, he began to put his subjects on canvas. The result is a hauntingly beautiful and remarkably real 360-degree panorama, set in an early morning mist and depicting most of the wildlife that calls the Everglades home. Every variety of native duck, egret, heron, and crane can be found somewhere on these walls. Owls, jays, and ospreys also make an appearance, as do deer, opossums, a marsh hare, raccoons, alligators, and a black bear with her cub. The mural is one continuous scene. Shepherd had to precisely measure and cut the canvas to fit around windows, cabinets, and the doorway. You almost feel as though you're standing in the middle of a cypress bay head at daybreak.

The inn has been at the center of life in Clewiston throughout the town's history. During World War II, the British Royal Air Force trained cadets at nearby Riddle Field. The Clewiston Inn was the flyboys' favorite hangout. The inn's caretakers have done an admirable job of adhering to the ambiance of that grand era.

This area's biggest attraction is what the Seminole Indians called the "Big Water." More than 730 square miles in area and 35 miles in diameter, Lake Okeechobee is a virtual inland sea. It is the second largest freshwater lake wholly within the United States' boundaries. To avid anglers, it is paradise. They come here for largemouth bass, bluegill, speckled perch, and Okeechobee catfish.

On September 16, 1928, tragedy struck Lake Okeechobee when a hurricane with 160-mile-per-hour winds crossed the lake from the Atlantic Ocean. The hurricane's front winds pushed the water in Lake Okeechobee to the north, flooding the town of Okeechobee. As it passed over, moving west, the winds from the backside of the hurricane pushed the water back south and flooded Pahokee, Belle Glade, and Clewiston. The Clewiston Inn survived but nearly two thousand people around Lake Okeechobee drowned. Rescuers continued to find bodies weeks after the storm. Many of them were Bahamian migrant workers, and there was no way to identify them. In response to that disaster, in the early 1930s, the US Army Corp of Engineers built 140 miles of forty-foot-high levees around the lake, which you will see if you are driving east out of Clewiston.

Entrance to Briny Breezes

BRINY BREEZES

Population: 578

*B*riny Breezes—The Little Trailer Park That Could. The reason it could is because it sits on prime beach property, on Highway A1A, fifteen miles south of posh Palm Beach.

By the 1920s, the price of a Ford Model T had dropped to under $300 (down from $850 when it was introduced in 1909). That changed vacationing forever. Roads were being paved to all corners and now everyday folks could take automobile trips—and they did—in droves. Those early "tin-can tourists" lived and camped out of their automobiles, and campgrounds sprung up to accommodate them. In the 1930s, the land that Briny Breezes was built on was a strawberry pasture, until farmer Ward Miller figured out that he could make more money parking cars and trailers on it than picking strawberries. In the 1950s, he began selling lots outright to regulars and by 1963 the property was owned entirely by residents, who decided to incorporate as the town of Briny Breezes. In 2005, developer Ocean Land Investments offered to buy all forty-two acres of Briny Breezes, for what amounted to about $1 million per trailer lot. It stirred quite a debate among the mostly-retiree residents, but in 2007 the deal fell through. Today, Briny Breezes residents are still there, and they seem content with that.

Lovegrove Gallery & Gardens, Matlacha

MATLACHA, BOKEELIA, PINELAND, ST. JAMES CITY

Population: Matlacha 620; Bokeelia 1,420; Pineland 309; St. James City 3,437

*S*tate Road 78 takes you across the only bridge that connects mainland Fort Myers to Pine Island. But before reaching the island you will pass through the curious little mile-long village of Matlacha (pronounced Mat-la-shay), a place so splashed in bright colors it is as if LeRoy Neiman and Andy Warhol went on a graffiti binge. Matlacha resides on the tiny stepping-stone islands along the bridge to Pine Island. Fishing boats bob up and down at their moorings behind restaurants, gift shops, and galleries that line both sides of the highway. For many decades prior to the completion of the bridge in 1927, local fishermen had worked these exceptionally fertile fishing grounds in the pass. When the bridge was built some of them put up squatter's shacks alongside it. Before long, it evolved into the village of Matlacha. Fishing is still big here. They even call the SR 78 bridge the "Fishingest Bridge in the World."

Matlacha has become an artist's enclave as well, with dozens of galleries and artists' studios. Many of Leoma Lovegrove's vivid, large-scale acrylic paintings depict Florida wildlife, but she has a thing for musicians too—particularly The Beatles. Her Lovegrove Gallery is filled with spectacular original art, and is a must-see, as is her (octopus'?) garden out back. Next door, Wild Child Gallery features work from more local artists who work in a variety of mediums: painting, sculpture, photography, and jewelry design. Across the street at tiny Elena's the owner has been creating her own unique style of island jewelry for more than twenty-five years.

Bert's Bar and Grill, Matlacha

Matlacha's oldest eats and entertainment spot—Bert's Bar & Grill—has been a fixture since the 1930s. In the 1940s, 1950s, and 1960s it was also a motel with a rowdy (and sometimes nefarious) reputation. Today, it is a great spot for live music and a grouper sandwich.

For good, hearty breakfast the Perfect Cup packs them in, and I can vouch for their blueberry pancakes.

When I stayed overnight, I was looking for lodging that matched the island's ambiance, and I found Matlacha Island Cottages, made up of four nicely renovated historic waterfront cottages. It has kitchenettes, as well as a backyard picnic area and private docks. Another option is the Bridgewater Inn, an eight-room motel built on pylons over the water. You can fish right from the front door of your room.

Tarpon Lodge, Pineland

Continue over the bridge and you will end up on seventeen-mile-long, three-mile-wide Pine Island—Florida's largest Gulf Coast island. SR 78 intersects Stringfellow Road, the island's main thoroughfare, which connects St. James City at its southern tip with Bokeelia at its northern tip. The straight two-lane road passes tropical groves and nurseries. Pine Island has a thriving subtropical exotic fruit and plant industry. Best known for its mangoes, which early settlers began growing here at the turn of the century, the island also supports pineapple, carambola (star fruit), papaya, loquat, and palm trees.

Bokeelia, at the north end, is a popular launching point for fishing expeditions. The waters that surround Pine Island regularly yield snook, cobia, snapper, and redfish, in addition to the granddaddy of them all—tarpon.

Bokeelia's Main Street dead-ends at Capt'n Con's Fish House. This was Bokeelia's first house, built by H. W. Martin in 1904. The smaller house on its west side was Bokeelia's first post office. Martin's wife ran the place as a boardinghouse for boat passengers and fishermen. To-

Bokeelia Art Gallery

day, the two-story wood-frame structure is Capt'n Con's gift shop, and the attached one-story building next door is its popular seafood restaurant.

The Bokeelia Art Gallery (formerly The Crossed Palms Gallery), a block east of Capt'n Con's, is an art lover's wonderland. Original owner and founder of Crossed Palms Gallery, Nancy Brooks, had a knack for seeking out exceptionally talented, undiscovered artists. In January 2020, Carol and Ed Garske bought the gallery from Nancy. They changed the name but have maintained the gallery's tradition of colorful paintings (much of it Florida nature-themed), eclectic sculpture, pottery, glass art, and whimsical pop art. And, most important to me, they still feature one of my very favorite Florida watercolor artists: David Belling. Belling's coastal landscapes capture the feel of this region of Florida in stunning detail like no other artist I have ever seen. When I look at his paintings, I always feel like I could step through the frame and be transported to that very location.

A few miles south of Bokeelia, wind down Pineland Road to Waterfront Drive. You will come across the restored 1926 Tarpon Lodge and Restaurant, a gracious retreat tucked away on the west side of the island overlooking the Pine Island Sound. The lodge has eight rooms in the main lodge and an additional twelve in the adjacent stilt house, plus a two-bedroom boathouse and a one-bedroom cottage. Its restaurant menu includes fresh seafood selections, steaks, plus burgers and crab cake sandwiches, and an exceptional blue crab and roasted corn chowder.

Waterfront Restaurant, St. James City

In St. James City, at the southern end of Pine Island, I have found another great small-town eatery—the Waterfront Restaurant, housed in St. James City's first schoolhouse. The school building was erected in 1887. It survived a fire in 1896 and was moved twice before settling in its current location. In the late 1940s, it became a fish camp. The wood-paneled interior has a rustic, old-Florida feel. The bar, in the original school's classroom, has a canoe hanging from the ceiling with hundreds of dollar bills taped to its hull. Once again, I recommend the grouper sandwich, but you will not miss with anything on their menu.

Pine Island has its own museum—Museum of the Islands—opened in 1990, just north of the intersection of Stringfellow Road and SR 78. History buffs will want to spend some time here to learn about this region's history. Some famous names in early Florida history have stopped at Pine Island. According to his logs, Ponce de Leon careened his ship along the western shore in 1513. He and his crew spent several days repairing the ship's hull, gathering wood, and collecting fresh water. He returned to Pine Island in 1521 and, during a skirmish here with the Calusa Indians, was shot with an arrow. His crew took him to Cuba to recuperate, but he died there as a result of his wound.

Much of Pine Island's history predates written record. The Calusa lived on Pine Island for more than a thousand years before Ponce de Leon came. They built huge shell mounds and dug elaborate canals across the island. The arrival of the Spanish ultimately brought on the Calusa's demise. They had no immunity to European diseases, most notably chickenpox. By the mid-1700s, they were all gone. Although the rumors are largely unsubstantiated, Pine Island Sound may have been a haven for pirates—including Brewster "Bru" Baker, who may have lived for a while near present-day Bokeelia, and Henri "Black" Caesar, reported to have camped on nearby Sanibel Island.

DON'T MISS
A visit to Lovegrove Gallery & Gardens

Heron at Ding Darling National Wildlife Refuge, Sanibel

SANIBEL, CAPTIVA

Population: Sanibel 7,401; Captiva 178

Sanibel and Captiva are so often mentioned in the same breath that many think they are one place. Granted, they are next to each other, and yes, you must drive through Sanibel to get to Captiva, however, they have distinctly different personalities.

Sanibel is famous for its gorgeous shell-strewn beaches and its casual (but still ritzy) boutiques, but also for its natural and historic sights.

If you can picture Sanibel Island as a fishhook—Lighthouse Beach Park would be at its (eastern) sharp tip. Here you will find the one-hundred-foot-tall iron-frame Sanibel Lighthouse that has guided ships since its completion in 1884. But it was almost lost before it ever went up. The lighthouse had been built in sections and brought down by ship from New Jersey. Just a few miles offshore from Sanibel, the ship ran aground and sank. Salvagers, or "wreckers," mostly from Key West, were able to retrieve the sections from the Gulf's floor, and eventually construction went forward as planned. It has been a National Landmark since 1972 and is still functional.

Four miles west you will find the Sanibel Historical Village and Museum, which opened in 1984 and consists of an impressive collection of ten relocated and restored 1910s–1930s Sanibel frame houses and buildings, including an 1896 schoolhouse and the original 1927 Baily General Store.

Local Sanibel shell-collecting club members started a museum project that took ten years to realize. Finally, in 1995, on property donated by the Sanibel pioneer Bailey family, the Bailey-Matthews Shell Museum opened its doors. The museum contains extensive exhibits on shellfish and has also become a renowned scientific and education resource.

Sanibel's paramount natural attraction is the J. N. Ding Darling National Wildlife Refuge, which occupies six thousand acres on the island's north end. Visitors can drive or hike through the refuge and see a wide variety of Florida wildlife, including alligators, turtles, otters, and raccoons. Bird watchers are in heaven here. Several hundred bird species make the refuge their home, among them pink-winged roseate spoonbills, blue herons, white ibis, egrets, owls, and ospreys. The refuge is named after political cartoonist Jay Norwood "Ding" Darling.

Sanibel Cottages, Sanibel

Darling won a Pulitzer Prize in 1924 and 1943 and later was head of the US Biological Survey. He was also founder of the National Wildlife Foundation. Darling spent his winters on Sanibel and Captiva and championed the cause of conservation and wildlife preservation here, long before it was fashionable. As far back as the 1920s, Darling's cartoons reflected his concerns about conservation. It was his efforts that led to Sanibel and Captiva both being declared wildlife sanctuaries by the state of Florida in 1948.

On one recent visit to Sanibel, I spent a morning kayaking the winding water trails and lagoons at the western end of Ding Darling National Wildlife Refuge. Once on the water I did not see another human being for the entire paddle—it seemed almost primeval. It was, however, lively. Fish were jumping all around me. I saw sea trout, redfish, and mullet. I had stuffed my camera in my dry bag, just in case I spotted something photo-worthy, and got one quick snap of an osprey searching for breakfast from his dead-limb perch. Ospreys have been on the Florida Fish and Wildlife's "Species of Special Concern" list for quite some time, but populations here are reportedly on the increase. Their common name is fish hawk because that is almost all they eat. I read an interesting fact about them that speaks to their intelligence and adaptability. Right after they snatch a fish out of the water, they spin it around between their claws so that the fish's head faces forward for aerodynamic advantage, or maybe they just want the fish to see where it is going.

Remote Florida tropical islands where you can truly "get away from it all," while still arriving by car, are a rare commodity. Captiva Island is a hardy holdout. To get any more remote you will need a boat, or a seaplane, or be an exceptionally good swimmer. Once you cross the short bridge that spans Blind Pass, between Sanibel and Captiva, there is a noticeable shift in the vibe. Captiva is more wildly vegetated, more rustic, and less populated. It is almost Polynesian in its tropical-ness. Dense flora—sea grapes, frangipani, crotons, spiny aloe, and all varieties of palm including sable, coconut, royal, butterfly, and cabbage—inhabit the island.

One-block-long Andy Rosse Lane qualifies as Captiva's "downtown," with the Captiva Island Store (originally a circa 1900 school-

Beach swing, Captiva

house) at one end, and the Mucky Duck—a British-style pub and restaurant on the beach—at the other end. In-between there are a few funky art galleries and shops. My favorite is the Jungle Drums Gallery, which features original wildlife-theme art, sculpture, and furniture, much of it created by the gallery's owners Jim and Kathleen Mazzotta.

There is no shortage of terrific restaurants on both islands. The Mucky Duck has a varied menu ranging from burgers to a very tasty Duck a l'Orange.

One of my regular Captiva restaurants, the Sunshine Seafood Café, recently relocated to new larger digs on Andy Rosse Lane. Its Pan-Asian/Floribbean menu features outstanding wood-grilled entrees like yellowfin tuna au poivre with red wine and pepper demi-glace, wood-grilled blackened salmon with mango/pineapple sauce, and paella.

A kid's favorite eatery is the Bubble Room, loudly decorated as a cross between a circus and a restaurant. It's known for their towering desserts.

Just over the Sanibel side of the Blind Pass Bridge and right on the beach (next to Castaways Cottages) is my perennial favorite, The Mad Hatter Restaurant. Its mouth-watering entrees include walnut and cherry pesto-crusted rack of lamb, pan-seared panko and black truffle-crusted scallops, and an amazing seafood bouillabaisse.

And then there is Doc Fords Rum Bar and Restaurant, there are two—one on Sanibel and one on Captiva. Before he was a popular novelist, Pine Island resident Randy Wayne White was a much in demand charter light-tackle fishing guide working the waters in and around Pine Island Sound, Boca Grande, Cayo Costa, Captiva, and Sanibel. He knows fish, particularly local fish. So perhaps it was a natural progression for him to eventually end up in the seafood restaurant business. Doc Ford's original Sanibel Rum Bar & Grill (named for Randy Wayne White's adventure-mystery series protagonist) opened in 2003 as a joint venture with a couple other investors, and like White's other endeavors, has been a resounding success. Many patrons come the first time because they're Randy Wayne White fans, but they come the second time (and third and fourth) because the food is so good. Doc Ford's menu leans toward the tropical, Central and South American, Cuban, and Caribbean. I have several regular favorites: banana leaf snapper, island style shrimp and grits, and then the one thing I must get every single time: Yucatan shrimp—steamed peel-and-eat shrimp in a spicy chili, cilantro, garlic, key lime juice, and butter sauce. It comes with fresh baked crusty French bread to soak up the remaining sauce after the shrimp have been devoured.

I have two favorite Captiva and Sanibel lodgings, and both are low-key and beach casual.

'Tween Waters Inn straddles Captiva Island's narrowest point, between the Gulf of Mexico and Pine Island Sound, just north of the Blind Pass Bridge. The inn has a long history. Captiva's first settlers arrived in the late 1800s and early 1900s, long after the pirates who frequented these waters had been vanquished. One settler was Dr. J. Dickey from Bristol, Virginia. Dickey visited Captiva on a fishing trip in 1900, and then returned with his family in 1905. Since there were no schools on Captiva, Dickey also brought along a tutor, Miss Reba Fitzpatrick, to educate his children. He built a schoolhouse with living quarters for Miss Reba upstairs. Mr. and Mrs. Bowman Price, friends of the Dickeys from Bristol, purchased the schoolhouse and surrounding property in 1925. In 1931, they converted the old school into the 'Tween Waters Inn. Over the years, the Prices added cottages to accommodate new visitors who arrived every winter. In the late 1940s, they floated army barracks across the sound from Fort Myers to add more cottages. Some famous people made 'Tween Waters their winter retreat. Anne Morrow Lindbergh, prolific author

Lindbergh Cottage at 'Tween Waters Inn, Captiva

and wife of Charles Lindbergh, stayed here in the 1950s. She wrote one of her best known works, *Gift from the Sea*, while on Captiva. Cartoonist "Ding" Darling frequented 'Tween Waters too. He would rent two cottages: #103 as his room and #105 as his studio. I have stayed in the Lindbergh Cottage, #104, that faces the Gulf and the beach across the road, and it was thoroughly charming. 'Tween Waters Inn offers studio and suite hotel rooms, plus nineteen individual cottages, a marina, and a restaurant.

The Castaways Cottages (which is now owned by 'Tween Waters Inn) sits just across Blind Pass on the Sanibel (south) side. Nothing fancy, just simple 1940s- and 1950s-era, wood-frame beach cottages and duplex cottages with screen porches and worn wood floors. Ten of the thirty units are right on the beach. I like to stay here when I bring my kayak because it's an easy paddle to Ding Darling National Wildlife Refuge from their dock on the Pine Island Sound side.

Do a little back road exploring on Captiva and you will eventually run across another quaint piece of Captiva history—the Chapel by the Sea. Captiva's earliest settler William Binder built this tiny white chapel on Chapin Road in 1901, originally as a schoolhouse. Binder was shipwrecked off Captiva in 1885 and was the first to file a homestead claim on the island. Next to the chapel, the Captiva Cemetery is shaded by gumbo-limbo trees. The high spot shared by the chapel and cemetery is an ancient Calusa Indian shell midden.

DON'T MISS

Seeing the Chapel by the Sea and the old Captiva Cemetery

Paradise Found Restaurant, Goodland

GOODLAND

Population: 437

From the top of the State Road 92 bridge crossing over Goodland Bay at the western edge of the Ten Thousand Islands, you get a brief glimpse at Marco Island's high-rise beach condos on the horizon, five miles away. But veer sharply left immediately after crossing that bridge and you will find yourself in a completely different world—the tiny fishing community of Goodland.

A few homesteaders settled here at "Goodland Point" back in the late 1800s, but more people started coming eighty years ago after the first Goodland bridge, an old wooden swing bridge, was built in 1935. In contrast to the beach side of Marco Island, Goodland has not grown much since then, and that is the way folks here like it. What it lacks in size, it makes up for in personality.

Today, as then, fishing is the main draw, and to keep those visitors (and the few locals) watered and fed, there are four notable bar and grills, all serving good local fresh seafood.

Panther Crossing Sign, Goodland

The first one you come to is Stan's Idle Hour. Owner Stan Gober was Goodland's Renaissance man: restaurateur, singer/songwriter, stand-up comic, and festival promoter. Stan's Idle Hour has been hosting Goodland's Annual Mullet Festival every January (usually the third weekend) since the 1980s. The event culminates in the crowning of that year's "Buzzard Lope Queen." "Buzzard Lope" is named for a Stan Gober song and the local's favorite dance. Sadly, Stan passed away in 2012, but his legend lives on. The bridge over to Goodland was recently renamed the Stan Gober Memorial Bridge, and a Stan Look-A-Like contest was added to the annual Lobsterfest in March. Stan's offers a wide assortment of fresh seafood platters (fried, blackened, broiled, and sautéed) and shrimp, catfish, oysters, scallops, and blue crab. They will also happily cook what you catch and bring them.

A one-block stroll up the road from Stan's will bring you to the Little Bar Restaurant. The sign says "New Little Bar and Restaurant" but most of the decorations and accoutrements inside are relics salvaged from old bars around the country by Little Bar founder Ray Bozicnik, which makes the place interesting to browse through. Bozicnik opened Little Bar in 1978, and his son Ray operates it today. Their extensive menu includes all the usual seafood dishes plus a couple you cannot always find easily: frog's legs and soft-shell crab. For an appetizer check out the grouper balls (who knew?).

Keep walking up the road a little further to find Paradise Found, which opened in 2019. The building was known as the Old Marco Lodge, built originally as a residence in 1869 and relocated from a few blocks away in 1965. It is seafood bar and grill fare: peel-and-eat shrimp, fish tacos, gumbo—all good.

Pelican across from Crabby Lady Restaurant, Goodland

Cross the parking lot next door, and across from the trailer park you will come to Crabby Lady (do not worry—she is nice). Like the others, Crabby Lady is seafood-centric but if I must pick a favorite, this is it. It's a little further off the beaten path but still waterfront, and the food is excellent. As the name implies, it's big on crab here and Joe's crab balls, stuffed with fresh blue crab, are the bomb!

DON'T MISS
Fresh seafood at the Crabby Lady restaurant

City Seafood Market, Everglades City

EVERGLADES CITY, CHOKOLOSKEE

Population: Everglades City 421; Chokoloskee 268

*F*lorida's netherworld Everglades is the largest subtropical wilderness in the United States, occupying much of the southern end of the peninsula. Technically, it is an immensely broad river, in some places nearly three-quarters the width of the state. The "river" trickles south, primarily out of Lake Okeechobee. With only a fifteen-foot drop in elevation from Okeechobee to Florida Bay, the flow is nearly imperceptible. Although most of the Everglades is underwater, it is seldom more than a foot deep. Water evaporating from the Everglades supplies most of the southern portion of the state's rainfall. Scientists call it the hydrologic cycle—a perpetual rain-generating machine. At one time this Everglades system was considerably larger than it is now, but canals have drained and diverted much of the water from its northern and central sections to the state's heavily populated southeast coast.

Everglades National Park encompasses only the lower fifth—about 1.4 million acres—of the entire Everglades. The lower east-west stretch of US Highway 41/Tamiami Trail marks the park's northern boundary. Another 720,000 acres on the north side of US Highway 41/Tamiami Trail were designated the Big Cypress National Preserve in 1974. In 1989, President Bush signed into law the Everglades National Park Protection and Expansion Act, enlarging Everglades National Park by an additional 170,000 acres on its east side.

From the Tamiami Trail/US Highway 41, the Everglades appears to be just an endless expanse of saw grass, slash pine bay heads, and swamp. Closer observation reveals that it is brimming with wildlife. More than three hundred species of birds call the Everglades home: among them, ospreys, bald eagles, blue herons, great egrets, wood ibis, anhingas, pink roseate spoonbills, and purple gallinules. One of the rarest—the Everglades snail kite—lives here too and feeds exclusively on apple snails.

There is far less chance that you will see a Florida panther, the state mammal, although this is its natural habitat. Park rangers estimate that there are less than 150 of these beautiful animals left in the wild. It is also unlikely that you will see any of the few crocodiles that live in a remote southeast section of the park. Everglades National Park is the only place in the United States where they coexist with their broader-snouted relatives, alligators. In contrast, alligators can be found throughout the state, and in vast numbers in the Everglades. Placed on the Endangered Species List in the late 1960s, these prehistoric reptiles made an astounding comeback and were removed from the list in 1987.

Turn of the (previous) century federal and state leaders saw the Everglades as a colossal nuisance—a swamp that needed to be drained. This was a popular enough opinion in 1904 that Governor Napoleon Broward was elected on a platform of promising to do just that. Dredging and canal building efforts to drain the Everglades began in 1906 and continued in earnest into the late 1920s, during which time a series of canals were built to redirect water from Lake Okeechobee over to developing cities on the Atlantic Gold Coast. The adage about buying or selling swampland in Florida has its origins here. Governor Broward generated much publicity with his plans to reclaim the Everglades, and plots of "swampland" began to sell like hotcakes. Of course, as it turns out, these properties were worthless to the hapless buyers. Then in 1928, one of the most devastating hurricanes in Florida's history cut across Lake Okeechobee, flooding the towns on its perimeter and killing nearly two thousand people. Congress' answer to that tragedy was the River and Harbor Act of 1930, which authorized the US Army Corps of Engineers to build forty-foot-high levees around the entire southern shoreline and portions of the northern shoreline of Lake Okeechobee to contain future hurricane flooding. What they did not understand was that in doing so they were constricting the heart that pumped water through the Everglades. In what seems like a contradiction today, only four years later Congress authorized the Everglades National Park Project. It would take thirteen additional years before the park was created.

By the mid-1940s, some people began to recognize the vital role the Everglades played in the climatological and ecological balance of the state. Without question the most valiant of them was *Miami Herald* columnist and author Marjory Stoneman Douglas. Her book *The Everglades: River of Grass* was published in 1947, the same year Everglades National Park finally opened (note: it is still in print today, published by Pineapple Press). For the next fifty years she fought vigorously against human encroachment on the Everglades. In the 1960s, while in her late seventies, she became involved with the Audubon Society of Miami's efforts to halt the building of an international airport in the Everglades. Society members pleaded with her to start an organization that would unite the efforts of those concerned with the fate of the Everglades. She did and named it Friends of the Everglades, an organization that is today one of the most powerful voices for the area's preservation. Proving that good people do not always die young, Marjory Stoneman Douglas passed away in 1998 at the age of 108.

Prior to 1923, Everglades City, southeast of Naples, had been a sleepy fishing village and trading outpost. Barron Collier put it on the map when he made it the Collier County seat, as well as the location of his company from which trail construction operations of the Tampa-to-Miami "Tamiami" Trail took place. Construction on the trail had first begun in 1915, but by 1922 the state of Florida had run out of funds needed to complete the last section from Naples to Miami, across the Everglades. Barron Collier, originally from Tennessee, had made millions with his New York City Consolidated Street Railway Advertising Company. He reinvested his earnings in real estate and development, and by the early 1920s had accumulated more than a million acres in southwest Florida, making him the largest single land-owner in the state at that time. The Tamiami Trail was crucial to the appreciation of Colliers's real estate holdings, so he proposed an idea to the state: if they would divide Lee County and create a new south-ern county, he would finance and oversee the completion of the trail through the Everglades. They agreed (and named the county Collier). It took five years of digging, dredging, and blasting but on April 26, 1928, the Tamiami Trail officially opened.

The Tamiami Trail impacted the Everglades in many ways. Back in the 1930s, it revealed some of the mystery of the place to anyone with a Model T. What had once been an expedition to cross the state was now a mere day's drive. What the trail's constructors had not anticipated was the choking environmental effect it would have. Like the Lake Okeechobee levees, the trail (and later its cousin to the north, Alligator Alley) was essentially an enormous Everglades-wide dam that halted the almost imperceptible flow of water south. It also cut off much of the Everglade's (nonbird) wildlife's ability to migrate. Much work has been done in recent years to channel water beneath the highways, and to add wildlife tunnels. Hopefully, these efforts prove effective, and not too late.

After Hurricane Donna thrashed Everglades City in 1960, Collier pulled the last of his interests out of the town. The county seat moved to Naples, and Everglades City settled back into the quiet fishing vil-lage that it once was, and still is today.

The Everglades City's proud centerpiece was the Rod and Gun Club—a three-story clapboard lodge that overlooked the Barron River. The city's original founder, W. S. Allen, built it in 1850. Sec-ond owner George W. Storter enlarged it to accommodate hunters, sport fishermen, and yachting parties that were coming to the Ev-erglades in increasing numbers each winter. Barron Collier bought it in 1922 and operated it as a private club for his fellow industrial magnates and political dignitaries. Framed newspaper articles and photographs on the entrance hallway walls chronicle visits from such luminaries as Herbert Hoover, Franklin D. Roosevelt, Dwight and Mamie Eisenhower, and Richard Nixon. Ghostly fishing and hunting trophies—a sawfish bill, a gaping shark's jaw, a stretched alligator hide, deer and wild boar heads, an assortment of game fish, festoon the dark wood-paneled walls in the lobby. The Rod and Gun Club is a place that I have championed for its historical significance in prior editions of *Visiting Small-Town Florida*, but sadly, it has declined over the last few years. I suggest visiting for its historical significance, but I cannot recommend you eat or stay there.

Thankfully, there is another Everglades City lodging option: the Ivey House Bed & Breakfast, with modern hotel rooms, a cottage, and a restaurant in their restored circa 1928 lodge. It's also a good place to book fishing charters and rent kayaks.

I found a great place to eat lunch too: City Seafood. Some of this area's best seafood can be found in this unlikely-appearing ramshackle building sitting on the banks of the Barron River. In addition to the more conventional grouper, oysters, scallops, and shrimp, they also serve excellent Everglades' delicacies like fried frog legs, cracked conch, soft-shell blue crab, and gator tail (which you know is fresh because there are alligators everywhere here).

Adventurous visitors should bear in mind that there are only two seasons here: "mosquito" and "nonmosquito," which roughly coincide with the wet and dry seasons. Nonmosquito/dry is from December through March. Those who live here year-round are hardy souls indeed, but they live in an amazing, other-worldly place that can be explored by canoe or kayak. One of the best ways to see the back country is on an airboat ride. Two locally owned outfitters: Captain Doug's Airboat Tours and Speedy Johnson's Airboat Rides have been operating out of Everglades City for decades. Except for those that park rangers use for patrolling, airboats are not allowed in Everglades National Park. They are, however, allowed in the Big Cypress National Preserve. Everglades City sits on the border between the two, so the airboat tours go north, east, or west.

On the town circle you will find the Museum of the Everglades in the Historic Laundry Building (restored in 1997). Built in 1927, it was one of Barron Collier's company-town buildings and remained a commercial laundry through World War II. In 2001, it was added to the National Register of Historic Places. The museum opened in 1998. A collection of Calusa and Seminole artifacts, as well as old photographs chronicling the town's evolution, are on permanent display. Also on display is some of the original laundry equipment dating back to the 1940s, including a giant centrifugal dry cleaner. There are also rotating exhibits of work by local artists, artisans, and photographers.

Highway 29 continues south out of Everglades City down to Chokoloskee Island. Archaeologists tell us that coastal mound dwellers inhabited Chokoloskee and the surrounding islands more than two thousand years ago and possibly as far back as ten thousand years. These inhabitants left relics remarkably like those left by Central American Mayans, which has led to speculation that they may have communicated with and traded with the Mayans. More recently, Chokoloskee was a refuge for the Seminole Indians forced out of Central Florida during the Seminole Wars. Chief Billy Bowlegs lived here in the mid-1800s.

About the same time W. S. Allen was developing Everglades City, Ted Smallwood was settling Chokoloskee. He began farming there in

Historic Ted Smallwood Store, Chokoloskee

1896, and in 1906 he turned his home into a trading post that grew into a full-time store and post office. Smallwood traded with the Seminoles, fishermen, fur traders, and other early settlers on the island. By 1917, the store had outgrown his house, so he built a larger facility on the water's edge. In 1924, a violent storm blew four feet of water into the store and shifted its foundation. The following year, he raised the building on wooden pilings, just in time to weather the severe 1926 hurricane.

In 1974, the Smallwood Store was placed on the National Register of Historic Places. It was still an active store up until 1982. Today, Lynn Smallwood, Ted's granddaughter, owns it. In 1990, she began restoring the building as a museum.

From the front door, you can see straight through to the back door and porch, which looks out over the water. The interior of the store looks much the same as it did for the better part of the twentieth century. Wall shelves hold staple goods and supplies that were typical of the store's inventory. A life-size likeness of Ted Smallwood sits in his favorite rocking chair. With his bushy mustache, tall hat, and glasses, he could be Teddy Roosevelt's twin. The store's original furnishings are still here. There's a long counter that runs the length of one wall with old books and photographs from Chokoloskee's bygone era on display. Decades of elbows leaning on the countertop have worn its edge smooth and rounded. One room serves as a memorial to one of this area's most intriguing characters, Totch Brown, who lived near here for three-quarters of a century. He made a living as a fisherman and gator trapper and even admitted to having been an occasional marijuana smuggler in the early 1970s. The store has been restored, but (except for Ted) it is not a re-creation. This is the real thing.

In Chokoloskee I found another one of those middle-of-nowhere breakfast-lunch-diner jewels, the Havana Café of the Everglades, serving terrific, authentic Cuban food.

DON'T MISS
The Historic Ted Smallwood Store

Historic Ochopee Post Office

OCHOPEE

Population not listed on census

*F*or driving across the Everglades, I find the Tamiami Trail/Highway 41 slower but much more scenic than Alligator Alley (I-75). I have always got an eye out for a skunk ape, Florida's version of Bigfoot, or perhaps the even more elusive Florida panther. I have yet to see either, but I am still hopeful. One thing you can spot (but do not blink or you will miss it) is the Ochopee Post Office. It is a corrugated tin shed, hardly bigger than an outhouse, and has the distinction of being the smallest official post office in the United States. The tiny building was originally an irrigation pipe shed for a tomato farm. A 1953 fire burned Ochopee's previous general store and post office to the ground. Postmaster Sidney Brown hurriedly put the pipe shed into what he assumed would be temporary service. But it served its purpose so well that no one saw reason to replace it. Tourists stop here regularly just to get the Ochopee 34141 postmark on their mail.

Skunk Apre Research Headquarters

I first heard about the skunk ape when I was a kid, in the late 1960s– early 1970s. It was described as an ape-like animal that walked upright and lived in the swamps. It was so named because, reportedly, you could smell him long before you saw him. There was some historical precedent: Seminole Indian folklore referenced a similar creature they called Esti Capcaki. No doubt, interest had escalated after the Patterson–Gimlin Bluff Creek, California Bigfoot film footage came out in 1967, but the skunk ape was supposedly smaller than Bigfoot. Of all the mystery cryptid primate sightings, the skunk ape might be the most valid. Monkeys are spotted in the wild in Florida all the time. There was a monkey that we all saw regularly for years that lived in the trees on the creek that ran beside my childhood neighborhood. Through the1950s and 1960s, roadside tourist attractions were commonplace in Florida, and caged animals were often the draw: bears, bobcats, monkeys, and yes, chimpanzees. Also, John Ringling had moved his entire Ringling Bros. and Barnum & Bailey Circus operation from Bridgeport, Connecticut, to Sarasota in 1927, where it remains. Some of the animals from these places would escape occasionally, and Florida's tropical climate and landscape made an ideal place for them to thrive and breed. Chimpanzees, their close cousin bonobos, and orangutans (all members of the great ape family) can grow to five feet tall. Chimps can reach 150 pounds and orangutans 190 pounds. And all three can, and do, walk upright. Interest in the Florida skunk ape had fizzled by the late 1970s but reenergized briefly in 2000 when the Sarasota sheriff's department received an anonymous letter and photographs purportedly taken near Myakka State Park southeast of Sarasota. The photos are relatively clear and show an upright hairy primate behind some palmetto bushes. Frankly, it looks a lot like an orangutan or a large chimp.

And now the skunk ape is back! With renewed Bigfoot interest, sightings are happening again, and the Everglades has become a skunk ape hotspot. A little over a mile east of the Ochopee Post Office, you will find life-long Everglades' resident Dave Shealy's Skunk Ape Research Headquarters, with everything "skunk ape": books, videos, T-shirts. I love this place and stop in every time I drive by. Do not be swayed by the touristy appearance. Dave is a serious skunk ape devotee—he tracks them, collects scat samples, and claims to have seen them on four occasions and photographed them twice.

Do I think the skunk ape exists? Well, I have never seen one, so I think the best I can say is that I hope so.

Across the highway and down the road a few hundred yards from the Ochopee Post Office you will find Joanie's Blue Crab Café. In 1987, Joanie Griffin and her husband Carl (now passed away) purchased this old roadside Florida cracker house, which had previously seen use as a barn and as an office for an oil company. They turned it into an Everglades diner, but it is as much a museum of swamp eclectia

Joanie's Blue Crab Café

as it is a place to eat. You will be sharing your meal with alligator heads and all manner of taxidermized swamp creatures. As for the menu, Joanie's specializes in things that were swimming (or crawling or hopping) around in the Everglades the day before: frog legs, soft shell blue crab, and alligator tail. They offer oysters, shrimp, blackened catfish, and crab cakes as well. I've opted for the fried gator bites salad, which is a full meal, and comes with another of Joanie's specialties: crispy, spicy Seminole Indian fry bread.

DON'T MISS
The Ochopee Post Office (and have your
camera ready in case you spot a skunk ape!)

Alabama Jack's, Card Sound

CARD SOUND, ALABAMA JACK'S

Population not listed on census

Most people, who drive down to the Keys, assume there is only one route between Homestead and Key Largo: US Highway 1. But there is a detour. It's longer, but if you're hungry for conch fritters, blue crab cakes, or a grilled fish sandwich, then it's a detour worth taking. On the way out of Homestead, watch for Card Sound Road (Highway 997/905A) to your left. Follow it and enjoy the scenery and solitude for the next twelve miles. If you are heading back north from the Keys, turn right on 905 just north of Key Largo. On an old barge, right at the base of the Card Sound Bridge, you will find the quintessential backwater-Florida, open-air dive bar and grill called Alabama Jack's. Do not be scared off by the rustic appearance. Yep, it is a popular biker hangout, but the food's good and the folks that run it are friendly.

241

The barge has been here since 1947, and it became Alabama Jack's sometime between then and 1953, depending on which history book you read. Apparently, "Alabama" Jack Stratham was from Georgia, and a construction worker, who reportedly worked on the Empire State Building. Somebody in a construction crew mistook his accent (yes, there is a difference between Alabama and Georgia accents) and the nickname stuck. After Stratham died in 1977, Alabama Jack's changed hands a couple times, and in 1981 Phyllis Sague bought it. Today, her son, Mike, and daughter, Raquel Dickson, run it.

Conch fritters have been a long-time Alabama Jack's specialty, and their grilled mahi is a favorite of mine. Last time I was there I had it in their tacos. They also offer steamed peel-and-eat shrimp, crab cakes, conch salad, smoked fish (whatever is fresh-caught that day), and a spicy conch chowder.

Monument to the 1935 hurricane, Islamorada

ISLAMORADA

Population: 6,317

The Florida Keys sit on top of the only living coral reef in the continental United States. Here, particularly in the northern Upper Keys, visitors come for the world-class fishing and scuba diving. Islamorada, at the center of the Upper Keys, is best known as Florida's big game "Sport Fishing Capitol," where avid fishing enthusiasts from around the world go after blue marlin, sailfish, swordfish, wahoo, tuna, and dolphin (not the mammal dolphin, the fish dolphin, also known as mahi or dorado). Although spring and summer are peak seasons, you can fish here year-round. Legendary sport fishermen like Ernest Hemingway, Zane Grey, and Ted Williams fished these waters and helped make Islamorada famous. But Islamorada, along with Plantation Key to the north and Lower Matecumbe Key and Long Key just south, share a nightmarish chapter in their history. On Labor Day in 1935, the most powerful hurricane ever to strike the continental United States blasted across these islands with almost no warning.

Three pioneer families—the Russells, the Pinders, and the Parkers—sailed to Upper Matecumbe Key (Islamorada) in the mid- and late-1800s from the Bahamas. These Anglo-Bahamian settlers were called "Conchs," after the shellfish that was such a staple in their diet. They built their homes from driftwood, planted pineapple and key lime groves, and fished. In 1905, their island outpost became connected with the rest of civilization when Henry Flagler built his railroad through here on its way to Key West. As a result, a few hotels and vacation homes went up on Islamorada.

In 1935, the Upper Keys would become the setting for one of Florida's most terrifying events. On September 1, 1935, locals on Lower Matecumbe Key and Upper Matecumbe Key were boarding up their homes in preparation for a tropical storm that was crossing the Bahamas. Weather forecasters were predicting that it would pass south of Key West, but by the morning of September 2, Labor Day, barometers on both Matecumbe Keys were dropping rapidly. That meant that the storm had veered northeast and was gaining strength.

In the summer of 1935, the Veterans Administration had hired 680 unemployed World War I veterans and sent them to the Upper Keys to build Highway 1's roadway and bridges. The press referred to them as "bonus-marching veterans" because they had marched on Washington, DC, to protest that they could not get jobs after returning from the war and wanted their war bonuses accelerated. The roadwork veterans were living in three construction camps on Upper and Lower Matecumbe Keys. About two-thirds of them had gone to Miami or Key West for that Labor Day holiday. Those who remained met a horrible fate.

By nightfall, the winds were howling, and it was apparent that this would be a big one. Families huddled in their wood-frame "conch" bungalows and storm shelters. At 8:30 PM, the barometer read an all-time Northern Hemisphere record low pressure of 26.35 millibars.

The hurricane cut a swath right through Upper Matecumbe. Winds blew to 260 miles per hour. A twenty-foot-tall tidal wave swept over the islands, ripping whole houses, with families in them, off their foundations. Roger Albury and his nine family members were in their eight-room Tavernier house when the wave picked it up and carried it more than two hundred feet.

Seventeen-year-old Bernard Russell and his family sought shelter in his father's Islamorada lime packinghouse. When flood waters came pouring in, they tried to escape to higher ground. Clinging desperately to each other, they pushed out of the packinghouse and were instantly blown apart. Bernard's sister and his young nephew were torn from his hands. Of the sixty members of the extended Russell family, only eleven survived the hurricane.

Earlier in the day, an eleven-car passenger train had left Miami to try to evacuate the Upper Keys residents and World War I veteran road workers who were working there. The train reached Islamorada right when a wall of water struck, blasting each of the one-hundred-ton passenger cars right off the tracks. Only the locomotive remained upright. It was the last train to travel these tracks. Flagler never rebuilt his railroad.

Ultimately, 408 bodies were counted, but the actual death toll was probably twice that. All of the war veteran road workers who had stayed on the islands were killed. Months after the storm, remains of victims' bodies were still being recovered. Thirty years later, while dredging on an outlying key near Islamorada, a developer found an automobile with 1935 license plates and five skeletons inside.

While doing research for the first edition of *Visiting Small-Town Florida* at the Islamorada-Helen Wadley Branch Library I came across, in their archives, a scathing newspaper editorial entitled "Who Murdered the Vets?" written on September 17, 1935, by Ernest Hemingway. Hemingway was living in Key West at the time and had gone to the Upper Keys with crews to assist in the rescue efforts two days after the disaster. His article was an angry indictment of the newly formed Veterans Administration for sending the veterans down to the Keys to work during the most dangerous time of year—hurricane season. It reads in part, "Fishermen such as President Herbert Hoover, and President Roosevelt, do not come to the Florida Keys in hurricane months. . . . There is a known danger to property. . . . But veterans, especially the bonus-marching variety, are not property. They are only human beings; unsuccessful human beings and all they have to lose are their lives. They are doing coolie labor, for a top wage of $45 a month and they have been put down on the Florida Keys where they can't make trouble."

The long and painful process of rebuilding began immediately after the storm had passed and the bodies were buried. Young Bernard Russell, who had seen his family all but wiped out, remained on the island. He started his own cabinet-building/carpentry business and later founded Islamorada's first fire rescue department. In a 1991 *St. Petersburg Times* interview, he said, "The thing I have always asked myself is this: 'Why was I spared? Why am I still here?' I saw great big robust he-men, dead on the ground. I saw little skinny children who survived. How do you put that together in your mind? I must think the Lord might have a purpose for me. I might be needed."

At mile marker 81.8 you will find the 1935 hurricane monument. It's also a tomb that contains the cremated remains of some of the storm's victims. A plaque at the base of the twelve-foot-tall coral keystone monolith reads, "Dedicated to the memory of the civilians and war veterans whose lives were lost in the hurricane of September Second, 1935."

Entrance to the historic Cheeca Lodge grounds is right next door (at mile marker 82) to the hurricane monument. Original owner, Clara Downey, called it the Olney Inn (after her hometown Olney, Maryland) when she opened in 1946. There were just twenty-two cottages then. One of the Olney Inn's first guests was President Harry Truman, setting the stage for the resort to become a popular retreat for politicians, sports figures, and movie stars for decades to come. The name changed to Cheeca Lodge in the 1960s when Cynthia and Carl Twitchell purchased it and added the lodge, ocean-front villas, and a golf course. "Chee" was Cynthia's nickname, and the "ca" came from "Carl." In 2005, the current owners, the Johnson family, did a $30 million renovation, and in 2009 rebuilt the main lodge.

Among the first buildings that the original Conchs built on Islamorada was a church, built in 1890, and a schoolhouse, built in 1900, on property that is now part of the Cheeca Lodge compound. Next to the church they established a small cemetery. The 1935 hurricane destroyed the schoolhouse and the church, but the Pioneer Cemetery remains. Looking out of place among the beach loungers and rental Hobie Cats, the tiny cemetery is surrounded by a low white picket fence. Only eleven gravesites are marked, but there are more without names. In the center, a life-size statue of an angel marks the grave of Etta Dolores Pinder (1899–1914). Tossed a thousand feet in the mighty winds of the 1935 hurricane, the angel, with one wing broken and a hand missing, nevertheless stands tall. A historical marker in one corner of the cemetery reads: "This cemetery memorializes the determination and vision of over fifty pioneer Anglo-Bahamian Conchs who labored to settle and organize the first community on Matecumbe Key. Descendants of three pioneer families, the Russells who homesteaded in 1854, the Pinders in 1873, and the Parkers in 1898, are buried on this land."

Another more recent piece of Islamorada history can be found just south at mile marker 81.2. In 1947, Sid and Roxie Siderious bought an Islamorada roadside diner and motel called the Rustic Inn, which had been built in 1928. It was one of the few structures still standing after the Labor Day 1935 hurricane. The Siderious's renamed it The Green Turtle Inn and specialized in cooking and serving locally fished turtle. The Green Turtle became famous for turtle steaks and turtle soup. At that time, sea turtles were plentiful in the Keys, and no one thought of them as endangered.

The Siderious's were energetic entertainers, regularly throwing parties, often with celebrities in attendance. That atmosphere set a Green Turtle Inn standard that would outlive their ownership. The Green Turtle had several subsequent owners through the years, but perhaps the most colorful was Henry "Bastille" Rosenthal, a famous magician who had performed around the world. Rosenthal owned and ran the Green Turtle Inn for several decades, and on occasion he would perform impromptu for his dinner patrons.

In Christopher Columbus's day, sea voyagers routinely captured sea turtles and kept them live on ship. Sea turtles can go months, even a year, without eating anything and survive, making them an ideal food source for long voyages. As recently as the 1960s, they were still being harvested as food, but thankfully by the 1970s most, and eventually all, sea turtle species were declared endangered and protected. Of course, today the Green Turtle does not serve sea turtle, however they do serve farm-raised freshwater snapping turtle stew.

You will not see a sign for The Hungry Tarpon from US Highway 1/A1A. Instead, turn off at the sign for "Robbie's Marina" just across the Lignumvitae Channel Bridge over to Lower Matecumbe Key. Be careful not to run over any of the iguanas that are always sunning themselves on the side of the road. Park and wander through the open-air bazaar where artists sell paintings, sculptures, jewelry, and all manner of tropical-themed knickknacks. Robbie's has a kind of hippie-commune feel to it that fits with the Keys. It is also a good place to rent a kayak or put your boat in the water. Keep wandering toward the docks until you find The Hungry Tarpon. You'll see people hand-feeding the tarpons from the dock. On my last visit I breakfasted on fried fresh mahi and grits. It came with two fried eggs, and perhaps the biggest and most buttery biscuit I have ever eaten.

It is difficult to get far off the beaten path down here since there is only one path from Key Largo south—US Highway 1, also known as the Overseas Highway. However, this makes it easy to give directions using mile markers. Add two digits to the end of the mile marker number and that is the street address.

DON'T MISS
Fish and grits for breakfast at the
Hungry Tarpon Restaurant at Robbie's Marina

Key deer, Big Pine Key

BIG PINE KEY, NO NAME KEY

Population: 4,887 (people), current Key deer population approximately 900

*H*enry Flagler was seventy-five years old in 1905 when he began construction extending his Florida East Coast Railroad beyond the southern reaches of the mainland. When word came that a shipping canal was to be dug across Panama, Flagler decided that his railroad must go all the way down to Key West. That would make it the nearest rail terminal to the canal, by three hundred miles. Most considered the idea of building a 150-mile railroad—that would skip across tiny coral islands, elevated over water—merely the preposterous dream of a crazy old man. It took seven years (four longer than they had first estimated), but on January 22, 1912, the first official train arrived in Key West, with eighty-two-year-old Henry Flagler aboard. Fifteen months later he died. Arguably, Flagler's

"Over the Sea Railway" still stands today as Florida's most astounding engineering feat. Twenty-five years later US Highway 1 would be paved across that same path.

One of the best places to see what remains of Flagler's railroad is at Bahia Honda Key State Park just north of Big Pine Key. Railroad tracks run beneath a ninety-foot-high, now-abandoned US Highway 1 bridge that was completed in 1938. Until recently you could walk right up to the top of the broken off bridge and gaze down ninety feet below at sea turtles, leopard rays, and sharks cavorting in the emerald water. Still, you can walk partway up and get a spectacular elevated view. The park is also popular with bird watchers (particularly for viewing shore birds on the flats that extend out from the beach), and for camping— but make your reservation well in advance.

Big Pine Key, the largest island in the Lower Keys, could be Florida's answer to the Galapagos Islands. Along with its northwest appendage, No Name Key, it is home to a number of rare and endangered birds, reptiles, and mammals—including the seldom-sighted, short-eared Lower Keys marsh rabbit (rumored to actually swim between the islands occasionally). Big Pine Key's best-known and most-endangered inhabitant is the petite Key, or toy, deer. Key deer are the smallest race of North American deer and are indigenous to the Lower Keys; nearly the entire population is found on Big Pine and No Name Keys. The typical adult weighs between forty and seventy pounds and stands less than two-and-half feet tall at the shoulder. Disproportionately large ears and brown eyes add considerably to the deer's "cuteness" quotient. Unfortunately, their adorableness may be one of the factors contributing to their demise.

For the most part, commercial development did not come to Big Pine Key until the late 1960s, but there had been small settlements here and on No Name Key for more than a hundred years. Some of the people who lived here in the mid-1800s were fishermen and spongers, but most came to harvest buttonwood trees—found in the lower and wetter areas of the island, for charcoal. Key West, thirty miles south, was at the height of its wreckers "golden era" and Big Pine Key charcoal was much in demand as a fuel source. But nothing lasts forever. At the end of the nineteenth century, with the construction of lighthouses in the Lower Keys to warn ships away from reefs, the wrecking industry died a quick death. Big Pine Key's buttonwood charcoal business soon followed suit.

In 1905, Henry Flagler started building his Overseas Railroad and began connecting the dots of the Keys. It rolled across Big Pine Key in 1911 and ended in Key West in 1912. But the horrendous Labor Day hurricane of 1935 brought an end to the Overseas Railroad. By 1938, the Overseas Highway had been paved to Key West, reusing many of Flagler's railway bridges. But Big Pine Key and No Name Key were largely unaffected. The islands' few inhabitants were mostly fishermen or rumrunners left from the Prohibition era and seeking anonymity.

In 1957, the US Fish and Wildlife Service established the National Key Deer Refuge on Big Pine and No Name Keys. Hunters had nearly wiped out the Key deer population: there were fewer than fifty deer in 1949. First refuge manager and local hero Jack Watson fought vehemently for their survival and is credited with saving them, almost single-handedly, from extinction. He battled poachers like the sheriff in a Wild West town, sometimes resorting to sinking their boats and torching their pickup trucks. Watson retired in 1975, and three years later the Key deer population had soared to four hundred.

Sadly, those numbers declined over the subsequent two decades. Loss of habitat, unusually low birth rates (Key deer rarely have multiple births), and automobile strikes are the most often-cited reasons. When I visited Big Pine Key and No Name Key in 1998, there were fewer than three hundred deer left on the islands (counted in 1997). Recently, there has been significant progress in the effort to bolster the Key deer's population. The highest count in recent years put their numbers as high as one thousand. Despite this improvement, they are still at great risk. More than half of those that die each year are killed by automobile strikes. Handfeeding exacerbates the problem. These little guys are so cute that people get out of their cars to feed them. The deer are quick learners, and before long they start running out to cars and invariably get hit. The fine for feeding a Key deer is $250. As of 2016, they have yet another threat: an infestation of New World screwworm. Estimates are that screwworm has killed about 10 percent of the population. Biologists with the US Fish & Wildlife Service have been working diligently to administer an antiparasitic to both infected and potentially infected deer. They have also enlisted the help of Big Pine Key residents in identifying sick deer and notifying Fish & Wildlife Service via their Key Deer Hotline.

Publicizing the National Key Deer Refuge is a double-edged sword: the value of increased awareness of the Key deer's plight, weighed against the potential for more traffic. Every person I have ever spoken to in the community has brought up something about the importance of driving slowly and carefully. The local police do their part. They write speeding tickets for just one mile per hour over the limit.

A likely place to spot other wildlife (in addition to Key deer) is Big Pine Key's Blue Hole. In the 1930s, road construction crews mined the hard oolitic limestone that makes up Big Pine Key. They extracted most of what they needed from one quarry near the center of the island, a place now called the Blue Hole (although it's actually green). It's one of the few spots in all the Lower Keys where a substantial amount of fresh rainwater collects, and it is a crucial source of drinking water for the island's wildlife, particularly Key deer. This is an extremely popular spot for bird watchers. Expect to see lots of waterfowl, and alligators too. A short loop trail leads into the hammock to a viewing platform on the back side of the Blue Hole. I am impressed at how determined the plant life is around here. Buttonwood, palmetto, slash pines (for which Big Pine Key was named), and gumbo-limbo trees grow right out of the rock with virtually no topsoil. A variety of orchids and air plants use both living and fallen trees as hosts. Key Deer Boulevard cuts a northern path through hardwood hammocks and pinelands, bisecting the largest of the designated Key Deer Refuge areas. Parking for the trailhead for the Blue Hole is three miles north of US 1 on Key Deer Boulevard.

Another good place to see a Key deer is on No Name Key (adjacent to Big Pine Key), particularly around sunset. The first time I saw one was on No Name Key. It was a doe about the size of a springer spaniel. She sauntered across the road up ahead of me, stopped for a moment to scratch one of her oversize ears with a hind hoof, took an uninterested glance at me, then trotted off into the woods.

On your way to No Name Key (follow the signs up Wilder Road), stop in at the No Name Pub, just on the Big Pine Key side of the bridge

No Name Pub, No Name Key

over to No Name Key. Watch carefully for it on the left. Mangroves and cactus half conceal the clapboard building, but a hand-painted sign nailed to a palm tree tells you it's there.

Built in 1936, the No Name Pub was originally a Cuban trading post and general store. It is also reputed to have been a smuggler's hangout/hideout and a brothel. Since the mid-1970s, it's been a bar and restaurant, the oldest on the island. Inside, the No Name Pub upholds the Keys' dive-bar-decor tradition of stapling signed and dated dollar bills on the walls and ceiling. Patrons have also carved their initials in the bar, which was built from salvaged scrap from the old wooden No Name Key Bridge (now replaced with a sturdier concrete crossing). This place also has some of the best pizza in the Keys.

DON'T MISS:
The No Name Pub. And please watch out for the Key deer.

APPENDIX

NORTH REGION

FLORA-BAMA/PERDIDO KEY
**Flora-Bama Lounge &
Oyster Bar**
17401 Perdido Key Drive
Perdido Key, FL 32507
(850) 492-0611
florabama.com

MILTON, BAGDAD
**Arcadia Mill Archaeological
Site and Museum**
5709 Mill Pond Lane
Milton, FL 32583

Arcadia Homestead
4755 Anna Simpson Road
Milton, FL 32583
historicpensacola.org/explore
  -arcadia-mill

**Milton Railroad
Depot Museum**
5003 Henry Street
Milton, FL 32572
wfrm.org

Imogene Theater
6866 Caroline Street
Milton, FL 32570
santarosahistoricalsociety.com

Bagdad Historical Museum
4512 Church Street
Bagdad, FL 32583

Blackwater Bistro
5147 Elmira Street
Milton, FL 32570
blackwaterbistro.com

Milton Quality Bakery
6727 Caroline Street
Milton, FL 32570
miltonqualitybakery.com

DEFUNIAK SPRINGS
Walton-DeFuniak Library
3 Circle Drive
DeFuniak Springs, FL 32435
(850) 892-3624
co.walton.fl.us/461/DeFuniak
  -Springs-Library

Hotel DeFuniak
400 East Nelson Avenue
DeFuniak Springs, FL 32433
(850) 892-4383
hoteldefuniak.net

The Little Big Store
35 North 8th Street
DeFuniak Springs, FL 32435
(850) 892-6066

Café Nola
400 East Nelson Avenue
DeFuniak Springs, FL 32433
(850) 892-4383
cafenola.net

Bogey's Bar & Restaurant
660 Baldwin Avenue
DeFuniak Springs, FL 32433
(850) 951-2233
bogeysrestaurant.net

Nook & Cranny
676 Baldwin Avenue
DeFuniak Springs, FL 32433
(850) 865-2976

The Perla Baking Company
766 Baldwin Avenue
DeFuniak Springs, FL 32435
(850) 564-3030
perlabakingco.com

**Walton County
Heritage Museum**
1140 Circle Drive
DeFuniak Springs, FL 32435
(850) 951-2127
waltoncountyheritage.org

TWO EGG
Directions: from I-10 Exit #152,
just east of Marianna, drive north
on Highway 69 for fifteen miles to
Highway 69A.

QUINCY
**Gadsden Art Center
& Museum**
13 North Madison Street
Quincy, FL 32351
(850) 875-4866
gadsdenarts.org

**McFarlin House
Bed & Breakfast**
305 East King Street
Quincy, FL 32351
(850) 875-2526
mcfarlinhouse.com

Allison House
215 North Madison Street
Quincy, FL 32351
(850) 875-2511
allisonhouseinn.com

The White Squirrel Inn
234 East King Street
Quincy, FL 32351
(850) 615-3006
whitesquirrelinn.com

HAVANA
Wanderings Décor & More
Poppy's Coffee & More
312 First Street Northwest
Havana, FL 32333
(850) 539-7711
thewanderings.com

**McLauchlin House
Weezies Cottage Home Decor**
201 First Street Northwest
Havana, FL 32333
(850) 539-9001

Planters Exchange
204 Second Street, Northwest
Havana, FL 32333
(850) 539-6343
theplantersexchange.com

Havana History & Heritage Society Shade Tobacco Museum
204 Second Street Northwest
Havana, FL 32333
(850) 270-7315
havana-history--heritage-society
    .portalbuzz.com

Oscar's Pizza
211 First Street Northwest
Havana, FL 32333
(850) 539-3036

Havana Trading Company
208 First Street Northwest
Havana, FL 32333
(850) 347-1950

Gocki's at Havana Trading Company
208 First Street Northwest
Havana, FL 32333
(850) 616-1364

MONTICELLO
Monticello Opera House
185 West Washington
Monticello, FL 32345
(850) 997-4242
monticellooperahouse.org

The Daffodale House Bed & Breakfast
620 West Washington Street
Monticello, FL 32344
(850) 997-1111
daffodaleestate.com

The Cottage Bed & Breakfast
295 West Palmer Mill Road
Monticello, FL 32344
(850) 342-3541
the-cottage-bed-breakfast
    .panhandle-florida.com

1872 John Denham House Bed and Breakfast
555 West Palmer Mill Road
Monticello, FL 32344
(85) 933-0456
johndenhamhouse.com

Rev Café
180 South Jefferson Street
Monticello, FL 32344
(850) 629-0138
revuprevdown.com

GRAYTON BEACH
Red Bar
70 Hotz Avenue
Grayton Beach, FL 32459
(850) 231-1008
theredbar.com

Chiringo
63 Hotz Avenue
Grayton Beach, FL 32459
(850) 534-4449
chiringograyton.com

The Zoo Gallery
89 Hotz Avenue
Grayton Beach, FL 32459
thezoogallery.com

Tribe Kelly Surf Post
99 Hotz Avenue
Grayton Beach, FL 32459
(850) 533-4019
tribekelleysurfpost.com

Hibiscus Coffee & Guest House Bed & Breakfast
85 DeFuniak Street
Grayton Beach, FL 32459
(850) 231-2733
hibiscusflorida.com

SEASIDE
Seaside Cottage Rental Agency
27 Quincy Circle
Santa Rosa Beach, FL 32459
(866) 966-2565
www.cottagerentalagency.com

Great Southern Cafe
83 Central Square
Seaside, FL 32459
(850) 231-7327
thegreatsoutherncafe.com

Bud & Alley's
2236 East County Road 30A
Seaside, FL 32459
(850) 231-5900
budandalleys.com

The Shrimp Shack
2236 East County Road 30A
Seaside, FL 32459
(850) 231-3799
sweetwilliamsltd.com/shrimp_shack
  .asp

30A Songwriters Festival
30asongwritersfestival.com

ROSEMARY BEACH
Rosemary Beach Vacation Rentals
78 North Barrett Square
Rosemary Beach, FL 32461
(866) 348-8952
rosemarybeach.com

The Rosemary Beach Inn
78 Main Street
Rosemary Beach, FL 32461
(844) 865-5783
therosemarybeachinn.com

The Pearl Hotel
63 Main Street
Rosemary Beach, FL 32461
(877) 935-6114
thepearlrb.com

Restaurant Paradis
82 South Barrett Square
Rosemary Beach, FL 32461
(850) 534-0400
restaurantparadis.com

The Summer Kitchen Café
78 Main Street
Rosemary Beach, FL 32461
(85) 213-0521
thesummerkitchencafe.com

MEXICO BEACH
Mexico Beach Community Development Council
mexicobeach.com

City of Mexico Beach
mexicobeachgov.com

APALACHICOLA
Gibson Inn
51 Avenue C
Apalachicola, FL 32320
(850) 653-2191
www.gibsoninn.com

Consulate Suites
76 Water Street
Apalachicola, FL 32320
(850) 653-1515
(877) 239-1159
consulatesuites.com

Coombs House Inn
80 Sixth Street
Apalachicola, FL 32320
(850) 653-9199
(888) 244-8320
coombshouseinn.com

Owl Café
15 Avenue D
Apalachicola, FL 32320
(850) 653-9888
owlcafeflorida.com

Apalachicola Seafood Grill
100 Market Street
Apalachicola, FL 32320
(850) 653-9510

Up the Creek Raw Bar
313 Water Street
Apalachicola, FL 32320
(850) 653-2525
upthecreekrawbar.com

Tamara's Café
71 Market Street
Apalachicola, FL 32320
(850) 653-4111
tamarascafe.com

Richard Bickel Photography Gallery
81 Market Street
Apalachicola, FL 32320
(850) 653-3900

John Gorrie Museum State Park
46 6th Street
Apalachicola, FL 32320
(850) 653-9347
floridastateparks.org/parks-and
  -trails/john-gorrie-museum
  -state-park

ST. GEORGE ISLAND
Resort Vacation Properties
61 West Gulf Beach Drive
St. George Island, FL 32328
(877) 272-8206
resortvacationproperties.com

Collins Vacation Rentals, Inc.
60 East Gulf Beach Drive
St. George Island, FL 32328
(877) 875-9062
collinsvacationrentals.com

St. George Lighthouse and Museum
2B East Gulf Beach Drive
St. George Island, FL 32328
(850) 927-7745
stgeorgelight.org

Paddy's Raw Bar
240 East 3rd Street
St. George Island, FL 32328
(850) 927-2299
paddysrawbar.com

Blue Parrot Oceanfront Café
68 West Gorrie Drive
St. George Island, FL 32328
(850) 927-2987
blueparrotsgi.com

Island Dog Beach and Surf Shop
160 East Pine Avenue
St. George Island, FL 32328
(850) 927-2600
sgislanddog.com

CARRABELLE
Carrabelle Junction
88 Tallahassee Street
Carrabelle, FL 32322
(850) 697-9550

SOPCHOPPY
Sopchoppy Worm Gruntin' Festival
wormgruntinfestival.com

Sopchoppy Grocery
60 Rose Street
Sopchoppy 32358
(850) 962-2231

Sand and Soul Designs
118 Municipal Avenue
Sopchoppy, FL 32358
(850) 556-3081

Sopchoppy Depot Museum
34 Railroad Avenue
Sopychoppy, FL 32359

WAKULLA SPRINGS
Wakulla Springs Lodge at Edward Ball/Wakulla Springs State Park
550 Wakulla Park Drive
Wakulla Springs, FL 32327
(850) 421-2000
(855) 632-4559 reservations
thelodgeatwakullasprings.com

ST. MARKS
Riverside Café
69 Riverside Drive
St. Marks, FL 32355
(850) 925-5668
riversidebay.com

Cooter Stew Cafe
859 Port Leon Drive (Highway 363)
St. Marks, FL 32355
(850) 925-9908

Sweet Magnolia Inn
803 Port Leon Drive (Highway 363)
St. Marks, FL 32355
(850) 755-3320
sweetmagnoliainn.com

WHITE SPRINGS
Stephen Foster State Folk Culture Center
11016 Lillian Saunders Drive/
    US Highway 41
White Springs, FL 32096

(386) 397-4331
floridastateparks.org/parks-and
   -trails/stephen-foster-folk-culture
   -center-state-park

Florida Folk Festival
floridastateparks.org
   /FloridaFolkFestival

American Canoe Adventures
10610 Bridge Street
White Springs, FL 32096
(386) 397-1309
aca1.com

FERNANDINA BEACH
Fairbanks House
Bed & Breakfast
227 South Seventh Street
Fernandina Beach, FL 32034
(904) 277-0500
fairbankshouse.com
(904) 277-0500
(888) 891-9880

Addison on Amelia
Bed & Breakfast
614 Ash Street
Fernandina Beach, FL 32034
(904) 277-1604
(800) 943-1804
addisononamelia.com

Florida House Inn
22 South Third Street
Fernandina Beach, FL 32034
(904) 491-3322
floridahouseinn.com

Amelia Island Williams House
Bed & Breakfast
103 South Ninth Street
Fernandina Beach, FL 32034
(904) 277-2328
(800) 414-9258
williamshouse.com

Elizabeth Pointe Lodge
98 South Fletcher Avenue
Fernandina Beach, FL 32034
(904) 277-4851
elizabethpointelodge.com

España Restaurant
22 South 4th Street
Fernandina Beach, FL 32034
(904) 261-7700
espanadowntown.com

Timoti's Seafood Shak
21 North 3rd Street
Fernandina Beach, FL 32034
(904) 310-6550
timotis.com

Crab Trap
31 North 2nd Street
Fernandina Beach, FL 32034
(904)-261-4749
ameliacrabtrap.com

Joe's 2nd Street Bistro
14 South 2nd Street
Fernandina Beach, FL 32034
(904) 321-2558
joesbistro.com

ST. AUGUSTINE

Agustin Inn
29 Cuna Street
St. Augustine, FL 32084
(800) 248-7846
agustininn.com

**Bayfront Marin House
Bed & Breakfast**
142 Avenida Menendez
St. Augustine, FL 32084
(904) 824-4301
bayfrontmarinhouse.com

Carriage Way Bed & Breakfast
70 Cuna Street
St. Augustine, FL 32084
(904) 829-2467
carriageway.com

**Casablanca Inn
Bed & Breakfast**
24 Avenida Menendez
St. Augustine, FL 32084
(904) 829-0928
casablancainn.com

Casa de Solona
21 Aviles Street
St. Augustine, FL 32084
(904) 824-3555
casadesolana.com

**Casa de Suenos Bed &
Breakfast**
20 Cordova Street
St. Augustine, FL 32084
(904) 824-0887
casadesuenos.com

Cedar House Inn
79 Cedar Street
St. Augustine, FL 32084
(904) 829-0079
cedarhouseinn.com

**Inn on Charlotte Street
Bed & Breakfast**
52 Charlotte Street
St. Augustine, FL 32084
(904) 829-3819
innoncharlotte.com

Kenwood Inn
38 Marine Street
St. Augustine, FL 32084
(904) 824-2116
thekenwoodinn.com

Old Powder House Inn
38 Cordova Street
St. Augustine, FL 32084
(904) 824-4149
oldpowderhouse.com

**Saragossa Inn
Bed & Breakfast**
34 Saragossa Street
St. Augustine, FL 32084
(904) 808-7384
saragossainn.com

**St. Francis Inn Bed &
Breakfast**
279 St. George Street
St. Augustine, FL 32084
(904) 299-0646
stfrancisinn.com

**Victorian House
Bed & Breakfast**
11 Cadiz Street
St. Augustine, FL 32084
(904) 824-5214
victorianhouse-inn.com

**Westcott House
on the Bayfront**
146 Avenida Menendez
St. Augustine, FL 32084
(904) 825-4602
westcotthouse.com

Casa Monica Hotel
95 Cordova Street
St. Augustine, FL 32084
(904) 827-1888
casamonica.com

Catch 27
40 Charlotte Street
St. Augustine, FL 32084
(904) 217–3542
catchtwentyseven.com

The Floridian
72 Spanish Street
St. Augustine, FL 32084
(904) 829-0655
thefloridianstaug.com

Crucial Coffee Café
26 Charlotte Street
St. Augustine, FL 32084
(904) 810-2080

City Perks Coffee Company
15 St. George Street
St. Augustine, FL 32084
(904) 342-0556
cityperkscoffee.com

St. Augustine Coffee House
6 St George Street, Suite 107
St. Augustine, FL 32084
(904) 819-1644
staugustinecoffeehouse.com

Preserved (restaurant)
102 Bridge Street
St. Augustine, FL 32084
(904) 679-4940
striverestaurant.com/preserved
  -restaurant

La Herencia Café
4 Aviles Street
St. Augustine, FL 32084
(904) 829-9487

**Restaurant Café Sol
Brasileirissimo**
8 Aviles Street
St. Augustine, FL 32084
(904) 823-1371
cafesol.letseat.at

Bouvier Maps & Prints
11-D Aviles Street
St. Augustine, FL 32084
(904) 825-0920
jbouviermaps.com

Flagler College
74 King Street
St. Augustine, FL 32084
(904) 819-6220
flagler.edu

**Gonzalez-Alvarez House/
The Oldest House
Museum of St. Augustine
   History**
14 St. Francis Street
St. Augustine, FL 32084
(904) 824-2872
oldesthouse.org

Lightner Museum
75 King Street
St. Augustine, FL 32084
(904) 824-2874
lightnermuseum.org

Castillo de San Marcos
1 South Castillo Drive
St. Augustine, FL 32084
(904) 829-6506
nps.gov/casa/index.htm

O'Steen's Restaurant
205 Anastasia Boulevard
St. Augustine, FL 32080
(904) 829-6974
osteensrestaurant.com

**St. Augustine Lighthouse
& Museum**
81 Lighthouse Avenue
St. Augustine, FL 32080
(904) 829-0745
staugustinelighthouse.org

**St. Augustine Alligator Farm
Zoological Park**
999 Anastasia Boulevard
St. Augustine, FL 32080
(904) 824-3337
alligatorfarm.com

**KEATON BEACH
Hodges Park**
South end of Keaton Beach Road/
   Highway 460
taylorcountygov.com/residents
   /parks_and_recreation/parks.php

**STEINHATCHEE
Steinhatchee Landing Resort**
228 Highway 51 Northeast
Steinhatchee, FL 32359
(352) 498-0696
steinhatcheelanding.com

Roy's Restaurant
100 1st Avenue Southwest
Steinhatchee, FL 32359
(352) 498-5000
roys-restaurant.com

**HIGH SPRINGS
Adventure Outpost**
adventureoutpost.net
Lar Anderson
riverguide2000@yahoo.com
(386) 497-4214

Ginnie Springs Outdoors
7300 Ginnie Springs Road
High Springs, FL 32643
(386) 454-7188
ginniespringsoutdoors.com

Gilchrist Blue Springs State Park

7450 Northeast 60th Street
High Springs, FL 32643
(386) 454-1369
floridastateparks.org/parks-and
  -trails/ruth-b-kirby-gilchrist
  -blue-springs-state-park

Poe Springs Park

28800 Northwest 182nd Avenue
High Springs, FL 32643
(352) 264-6868
alachuacounty.us/Depts/pcl/Pages
  /Details.aspx?park=Poe Springs
  Park

O'Leno State Park

410 Southeast O'Leno Park Road
High Springs, FL 32643
(386) 454-1853
floridastateparks.org/parks-and
  -trails/oleno-state-park

Ichetucknee Springs State Park

12087 Southwest Highway 27
Fort White, FL 32038
(386) 497-4690
floridastateparks.org/parks-and
  -trails/ichetucknee-springs
  -state-park

Great Outdoors Restaurant

18587 High Springs Main Street
High Springs, FL 32643
(386) 454-1288
greatoutdoorsrestaurant.com

El Patio

18576 High Springs Main Street
High Springs, FL 32643
(386) 454-1330

Spins: Sweet & Savory

23677 West Highway 27
Highs Springs, FL 32643
(706) 840-2734
spinssweetandsavory.com

Consider the Lilies Thrift Shop

23560 Northwest Railroad Avenue
High Springs, FL 32643
(386) 867-5403

The Bird Nest Vintage Market

18568 High Springs Main Street
High Springs, FL 32643
(386) 454-2200

MICANOPY
Herlong Mansion Bed & Breakfast

402 Northeast Cholokka Boulevard
Micanopy, FL 32667
(352) 466-3322
herlong.com

Micanopy Historical Society Museum

607 Northeast Cholokka Boulevard
Micanopy, FL 32667
micanopyhistoricalsociety.com
(352) 466-3300

Micanopy Historic Cemetery

401 West Smith Avenue
Micanopy, FL 32667

Coffee n' Cream
201 Northeast Cholokka Boulevard
Micanopy, FL 32667
(352) 466-1101
micanopycoffeeshop.com

Old Florida Café
203 Northeast Cholokka Boulevard
Micanopy, FL 32667

**Pearl Country Store
and Barbecue**
106A NE Hwy 441
Micanopy, FL 32667
(352) 466-4025
pearlcountrystore.com

Gallery Under the Oaks
207 Northeast Cholokka Boulevard
Micanopy, FL 32667
(352) 466-9229

Micanopy Trading Outpost
205 Northeast Cholokka Boulevard
Micanopy, FL 32667
(352) 466-0010
micanopyoutpost.com

Delectable Collectables
112 Northeast Cholokka Boulevard
Micanopy, FL 32667
(352) 466-3327

Dakota Mercantile
114 Northeast Cholokka Boulevard
Micanopy, FL 32667
(352) 466-5005

**Paynes Prairie Preserve
State Park**
100 Savannah Boulevard
Micanopy, FL 32667
(352) 545-6000
floridastateparks.org/parks-and
-trails/paynes-prairie-preserve
-state-park

CROSS CREEK
**Marjorie Kinnan Rawlings
State Historic Site**
18700 South County Road 325
Cross Creek, FL 32640
(352) 466-3672
floridastateparks.org/parks-and
-trails/marjorie-kinnan-rawlings
-historic-state-park

The Yearling Restaurant
14531 County Road 325
Cross Creek, FL 32640
(352) 466-3999
yearlingrestaurant.net

EVINSTON
**Wood & Swink Store
and Post Office**
18320 Southeast County Road 225
Evinston, FL 32633
(352) 591-4100
woodandswink.org

MCINTOSH
McIntosh 1890s Festival
Friends of McIntosh
Post Office Box 436
McIntosh, FL 32664

(352) 591-4038
friendsofmcintosh.org

Antonio's Italian Restaurant
22050 North Highway 441
McIntosh/Micanopy, FL 32667
(352) 591-4141
antonios.co

CRESCENT CITY
Catfish Festival
rotaryclubcrescentcity.com

Sprague House Bed
and Breakfast Inn
125 Central Avenue
Crescent City, FL 32112
(386) 698-2622
spraguehouse.com

3 Bananas Restaurant and Bar
11 South Lake Street
Crescent City, FL 32112
(386) 698-2861
3bananas.com

ROSEWOOD
Directions: from the intersection
of Highway 24 and US Highway
19/98, at Otter Creek, drive
southwest on Highway 24 for
twelve miles to the historic marker
on the left.

CEDAR KEY
The Island Hotel
373 2nd Street
Cedar Key, FL 32625

(352) 543-5111
islandhotel-cedarkey.com

Cedar Key Bed & Breakfast
810 3rd Street
Cedar Key, FL 32625
(352) 543-9000
cedarkeybedandbreakfast.com

Harbour Master Suites
390 Dock Street
Cedar Key, FL 32625
(352) 543-9146
cedarkeyharbourmaster.com

Island Place Cedar Keys
550 1st Street
Cedar Key, FL 32625
(352) 543-5307
islandplace-ck.com

Old Fenimore Mill
Condominiums
11 Old Mill Drive
Cedar Key, FL 32625
(352) 543-9803
fenimoremill.com

Tony's Seafood Restaurant
597 2nd Street
Cedar Key, FL 32625
(352) 543-9143
tonyschowder.com

1842 Daily Grind & Mercantile
598 2nd Street
Cedar Key, FL 32625
(352) 543-5004

2nd Street Cafe
434 2nd Street
Cedar Key, FL 32625
(352) 477-5099
2ndstreetcafe.com

Steamers Clam Bar & Grill
420 Dock Street
Cedar Key, FL 32625
steamerscedarkey.com

Big Deck Raw Bar
331 Dock Street
Cedar Key, FL 32625
(352) 543-9992

The Tipsy Cow Bar and Grill
360 Dock Street
Cedar Key, FL 32625
(352) 543-5169

Bonish Studio and Bar
582 2nd Street
Cedar Key, FL 32625
patbonishphotography.com

Cedar Keyhole Artist Co-op and Gallery
457 Second Street
Cedar Key, FL 32625
(352) 543-5801
cedarkeyhole.com

Cedar Key Historical Society and Museum
609 2nd Street
Cedar Key, FL 32625
(352) 543-5549
cedarkeyhistory.org

Cedar Key State Museum
12231 Southwest 166th Court
Cedar Key, FL 32625
floridastateparks.org/parks-and
   -trails/cedar-key-museum-state
   -park

Cedar Key Railroad Trestle Nature Trail
Florida's Nature Coast Conservancy
Grove Street, just off State Road 24
floridasnaturecoastconservancy.org
   /projects/rr-trestle-nature-trail

Southern Cross Sea Farms
12170 State Road 24
Cedar Key, FL 32625
(352) 543-5980
clambiz.com

Cedar Key Old Florida Arts Festival
Third weekend in April
cedarkeyartsfestival.com

Cedar Key Seafood Festival
Third weekend in October
cedarkey.org/event/48th-annual
   -cedar-key-seafood-festival

YANKEETOWN
Blackwater Grill and Bar
6301 Riverside Drive
Yankeetown, FL 34498
(352) 441-5002
blackwater.restaurant

Chik'n'Butt Café
6621 Riverside Drive
Yankeetown, FL 34498

(352) 405-6670
the-dockside-tiki.business.site

CENTRAL REGION

DE LEON SPRINGS
De Leon Springs State Park
601 Ponce de Leon Boulevard
De Leon Springs, FL 32130
(386) 985-4212
floridastateparks.org/parks-and
   -trails/de-leon-springs-state-park

**Old Spanish Sugar Mill
Restaurant**
601 Ponce de Leon Boulevard
De Leon Springs, FL 32130
(386) 985-5644
oldspanishsugarmill.com

DUNNELLON
**Blue Gator Tiki Bar
and Restaurant**
12189 South Williams Street
Dunnellon, FL 34432
(352) 465-1635
blue-gator.com

Swampy's Bar and Grill
19773 East Pennsylvania Avenue
Dunnellon, FL 34431
(352) 547-4777
swampys.restaurant

Adventure Outpost
adventureoutpost.net
Lar Anderson
riverguide2000@yahoo.com
(386) 497-4214

OCKLAWAHA
Gator Joe's Beach Bar and Grill
12431 Southeast 135th Avenue
Ocklawaha, FL 32179
(352) 288-3100
gatorjoesocala.com

Ma Barker House
Carney Island Recreation &
   Conservation Area
13279 Southeast 115th Avenue
Ocklawaha, FL 32179
(352) 671-8560
mabarkerhouse.org

CASSADAGA
Cassadaga Hotel
355 Cassadaga Road
Cassadaga, FL 32706
(386) 228-2323
hotelcassadaga.com

Sinatra's Ristorante
355 Cassadaga Road
Cassadaga, FL 32706
(386) 218-3806
sinatras.us

**Cassadaga Spiritualist
Camp Bookstore**
1112 Stevens Street
Cassadaga, FL 32744
(386) 228-2880
cassadaga.org

INVERNESS
**Old Courthouse
Heritage Museum**
One Courthouse Square
Inverness, FL 34450

(352) 341-6428
citruscountyhistoricalsociety.org
/courthouse-museum.php

Stumpknocker's On the Square
110 West Main Street
Inverness, FL 34450
352-726-2212
stumpknockersonthesquare.com

Angelo's Pizzeria
301 West Main Street
Inverness, FL 34450
(352) 341-0056
angelosnypizza.com

Coach's Pub & Eatery
114 West Main Street
Inverness, FL 34450
(352) 344-3333
coachspubeatery.com

Cattle Dog Coffee Roasters
210B Tompkins Street
Inverness, FL 34450
(352) 726-7060
cattledogcoffeeroasters.com

Withlacoochee State Trail
3100 South Old Floral City Road
Inverness, FL 34450
(352) 726-0315
floridastateparks.org/parks-and
   -trails/withlacoochee-state-trail

MOUNT DORA
Lakeside Inn
100 North Alexander Street
Mount Dora, FL 32757

(352) 383-4101
lakeside-inn.com

Adora Inn Bed & Breakfast
610 North Tremain Street
Mount Dora, FL 32757
(352) 735-3110
adorainn.com

The Goblin Market Restaurant
330 Dora Drawdy Way
Mount Dora, FL 32757
(352) 735-0059
goblinmarketrestaurant.com

Windsor Rose English
Tea Room
142 West 4th Avenue
Mount Dora, FL 32757
(352) 735-2551
windsorrose-tearoom.com

Pisces Rising
239 West Fourth Avenue
Mount Dora, FL 32757
(352) 385-2669
piscesrisingdining.com

Piglet's Pantry Dog Bakery
400 North Donnelly Street
Mount Dora, FL 32757
(352) 735-9779
pigletspantry.com

Donnelly House
535 North Donnelly Street
Mount Dora, FL 32757
lodges.glflamason.org/Lodge/238

Segway of Central Florida
430 North Alexander Street
Mount Dora, FL 32757
(352) 383-9900
segwayofcentralflorida.com

Mount Dora Arts Festival
mountdoraartsfestival.org

Mount Dora Sailboat Festival and Regatta
mountdoraregatta.com

Mount Dora Seafood Festival
mountdoraseafoodfestival.com

Mount Dora Bicycle Festival
mountdorabicyclefestival.com

FLORAL CITY, PINEOLA, ISTACHATTA
Heritage Hall Museum with Museum Country Store
8394 East Orange Avenue
Floral City, FL 34436
(352) 726-7740
cccourthouse.org
/fcheritagemuseum.php

Ferris Groves
7607 South Florida Avenu
Floral City, FL 34436
(352) 860-0366
ferrisgroves.com

Shamrock Inn
8343 East Orange Avenue
Floral City, FL 34436

(352) 726-6414
shamrockinn-floralcity.com

Istachatta General Store (closed)
28202 Magnon Drive
Istachatta, FL 34636

CRYSTAL RIVER
Save the Manatee Foundation
savethemanatee.org

Fish and Wildlife Service Crystal River manatee rules
fws.gov/refuge/Crystal River/visit
/rules_and_regulations.html

Three Sisters Springs Park
123 Northwest Highway 19
Crystal River, FL 34428
(352) 586-1170
threesistersspringsvisitor.org

Crystal River Archaeological State Park
3400 North Museum Point
Crystal River, FL 34428
(352) 795-3817
floridastateparks.org/parks
-and-trails/crystal-river
-archaeological-state-park

Plantation on Crystal River
9301 West Fort Island Trail
Crystal River, FL 34429
(352) 795-4211
plantationoncrystalriver.com

Charlie's Fish House Restaurant and Seafood Market
224 US Highway 19
Crystal River, FL 34428
(352) 795-3949
charliesfishhouse.com

Cattle Dog Coffee Roasters
638 North Citrus Avenue
Crystal River, FL 34428
(352) 228-8818
cattledogcoffeeroasters.com

Franklin Anderson Gallery of Arts
659 North Citrus Avenue
Crystal River, FL 34428
(352) 697-2702
franklinandersongallery.com

Coastal Art Gallery
652 North Citrus Avenue
Crystal River, FL 34428
(352) 228-8800
coastalartgallery.net

OZELLO
Peck's Old Port Cove Restaurant
139 North Ozello Trail
Ozello, FL 34429
(352) 795-2806

HOMOSASSA
MacRae's Marina
5300 South Cherokee Way
Homosassa, FL 34448-4423
(352) 527-7540

Homosassa Public Boat Ramp
5424 South Cherokee Way
Homosassa, FL 34448
(833) 426-8687

The Freezer Tiki Bar
5590 South Boulevard Drive
Homosassa, FL 34448
(352) 628-2452

Shelly's Seafood & Fish Market
5380 South Boulevard Drive
Homosassa, FL 34448
(352) 503-6882
shellysseafood.com

Seagrass Waterfront Restaurant
10386 West Halls River Road
Homosassa, FL 34448
(352) 503-2007
seagrassresort.com

Crumps' Landing
11210 West Halls River Road
Homosassa, FL 34448
(352) 765-4942
crumpslanding.com

Yulee Sugar Mill Ruins Historic State Park
State Road 490
Homosassa, FL 34446
(352) 795-3817
floridastateparks.org/parks-and
 -trails/yulee-sugar-mill-ruins
 -historic-state-park

**Ellie Schiller Homosassa
Springs Wildlife State Park**
4150 S. Suncoast Boulevard
Homosassa, FL 34446
352-628-5343
floridastateparks.org/parks-and
   -trails/ellie-schiller-homosassa
   -springs-wildlife-state-park

CHASSAHOWITZKA
Chassahowitzka Hotel
8551 West Miss Maggie Drive
Chassahowitzka, FL 34448
(877) 807-7783
chazhotel.com

**Chassahowitzka River
Campground**
8600 West Miss Maggie Drive
Chassahowitzka, FL 34448
(352) 382-2200
chassahowitzkaflorida.com

WEEKI WACHEE SPRINGS
**Weeki Wachee Springs
State Park**
Intersection of Highway 19
   and Highway 50/
   Cortez Boulevard
Weeki Wachee, FL 34606
(352) 592-5656
weekiwachee.com
Kayak and stand-up paddle
   board rentals
(352) 597-8484
weekiwachee.com/kayaking
   -paddling-boating-in-weeki
   -wachee-springs-state-park

Becky Jack's Food Shack
8070 Cortez Boulevard
Weeki Wachee, FL 34607
(352) 610-4412
beckyjacks.com

ARIPEKA
**Norfleet Fish Camp Bait
and Tackle**
221 Osowaw Boulevard
Aripeka, FL 34607
(352) 666-2900

WEBSTER
**Sumter County
Farmer's Market**
524 North Market Boulevard
   (off Highway 471)
Webster, FL 33597
(352) 793-2021
sumtercountyfarmersmarket.com

TRILBY
**Little Brown Church
of the South**
37504 Trilby Road
Trilby, FL 33523
(352) 583-3310

DADE CITY
**Pioneer Florida Museum
& Village**
15602 Pioneer Museum Road
Dade City, FL 33523
(352) 567-0262
pioneerfloridamuseum.org

Sugarcreek Too Antiques
37836 Meridian Avenue
Dade City, FL 33525
(352) 437-4888

Lunch on Limoges
14139 7th Street
Dade City, FL 33525
(352) 567-5685
lunchonlimoges.com

Kafe Kokopelli
37940 Live Oak Avenue
Dade City, FL 33523
(352) 523-0055
kafekokopelli.com

Green Door on 8th
14148 8th Street
Dade City, FL 33525
(352) 437-5335
greendooron8th.com

Francesco's Restaurant & Pizzeria
14418 7th Street
Dade City, FL 33523
(352) 518-0009
francescosofdadecity.net

Coyote Rojo Mexican Restaurant
14016 7th Street, #4306
Dade City, FL 33525
(352) 437-5660

Olga's Bakery
14117 7th Street
Dade City, FL 33525
(352) 567-6211

Steph's Southern Soul Restaurant
14519 5th Street
Dade City, FL 33525
352-437-5907
stephssouthernsoul.com

Kumquat Festival
kumquatfestival.org
dadecitychamber.org/annual
-kumquat-festival

RICHLOAM
Richloam General Store
38219 Richloam Clay Sink Road
Richloam/Webster, FL 33597
(800) 915-8027
richloamstore.com

GROVELAND
James Barbecue
262 East Orange Street/
Highway 50
Groveland, FL 34736
(352) 557-4050

CHRISTMAS
Christmas Post Office
23580 East Colonial Drive/
Highway 50
Christmas, FL 32709
(800) 275-8777
postallocations.com/fl/christmas
/Christmas

Fort Christmas Historical Park
1300 N Fort Christmas Road
Christmas, FL 32709
(407) 254-9312
orangecountyfl.net/cultureparks
/parks

Jungle Adventures
26205 East Colonial Drive/
Highway 50
Christmas, FL 32709
(407) 568-2885
jungleadventures.com

OZONA
Molly Goodhead's Raw
Bar & Restaurant
400 Orange Street
Ozona, FL 34660
(727) 786-625
mollygoodheads.com

Ozona Pig Barbecue
311 Orange Street
Ozona, FL 34660
(727) 773-0744
theozonapig.com

Antiques and Uniques
303 Orange Street
Ozona, FL 34660
(727) 253-4976
antiquesanduniquesozona.com

ANNA MARIA,
HOLMES BEACH
Rod and Reel Pier and Café
875 North Shore Drive
Anna Maria, FL 34216

(941) 778-1885
rodreelpier.com

Duffy's Tavern
5808 Marina Drive
Holmes Beach, FL 34217
(941) 778-2501
duffystavernami.com

The Sandbar Restaurant
100 Spring Avenue
Anna Maria, FL 34216
(941) 778-0444
sandbar.groupersandwich.com

Beach Bistro
6600 Gulf Drive
Holmes Beach, FL 34217
(941) 778-6444
beachbistro.com

Eat Here Anna Maria Kitchen
5315 Gulf Drive
Holmes Beach, FL 34217
(941) 778-0411
eathereflorida.com

The Waterfront Restaurant
111 South Bay Boulevard
Anna Maria, FL 34216
(941) 778-151
thewaterfrontrestaurant.net

CORTEZ
Star Fish Company Market
and Restaurant
12306 46th Avenue West
Cortez, FL 34215

(941) 794-1243
starfishcompany.com

Tide Tables at Marker 48
12507 Cortez Road West
Bradenton, FL 34210
(941) 567-6206
tidetablescortez.com

Annie's Bait & Tackle
4334 127th Street West
Cortez, FL 34215
(941) 794-3580
anniesbaitandtackle.com

Florida Maritime Museum
4415 119th Street West
Cortez, FL 34215
(941) 708-6120
floridamaritimemuseum.org

Sea Hagg
12304 Cortez Road West
Cortez, FL 34215
(941) 795-5756
seahagg.com

YEEHAW JUNCTION
Desert Inn, Yeehaw Junction
Directions: at the junction of
SR 60, Highway 441, and the
Florida Turnpike

Osceola County
Historical Society
osceolahistory.org

SEBRING
Sebring International Raceway
113 Midway Drive
Sebring, FL 33870
(863) 655-1442
sebringraceway.com

Sebring Soda &
Ice Cream Works
201 Circle Park Drive
Sebring, FL 33870
(863) 417-8813
sebringsoda.com

Dee's Place
138 North Ridgewood Drive
Sebring, FL 33870
(863) 471-2228

Dimitri's Family Restaurant
Back Alley Bar and Grill at Dimitri's
2710 Kenilworth Boulevard
Sebring, FL 33870
dimitrisrestaurant.net

Chicanes Restaurant
3101 Golfview Road
Sebring, FL 33870
(863) 314-0348
chicanesrestaurant.com

Inn on the Lakes
3101 Golfview Road
Sebring, FL 33870
(863) 471-9400
innonthelakes.com

LAKE PLACID
Lake Placid Annual
Caladium Festival
Event location: Devane Park
115 West Interlake Boulevard
Lake Placid, FL 33852
(863) 465-4331
lpfla.com/caladium-festival-2

Caladium Arts and
Crafts Co-op
132 East Interlake Boulevard
Lake Placid, FL 33852
(863) 699-5940
caladiumarts.org

Toby's Clown School
and Museum
109 West Interlake
Lake Placid, FL 33852
(863) 465-2920
tobysclownfoundation.org

Glenda Jean's
Country Kitchen
204 North Main Avenue
Lake Placid, FL 33852
(863) 531-3476
glendajeanslp.com

Morty & Edna's
Craft Kitchen
231 North Main Avenue
Lake Placid, FL 33852
(863) 699-0600
mortyandednas.com

ARCADIA
Arcadia All-Florida
Championship Rodeo
2450 Northeast Roan Street
Arcadia, FL 34266
(800) 749-7633
arcadiarodeo.com

Arcadia Opera House
106 West Oak Street
Arcadia, FL 34266
(863) 494-9444

Wheeler's Goody Café
13 South Monroe Avenue
Arcadia, FL 34266
(863) 494-3909

SOUTH REGION
JENSEN BEACH
Elliott Museum
825 Northeast Ocean Boulevard
Jensen Beach/Stuart, FL 34996
(772) 225-1961
hsmc-fl.com/elliott-museum/

Florida Oceanographic Center
890 Northeast Ocean Boulevard
Jensen Beach/Stuart, FL 34996
(772) 225-0505
floridaocean.org

Gilbert's Bar House of Refuge
301 Southeast MacArthur Boulevard
Jensen Beach/Stuart, FL 34996
(772) 225-1875
hsmc-fl.com/house-of-refuge/

**Kyle G's Prime Seafood
& Steaks**
10900 South Ocean Drive
Jensen Beach, FL 34957
(772) 237-5461
kylegseafood.com

**Conchy Joe's Seafood
Restaurant & Bar**
3945 Northeast Indian River Drive
Jensen Beach, FL 34957
(772) 334-1130
conchyjoes.com

The Hoffmann
3825 NE Indian River Drive
Jensen Beach, FL 34957
(772) 444-3697
the-hoffmann.com

Crawdaddy's
1949 Northeast Jensen
   Beach Boulevard
Jensen Beach, FL 34957
(772) 225-3444
crawdaddysjensenbeach.com

Bunk House Coffee Bar
3181 Northeast West End Boulevard
Jensen Beach, FL 34957
(772) 261-8312
bunkhousecoffeebar.com

**BOCA GRANDE
The Gasparilla Inn & Club**
500 Palm Avenue
Boca Grande, FL 33921
(877) 764-1420
the-gasparilla-inn.com

The Innlet (motel)
The Outlet Restaurant
1251 12th Street East
Boca Grande, FL 33921
(855) 643-7557
theinnlet.com

The Anchor Inn
450 4th Street East
Boca Grande, FL 33921
(941) 964-5600
anchorinnbocagrande.com

The Pink Elephant
491 Bayou Avenue
Boca Grande, FL 33921
(941) 964-4540
the-gasparilla-inn.com/dining

The Inn Bakery
384 East Railroad Avenue
Boca Grande, FL 33921
(941) 855-9170
the-gasparilla-inn.com/dining
   /#inn-bakery

Temptations
350 Park Avenue
Boca Grande, FL 33921
(941) 964-2610
temptationbocagrande.com

**Miller's Dockside Bar
and Grill and Eagle Grille
Restaurant**
220 Harbor Drive
Boca Grande, FL 33921
(941) 979-6995
eaglegrille.com

South Beach Bar & Grille
760 Gulf Boulevard
Boca Grande, FL 33921
(941) 964-0765
southbeachbarandgrill.com

Fugate's
428 4th Street West
Boca Grande, FL 33921
(941) 964-2323

Boca Grande Outfitters
375 Park Avenue
Boca Grande, FL 33921
(941) 964-2445
bocagrandeoutfitters.com

**The Port Boca Grande
Lighthouse and Museum
at Gasparilla Island
State Park**
880 Belcher Road
Boca Grande, FL 33921
(941) 964-0375
floridastateparks.org/parks-and
    -trails/gasparilla-island-state-park

Gasparilla Island Lighthouse
220 Gulf Boulevard
Boca Grande, FL 33921
(941) 964-0060
barrierislandparkssociety.org

Whidden's Marina
190 1st Street East
Boca Grande, FL 33921
(941) 964-2878
whiddensmarina.com

CLEWISTON
Clewiston Inn
108 Royal Palm Avenue
Clewiston, FL 33440
(863) 983-8151
clewistoninn.com

BRINY BREEZES
Briny Breezes
5000 N. Ocean Boulevard
Briny Breezes, FL 33435
(561) 276-7405
brinybreezes.us

**MATLACHA, BOKEELIA,
PINELAND, ST. JAMES CITY**
Lovegrove Gallery & Gardens
4637 Pine Island Road Northwest
Matlacha, FL 33993
(239) 938-5655
leomalovegrove.com

Wild Child Gallery
4625 Pine Island Road Northwest
Matlacha, FL 33993
(239) 283-6006
wildchildartgallery.com

Elena's Gallery
4606 Pine Island Road
Matlacha, FL 33993
(239) 283-9658

Bert's Bar & Grill
4271 Pine Island Road
Matlacha, FL 33993
(239) 282-3232
bertsbar.com

The Perfect Cup
4548 Pine Island Road
Matlacha, FL 33993
(239) 283-4447

Matlacha Island Cottages
4760 Pine Island Road
Matlacha, FL 33993
(845) 652-3181
matlacha-cottages.com

Bridgewater Inn
4331 Pine Island Road
Matlacha, FL 33993
(239) 283-2423
bridgewaterinn.com

Capt'n Con's Fish House
8421 Main Street
Bokeelia, FL 33992
(239) 283-4300
captnconsfishhouse.com

Bokeelia Art Gallery
8315 Main Street
Bokeelia, FL 33992
(239) 738-5280
bokeeliaartgallery.com

Tarpon Lodge & Restaurant
13771 Waterfront Drive
Pineland, FL 33922
(239) 283-3999
tarponlodge.com

Museum of the Islands
5728 Sesame Drive
Pineland, FL 33922

(239) 283-1525
museumoftheislands.com

Waterfront Restaurant
131 Oleander Street
St. James City, FL 33956
(239) 283-0592
waterfrontrestaurant.com

CAPTIVA, SANIBEL
Lighthouse Beach Park
110 Periwinkle Way
Sanibel, FL 33957
(239) 472-0345

**Sanibel Historical Museum
and Village**
950 Dunlop Road
Sanibel, FL 33957
(239) 472-4648
sanibelmuseum.org

**Bailey-Matthews Shell
Museum**
3075 Sanibel Captiva Road
Sanibel, FL 33957
(239) 395-2233
shellmuseum.org

**J. N. "Ding" Darling National
Wildlife Refuge**
1 Wildlife Drive
Sanibel Island, FL 33957
(239) 472-1100
fws.gov/refuge/jn_ding_darling
Ding Darling Wildlife Society
    /Friends of the Refuge
dingdarlingsociety.org

Captiva Island Store
11500 Andy Rosse Lane
Captiva, FL 33924
(239) 427-2374
captivaislandstore.com

The Mucky Duck
11546 Andy Rosse Lane
Captiva Island, FL 33924
239-472-3434
muckyduck.com

Jungle Drums Gallery
11532 Andy Rosse Lane
Captiva, FL 33924
(239) 395-2266
jungledrumsgallery.com

Sunshine Seafood Café
11508 Andy Rosse Lane
Captiva Island, FL 33924
(239) 472-6200
captivaislandinn.com/captiva
   -island-restaurant/sunshine
   -seafood

The Bubble Room
15001 Captiva Drive
Captiva, FL33924
(239) 472-5558
bubbleroomrestaurant.com

The Mad Hatter Restaurant
6467 Sanibel Captiva Road
Sanibel, FL 33957
(239) 472-0033
madhatterrestaurant.com

**Doc Fords Rum Bar
and Restaurant**
2500 Island Inn Road
Sanibel, FL 33957
(239) 472-8311
docfords.com/sanibel-island

**Doc Fords Rum Bar
and Restaurant**
5400 South Seas Plantation Road
Captiva, FL 33924
(239) 312-4275
docfords.com/captiva-island

'Tween Waters Inn
15951 Captiva Drive
Captiva, FL 33924
(800) 223-5865
tween-waters.com

Castaways Cottages
6460 Sanibel Captiva Road
Sanibel, FL 33957
(800) 375-0152
castaways-cottages.com

Chapel by the Sea
11580 Chapin Lane
Captiva, FL 33924
(239) 472-1646
captivachapel.com

GOODLAND
**Stan's Idle Hour Bar and
Seafood Restaurant**
221 County Road 892/
   Goodland Drive
Goodland, FL 34145

(239) 394-304
stansidlehourgoodland.com

Little Bar Restaurant
205 Harbor Drive
Goodland, FL 34145
(239) 394-5663
littlebarrestaurant.com

Paradise Found
401 Papaya Street
Goodland, FL 34140
(239) 330-7773
paradisefoundrestaurant.com

Crabby Lady
123 Bayshore Way
Goodland, FL 34140
(239) 500-2722
crabbylady.com

**EVERGLADES CITY,
CHOKOLOSKEE**
Rod and Gun Club
200 West Broadway
Everglades City, FL 34139
(239) 695-2101
rodanguneverglades.com

Ivey House Bed & Breakfast
605 Buckner Avenue North
Everglades City, FL 34139
(239) 695-3299
iveyhouse.com

**City Seafood Market and
Restaurant**
702 Begonia Street
Everglades City, FL 34139

(239) 695-4700
cityseafood1.com

Captain Doug's Airboat Tours
905 DuPont Street
Everglades City, FL 34139
(877) 222-6400
captaindougs.com

Speedy Johnson's Airboat Rides
621 Begonia Street
Everglades City, FL 34139
(239) 695-4448
speedysairboattours.com

Museum of the Everglades
105 West Broadway Avenue
Everglades City, FL 34139
(239) 252-5026
colliermuseums.com/locations
    /museum-of-the-everglades

Historic Ted Smallwood Store
360 Mamie Street
Chokoloskee, FL 34138
(239) 695-2989
smallwoodstore.com

Havana Café of the Everglades
191 Smallwood Drive
Chokoloskee, FL 34138
(239) 695-2214

OCHOPEE
Ochopee Post Office
38000 Tamiami Trail/
    US Highway 41
Ochopee, FL 34141
(239) 695-2099

**Skunk Ape Research
Headquarters**
40904 Tamiami Trail/
    US Highway 41
Ochopee, FL 34141
(239) 695-2275
skunkape.info

Joanie's Blue Crab Café
39395 Tamiami Trail/
    US Highway 41
Ochopee, FL 34141
(239) 695-2682
joaniesbluecrabcafe.com

**CARD SOUND/
ALABAMA JACK'S**
Alabama Jack's
58000 Card Sound Road
Card Sound/Homestead, FL 33030
(305) 248-8741

ISLAMORADA
Cheeca Lodge
81801 Overseas Highway
Islamorada, FL 33036
Phone: (305) 664-4651
cheeca.com

The Green Turtle Inn
81219 Overseas Highway
Islamorada, FL 33036
(305) 664-2006
greenturtlekeys.com

Robbie's Marina Kayak Rental
77522 Overseas Highway
Islamorada, FL 33036
(305) 664-4878

robbies.com/kayak-and
    -paddleboard-rentals-tours.htm

**Hungry Tarpon Restaurant
at Robbie's Marina**
77522 Overseas Highway
Islamorada, FL 33036
(305) 664-0535
hungrytarpon.com

**BIG PINE KEY/
NO NAME KEY**
**Bahia Honda Key
    State Park**
36850 Overseas Highway
Big Pine Key, FL 33043
(305) 872-2353
floridastateparks.org
    /BahiaHonda

Big Pine Key Blue Hole
3 miles north of Overseas
    Highway/US 1 on
    Key Deer Boulevard
Big Pine Key, FL 33043

No Name Pub
30813 Watson Boulevard
Big Pine Key, FL 33043
(305) 872-9115
nonamepub.com

National Key Deer Refuge
fws.gov/refuge/National_Key
    _Deer_Refuge
Key Deer Hotline at
    (305) 470-6863 ext. 7

INDEX

ABOUT THE AUTHOR

Bruce Hunt is an award-winning writer, photographer, and third-generation native Floridian. He's authored eleven books on Florida travel and history. He has also written and photographed hundreds of articles for magazines and newspapers. For five years Hunt was a regular feature writer and photographer for *DuPont Registry Tampa Bay* magazine. His work has also appeared in the *St. Petersburg Times* (*Tampa Bay Times*), *Tampa Tribune*, the *Visit Tampa Bay Official Visitors Guide*, *Backpacker* magazine, *Rock & Ice* magazine, *Skydiving* magazine, *Florida Trend* magazine, *Growing Bolder* magazine, *Celebrity Car* magazine, *Coastal Living* magazine, and *Southern Living* magazine, among others.